THE OFFICIAL COMPANION

VOLUME ONE

FIREFLY: THE OFFICIAL COMPANION VOLUME ONE

ISBN 1 84576 314 9
ISBN-13 9781845763145

Published by Titan Books, a division of
Titan Publishing Group Ltd.
144 Southwark Street
London
SE1 0UP

First edition July 2006
2 4 6 8 10 9 7 5 3

Firefly: The Official Companion
Volume One

Based on the series created by Joss Whedon.

Acknowledgements
The publishers would like to thank the cast, crew and writers of *Firefly* for all their enthusiasm and cooperation with this book, particularly Joss Whedon. Thank you to the 'shiny' crew who conducted the interviews and wrote material for the book: Abbie Bernstein (Joss Whedon, Jewel Staite, Michael Fairman, Christina Hendricks, Shawna Trpcic, Carey Meyer, Greg Edmonson), Bryan Cairns (Adam Baldwin, Morena Baccarin, Gina Torres), Karl Derrick (Chris Calquhoun, Mike Gibbons, Jonathan A. Logan, Brennan Byers, Regina Pancake, Randy Eriksen, Chris Gilman), Tara DiLullo (Nathan Fillion, Ron Glass, Summer Glau, Alan Tudyk, Tim Minear, Loni Peristere). Thank you to Julie Thompson at still-flying.net, Barbara Johnson and Harry Harris for their help. Thank you also to Shawna Trpcic for allowing us to photograph her costume designs. Finally, thank you to Debbie Olshan and Jamie Waugh at Fox for all their support on this project.

Props and costumes courtesy of Karl Derrick.

What did you think of this book? We love to hear from our readers.
Please email us at: **readerfeedback@titanemail.com** or write to us at the above address.
You can also visit us at **www.titanbooks.com**

A CIP catalogue record for this title is available from the British Library.

Printed and bound in the USA.

firefly

THE OFFICIAL COMPANION

VOLUME ONE

Features and Interviews by Abbie Bernstein, Bryan Cairns,
Karl Derrick & Tara DiLullo

TITAN BOOKS

CONTENTS

INTO THE BLACK

An interview with Joss Whedon

Did *Firefly* wind up being about what it started out being about?

JOSS WHEDON: Ultimately, mostly yes. Because what it set out to be was a mixture of genres, a *Stagecoach* kind of drama with a lot of people trying to figure out their lives in a bleak and pioneer environment. There was one major sea change during the process and it came from [the network] Fox, which was obviously that they wanted it to be more an action-oriented drama. I wanted it to be the kind of show where guns would not be drawn often, so that when they were, it was that much more dire a thing. They wanted gunplay a-plenty and it was both a rhythmic and something of a moral adjustment to go, 'Okay, we're going to go a little more *Wild Bunch* than *Stagecoach*' [laughs]. I still got to have the things that I was looking for, the moments between people. Those are the things that people remember and love, and I explained early on, that the most important scene in the pilot ['Serenity'] is the scene of Kaylee eating that strawberry. That to me was the essence of the entire show. But when Mal came in and shot the agent [Dobson] in the head, it was really because he had no other choice. Reavers were coming; this was the most efficient thing to do. He did it very cold-bloodedly and that was on purpose, but not gratuitously. By the time we made the first episode ['The Train Job'], he kicked a guy into the ship's engine for a laugh. That's a bit of a change. I think if we had been able to do something without *any* adjustment, and that's very rare, it would have been somewhat quieter. But as it was, the integrity of the characters and the show and the rhythm and the feeling they had about each other was very much the show that I had originally intended; and the episodes that I had thought to do, that I now never will, were still very much in place. It was just a question of easing the audience into it with something a little more exciting than contemplative.

❖ Opposite: Meet the crew of Serenity.

❖ Below: *Firefly* creator Joss Whedon

You have previously said that most of your stories are about discovering strength or discovering what to do with strength. Which is *Firefly*?

It's interesting. I wouldn't have classified it as either, but it's definitely both and more. Because ultimately, *Firefly* is also about perhaps discovering strength through weakness, simply because the idea that these people could get through the day at all, make a living, avoid the Alliance and not get eaten is kind of a triumph. But it's a triumph because they have no power, which is of course different than strength. But because I had so many different people on so many different journeys, I would say that this sort of fits every mode. We have River, who is obviously the classic adolescent with power who is going to learn that she has it and how to control it, something we paid off in the movie; and Mal, who at this point in his life has rejected the idea of the power he had, even though he was a captain, because the power he used to have, a lot of it came from idealism and faith and momentum, and when that was kicked out of him, he's sort of empty. I would say, power is not what I was thinking about when I made the show. This is part of the difference between the show and the movie, because the show was really about what is it like to be the little guy, and the movie was, what is it like to be the little guy — in an awesome epic! Where you win! Because it's a movie! [laughs] And the paradigm adjustment for the movie is much greater than any that I had from the network.

When you were putting *Firefly* together, out of all of the people that you were working with at that time, how did you select Tim Minear as the other show-runner?

Through deceit and evil. I wish I were kidding. I had not intended to use Tim. I was desperate to use Tim. I had three people that I absolutely knew could run a show, and they were David [Greenwalt on *Angel*] and Marti [Noxon on *Buffy the Vampire Slayer*] and Tim [on *Angel*], and David and Marti already were show-runners. And I promised David Greenwalt, to his face, I would not take Tim away from him when I did *Firefly*. But I could not find anybody even remotely of the caliber of Tim, and somebody — a very smart person and a good friend — took me aside and

❖ Top: Cast and crew in the galley.

❖ Above: Joss Whedon and Morena Baccarin during filming.

❖ Right: Executive producer Tim Minear.

of a sudden, I had an even better reason to spend a lot of time on *Buffy* and *Angel* — I had no show-runners. So it really was difficult, because I just had so much work, but once I made the decision, once I knew I had to do it [laughs], it was so easy. And Tim had been dying to do it. And then all of a sudden, I had a second half. I mean, as much as anybody I've ever worked with, Tim had the same voice and came in at the very beginning, the way David did with *Buffy*, and informed the voice of *Firefly* so much and did so much of the great stuff. He was the guy I wanted, and I realized eventually that he was the guy I *needed*; and my god, from the first moment, he understood the show as well as any human being, and just brought so much to it that I think of it as though he were always a part of it. There was never a time when I hadn't hired him.

Was there a defined division of responsibilities, or did you both just jump in and handle whatever came up?

It really was just, 'Tag, you're it.' I obviously ended up with final say on all things, because that's how it worked, but I could leave anything in Tim's hands and know that it would come back to me the way it should. It was my show, in the sense of it was something I had been nurturing for years, and he didn't have to go through a lot of the incredibly painful casting process and stuff like that, but had I had to shuffle off this mortal coil or move to Gdansk and change my name, I would have had perfect confidence the show would be just about everything it could with only Tim on working it.

How did you select the writing and production staff?

Basically, the production staff as much as possible was made up of people that I knew and loved: ADs [assistant directors] and producers and people like that, I had used before. The big find was David Boyd, the DP [director of photography], whose style fit the show so perfectly, who is full of joy and energy and lit faster than anybody I'd ever worked with. Which was great, because we had a smaller budget than either *Buffy* or *Angel*, and we had to move as down and dirty as possible, and so it was a piece of luck. When a guy like that walks in a room, you feed off his energy, you know you've got a problem-solver. DPs come in two kinds — problem-solvers and the other kind. David lit environmentally, so you could turn around and shoot the other way. Very often, DPs can kill you. [Boyd's] stuff looked cinematic, just beautiful, but he always achieved it with as little work as possible. He thought the lenses were too clean and he knew I was going for that 1970s Western look, so he found some beautiful old lenses that caught flares off of everything and really helped the look of the thing. I brought a camera operator over from *Buffy* and sound people — anybody that I could spare, where

said, 'Be realistic. If you don't move Tim to *Firefly*, you will never see *Buffy* or *Angel* again. If you don't have a second-in-command who can control the set when you walk away from it, you never will. And the only way to make things even out is to put him on that show.' And it was true. And I didn't want to admit it, because I had made a promise and then I had to go back on it. And needless to say, David Greenwalt did not take that lightly, nor should he have. Not just because of that, there were many factors involved, but David left *Angel* [he went to ABC to produce *Miracles*] and then Marti had her baby right away, and all another show was dialed in enough that the show wouldn't suffer if the person moved. I brought them over, so that I would have that comfort factor.

As far as the writing staff, we did it the way you normally do it. We read scripts and we met with people. Jose [Molina] we had known for a while, as Howard Gordon's assistant and then as a writer. Tim is very active in following writers and nurturing writers. Obviously when we found Ben [Edlund], we grabbed him pretty quick, because he has a sensibility that's so left of center. Cheryl [Cain] had written a beautiful spec; and Brett [Matthews], who was my assistant, knew the show from being with me and from being a young writer himself, so he wrote one of the scripts. And we pilfered staff: we used Drew Greenberg and Jane Espenson from *Buffy*. The first year of a staff is always difficult. But we actually started out very strong and that's rare.

The two-hour episode 'Serenity' was originally conceived as the première, but it wound up airing last; Fox required you to make a new first episode, 'The Train Job'. Do you think *Firefly* would have been the same if the network had not made you reiterate the premise several times in different episodes?

You know, the only time it was egregiously difficult was obviously 'The Train Job'. And I still think that's a sweet episode. The fact of the matter is, I am a firm believer in reiterating the premise of any show anyway. Because you don't catch the first one every time. And I believe that for the first thirteen, you should always make it as easy as possible for people to come in and be told what's going on. If you have to tell them too much, maybe you're doing something wrong. But there are some things you can take for granted. If you see the Shepherd with his collar, you don't have to say, 'Look! He's a Shepherd, he's a man of God!' He's got the collar. You see Jayne — do you *have* to explain he's a mercenary? Not so much. There are certain things that we'd throw out there every time, but certain things do take care of themselves. I do believe that you should always explain the show kind of up-front, let people know what they're in for. 'The Train Job' was a bit more extreme, because we really had to assume people hadn't seen anything ever — and as it turned out, we would be right. It's the same thing I had to do for [the feature film] *Serenity*, except I only had a weekend to do 'The Train Job'. But I had Tim.

In the two-hour 'Serenity' episode, there are some shots that are almost like thought voiceovers — shots of the character's reaction outside the scene...

I wanted to be a little stylistically funky and people pretty much wanted me to turn that down, because it is a little odd, it throws some people. Every now and then, I wanted to be a little stylistically bizarre. I found [Steven Soderbergh's] *The Limey* an extremely influential film for me stylistically, and I've never really gotten away from it. I wanted the thing to feel like little found bits of footage that got stuck together, and I think it's a nice way to get into somebody's head, to hear them saying one thing and to

❖ Bottom: Serenity flying through space.

❖ Below: Bridge control panel detail.

see another. It's something I would have liked to have done more of, but again, the mission statement became, 'Tell the story, get people through it and earn your indulgence.'

Did you ever consider actually killing off a member of the crew in the opening episode?

No. No. No. Because you just can't do it — you want to do it [laughs] and I think about it every show I ever create — the fact of the matter is, it never doesn't get out. So it's too difficult. I wanted to create a world with all these people, and then I wanted to live with them. So that was my only mandate. I did intend to kill at least one of them at some point, suddenly and unexpectedly, because it is my nature to do so. And it's very much the nature of the show that things are pulled out from under you suddenly; that you can depend on nothing; that you are floating in the midst of nothing. But I wasn't planning to do that for a while.

Can you talk about the design of Serenity the ship?

The design of the ship is something that I worked on very hard and then [production designer] Carey Meyer worked on very hard. To me, the design of the ship was very crucial just in terms of the idea of a known space; the idea of, 'We live on this space, and here's where the rooms are, and here's why, and here's where the cargo bay is, and here's why,' and there are not fourteen hundred decks and a holodeck and an all-you-can-eat buffet in the back. It's very utilitarian. If you actually watch *Stagecoach*, they spend a long time introducing the stagecoach, because that space is very important. We did a lot of collaboration. I knew everything I was looking for and which space related to which character. We spent a lot of time talking about paint. Because you're going into this knowing you're going to spend most of your time on the ship, and every room represented either a feeling or a character. The engine room was rusty brown because that's very earthy and likable and real, and that's Kaylee's space — that was very deliberate. The hall next to it is very cool and blue, because that space doesn't really serve a purpose [laughs], except for action or suspense. Everything was done exactly like that. Obviously, the blue of the infirmary is like Simon.

Did you ever write scenes for certain parts of the ship that had to be moved to a different part because the mood of the scene didn't match the specific environment?

Not particularly. It wasn't like I ever made a huge mistake like I did on *Buffy* of putting a bedroom scene on a front lawn [in the episode 'Innocence'; the scene was reshot to take place inside a bedroom]. Ultimately, every space had that Serenity feel. It was beat-up but lived-in

and ultimately, it was home. Having said that, there certainly were specific things you could go for from one space to another, but we pretty much knew as we broke the story, that we said, 'We want to be here with this character, we want to be here with this one.'

The design used different influences, like the sliding doors and — you couldn't see them, we didn't build one, we only had little doors for them — but those tiny cubicles — I should say 'tubicles', you could only lie down in them — that are found in little Japanese hotels. Those sliding doors were influenced by that idea, the idea that there were a couple of cubicles even smaller than the ones that Simon and River and Book had.

When we designed the ship, the only thing I learned really was that you don't put the opening of a cargo ship in the front, because it really goes in the back, aerodynamically speaking [laughs], and that was a bit of awkward design that was my fault. But basically, once we created the environment for them to live in, Carey not only built it beautifully, he built the entire thing with ceilings, so that we could always look every which way *and* the entire thing was adaptable — you could pull it away or move something huge, so that you could get in and around everything. That meant the environment worked for us and there weren't a lot of adjustments that needed to be made. It was more like discovering, 'Oh! I can shoot here! I can shoot there! I can get behind these stairs!' It was a dream set, because there was always something interesting to look at, and it wasn't difficult to get there.

The crew's bunks being down ladders was a very important thing to me. I'm a huge believer in vertical space, and one of the reasons I loved doing the show, something that had dropped out of televised science fiction to an extent, was the idea of vertical space, because

❖ Top left: The galley.

❖ Top right: Joss watches a take on the monitor.

❖ Above: Relaxing between takes during the filming of 'Safe'.

❖ Opposite: The Alliance seal.

it's just easier to do things horizontally; everything's out on a soundstage and you can roll the cameras around. But we knew we were going to be carrying the cameras hand-held most of the time anyway. In fact, our Steadicam operator lamented at one point, 'I used to have a Steadicam for a job...' because we made him do so much hand-held. This was Bill Brummond. He was so damn steady holding the thing that a lot of his hand-held looked like Steadicam. I used to yell at him, 'What do I have to do — get behind you and tickle you? C'mon, make it dirty.'

Anyway, the idea of the ship was that you lived in it. And that's the same idea behind the camerawork: don't be arch, don't be sweeping — be found, be rough and tumble and docu and you-are-there.

We knew we were going to have to be on the ship a lot — like 'Objects in Space' — as an attempt to save some dough [laughs], because we didn't have any. In the case of the world, we always had to sort of build a little something or find a little something. In that sense, we were flying a little blinder, because we didn't know what we were going to be able to pull off or come up with. Something like 'Heart of Gold', which is very rustic, or 'Shindig', which is very old-fashioned but also modern and opulent — to create either of those is going to mean a lot of cheating, a lot of building and a lot of using what's already there. Carey Meyer, (who had worked with me on *Buffy* forever) again, like David Boyd, was endlessly inventive. Except I did have to tell him at one point, 'You have to stop using wine crates on every set,' because I was starting to notice [laughs] — but my god, they saved us a ton of money. The mall in 'The Message', where they go and get the dead body, was basically a piece of every set that we'd ever built that we still had, but it had a look of its own. He did an extraordinary job creating those worlds. But with exceptions, they were difficult to visualize, because you know, how much can we get away with? It's part of why I gave every planet Earth atmosphere and Earth tones, because quite frankly, I knew that I couldn't afford to make alien worlds. I didn't want to go to Yucca Flats every other episode and transform it into Bizarro World by making the sky orange.

A number of episodes conclude with a shot of Serenity flying away from us as a few guitar notes are played. Was this conceived as a signature shot for *Firefly*?

I didn't think of it as that, but it's not the 'Let's fly at camera in the *Back to the Future* shot' and it's not the warp speed end of *Star Trek* shot, 'It's a small ship, we've had some fun, but we're still all alone out here.' The guitar is very small. The idea of the instrumentation was to highlight the sparseness of their environment and the teeniness of them. So, yeah. It wasn't 'Let's have that — this will sum it all up,' but it does.

Four of your actors who had guest roles in *Firefly* — Andy Umberger as the Captain of the Dortmunder and Carlos Jacott as Dobson in 'Serenity', Jeff Ricketts as a Blue-Gloved Man in 'The Train Job' and 'Ariel' and Jonathan M. Woodward as Tracey in 'The Message' — were 'hat-trick' actors who all also appeared in both *Buffy* and *Angel*. Would you have had more hat-trick actors if *Firefly* had gone on longer?

I don't do it in order to do it, I do it because I have somebody I love and they fit a space. Carlos had actually read for Wash and when Alan [Tudyk] got Wash, it occurred to me that Carlos was that guy who can appear very menacing, but he's also the most disarming fellow in the world, so he worked perfectly for Dobson. I don't go into these things saying, 'We absolutely must,' but when you have a guy who's right, it saves you some time. Jonathan [Woodward] had worked on *Buffy* but not *Angel* yet when he did 'The Message'.

Were Niska and Saffron designed to be recurring characters?

Only if they worked. I mean, you want everybody to be so good that you want them to be ongoing. And that worked out. I didn't even close the door on Early, or for that matter, even Dobson. I planned to bring him back — when I couldn't, I brought him back in the comic. He got shot in the eye. In the show, he was going to have a whole run about how Mal had shot him in the eye and not killed him and how pathetic Mal was. It was going to be really funny.

What about the Blue-Gloved Men?

This was another change: they [the network executives] were very interested in the over-reaching arc. I wanted the show to play more episodically, because *Buffy* and *Angel* had gotten so caught up in their own mythos that *I* couldn't tell what was going on; and so I was like, 'Let's be very standalone,' and also because it reflected the sort of day to day pointlessness of these [*Firefly*] people's lives, not in a harsh way, just 'We got through today, now we have to get through tomorrow, so let's not be part of a grander scheme right away.' Eventually, we were going to build to it, because I think you have to, but [the network] wanted to bring that out sooner, so I created the Blue-Handed fellas for that purpose, so there was sort of the ticking clock of the thing following [the main characters]. I had not actually intended to use the same two actors. I wanted to indicate that there were a bunch of them, but nobody knew that [laughs], so when we had the Blue-Hand Men again, they had the same guys [Jeff Ricketts and Dennis Cockrum]. So I was like, 'Okay, apparently there's only two of them.' Because I was running three shows and so I missed that one, that fell between the cracks. That's not a diss on the actors, they did a great job,

but yeah, the original idea was that there would be these guys everywhere. Blue Sun [Corporation, the employer of the Blue-Gloved Men] was going to be a big thing, part of the whole Miranda thing, but the movie just didn't have room for that.

Interviews with the cast often give the impression that their characters really had a continued life beyond just 'action — cut.' Did you get that feeling from your cast on this?

I did. Here were very, very dedicated craftsmen, who were working on making it work and getting it right, but they lived their characters to such an extent that, yeah, sometimes the issue would become confused. I thought for a long time that Sean [Maher] was looking at all of us going, 'How did I get on board with these idiots?' Because he's very quiet and reserved. He's actually the sweetest guy in the world and was having a lot of fun, but I didn't know it for a while [laughs]. I thought he was just looking at us like, 'I'm smarter than them,' because he's got such incredible self-containment. But then, like Simon, he's just all mushy heart. Jewel's mom actually talked to me about what it was like when Jewel was playing Kaylee, that it was exciting for her to be playing somebody so optimistic and so full of love and life, because she had been cast in a different kind of role before that and it was like playing Kaylee opened her up, to an extent. Yeah, [the entire cast] embodied their characters to the point where I can't remember a time when those characters existed without those faces.

Did they ever discuss with you what allowed them to jump into it so wholeheartedly?

I don't know. Part of it was a feeling — there was a history to the thing, that if they had a question, there was an answer, or we would work out an answer, we would find it together. But I don't know how I got so many grossly talented people all in one place who really enjoyed what they were doing and really liked each other. I've worked with great ensembles every time out and I've been very lucky, but there was something going on here that was really different than anything I've seen on any set. Nobody ever went to their trailer — they all just wanted to watch each other. It's not something to be taken lightly. Or canceled.

(End of part 1. Continued in Volume 2.)

SERENITY

Written & Directed by Joss Whedon

JOSS WHEDON

The most difficult shot we did is in the pilot. It's Mal coming out of his quarters on the ladder. The camera is in his quarters and then goes up the ladder above him and into the hall. That required building a piece of the hall above his room and [director of photography] David and his guys designing a rig that they attached the camera to, that basically ran on tracks which they attached to the ceiling, so they could stick the camera all the way down in the room. Then I actually asked them to adjust it and the next day, they had completely reworked it so you went up the track and then they'd literally pull it with a rope, while someone was operating the head of the camera so that it could look down. It could go up and then go out again when he came up the hall, so that

it really felt like it was just hanging with him. And that kind of last-minute, low-rent but elaborate inventiveness to get that feeling of being there was something that I adored, that I got from everybody I worked with, and that I thrived on, because we were making something that felt very epic, but at the same time, it felt so little regional theatre, intimate, no-budge [no-budget], we are a little band of brothers, little artists having our moment. And that kind of energy is very rare in television. Usually somebody is stepping on it, and very often, it's the actors [laughs]. But again, in this case, they all were very much in the same spirit of 'How much can I bring to the party?' and not 'What's in it for me?'

TEASER

EXT. SERENITY VALLEY – NIGHT

Battle rages. Dead bodies, explosions — we see rapidfire images of bloody conflict. The INDEPENDENTS hold a narrow gulch that overlooks a desert valley, which the ALLIANCE troops swarm through, trying to take the position. From above, a small Alliance SKIFF flies by, strafing the ground and several men.

ANGLE: behind an outcropping:

are six soldiers, all in conference, sweaty, haggard, shouting over the din. Amongst them are SGT. MALCOLM REYNOLDS, clearly in charge, ZOE, his unflappable corporal, BENDIS, a terrified young soldier, and GRAYDON, an exhausted but tough radio operator. Around them, other soldiers are laid out, firing, keeping back the onslaught of Alliance troops.

GRAYDON
Sergeant! Command says air support is holding til they can assess our status!

MAL
Our status is that we need some gorramn air support! Get back on line and —

ZOE
That skiff is shredding us, sir —

GRAYDON
They won't move without a lieutenant's authorization code, sir —

Mal breaks past them, moves to a corpse of at least two days in officer's gear. He rips a rank symbol off the corpse's arm.

Hands it to Graydon, flipping it over so we can

SERENITY VALLEY

Production designer Carey Meyer: "Serenity Valley was in several places. In flashbacks, we had this interior that looked like an old decrepit church — it had parts of columns and an old Buddha. The exterior was in the deep San Fernando Valley, in Lake Los Angeles — where there is no lake. It's not easy to light, but you can get equipment in and it's a nice place to shoot because you can light it up and see a pretty large environment. Often, if you get to an exterior and your geography is not controlled or you have a very close horizon, you just can't afford to light it. So you try to find a space that has a high horizon that is close to you, where you can control the lighting. Even though it's still a big space, the valley essentially like a large bowl, where you can see the ground in front of you, light it and actually shoot it at night. It also was somewhere we could set off those large fireballs and have a lot of gunfire late at night and not disturb the community."

see a series of numbers and letters on the other side.

MAL
That's your code. You're lieutenant Baker, congratulations on your promotion, now get me air support!

Turns to the two other soldiers.

MAL (cont'd)
(to one)
Pull back just far enough to wedge 'em in here.
(to the other)
Get your squad to the high ground, you pick 'em off.

THE BROWNCOATS

Costume designer Shawna Trpcic: "We actually designed the Serenity battle before we designed Mal's individual look. That was a lot of [original *Firefly* designer] Jill Ohanesson's input. We went everywhere from chain mail to these red vests with the Asian closures and Civil War pants and torn-up rags for keeping warm. We had images from around the world, from wars in Genghis Khan's time to Civil War time, and captured a little bit of everybody's armor and everybody's layers to try to convey the homespun look of the Serenity battle."

❖ Above right: Costume designs for Mal and Zoe as Independent soldiers.

❖ Right: The Independents' rank symbols, including the lieutenant's patch Mal rips from the arm of a dead soldier.

❖ Above: The anti-aircraft gun Mal fires up.

ZOE
High ground's death with that skiff in the air.

MAL
That's our problem and thank you for volunteering.
(to the scared guy)
Bendis, you give us cover, we're going duck hunting.

A soldier falls back between them, dead.

MAL (cont'd)
(to all)
Just focus. Alliance said they were gonna waltz through Serenity Valley and we've choked 'em with those words. We've done the impossible and that makes us mighty. Just a little while longer, our angels'll be soaring overhead, raining fire on those arrogent cods, so you hold. You HOLD! Go.

Two of them scamper off, Bendis moving into position, back to the rock, ready to give cover fire but still scared shitless.

Mal and Zoe move over to a small cache of arms and he picks up a rifle.

ZOE
Really think we can bring her down, sir?

MAL
Do you even need to ask?

Unseen by her, he pulls a small cross from a

chain on his neck, silently kisses it, puts it back.

MAL (cont'd)
Ready?

ZOE
Always.
(shouts)
Bendis! BENDIS!

But he is too scared. Can't move.

ZOE (cont'd)
Rut it.

She pops up herself, firing a machine gun, strafing the area. A moment, and Mal goes, also firing, Zoe behind.

As they run to an anti-aircraft gun, three Alliance troops come into view.

They each shoot one but one gets in close to Mal and they tangle, Mal adroitly outfighting him, knocking him on his ass and moving on as Zoe follows, firing a burst into the gut without even stopping.

She reaches a little cover, throws herself down. He goes higher, for a clear view of the sky.

ANGLE: THE SKIFF

streaks through the night sky, firing short, deadly bursts. A single-person fighter, it looks like nothing so much as a boomerang.

Mal shoots the soldiers by the anti-aircraft gun, then jumps in and grabs it. There is much with buttons and dials and whirring and clicking. He sights up...

MAL
Give me a lock...

ANGLE: THROUGH THE SCOPE:

More of the skiff, but with calibrations and infravision and whatnot.

A moment, and Mal fires.

ANGLE: THE SKIFF

is hit direct, explodes, fragments of it coming straight for camera —

Mal bolts, slamming into Zoe and diving with her out of the way as a huge flaming chunk of skiff spins over them and into his position, exploding.

They hit the ground and roll, fire raining down around them.

ANGLE: behind the outcrop —

They return, Bendis still unmoving.

ZOE
Nice cover fire.

MAL
What's the status on —

But they see that Graydon is dead.

MAL (cont'd)
Zoe.

She starts pulling the radio off his corpse. Mal moves to Bendis, gets in his face.

MAL (cont'd)
Listen to me. Look at me! Listen. We're holding this valley. No matter what.

BENDIS
We're gonna die...

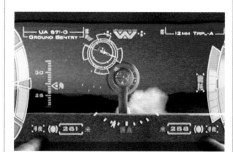

MAL
We're not gonna die! We can't die, Bendis, and do you know why? Because we are so very pretty. We are just too pretty for God to let us die, look at that chiseled jaw, come on...

BENDIS
I'm sorry...

Mal hears something — a growing roar. He smiles.

MAL
You won't listen to me, listen to that.

That's our angels, come to blow the Alliance right to the hot place.

Bendis hears it too. It changes him, hope suffusing his expression.

MAL (cont'd)
Zoe, tell the eighty second to —

ZOE
They're not coming.

Mal stops. Zoe lowers the radio.

ZOE (cont'd)
Command says it's too hot. They're pulling out. We're to lay down arms.

Mal is uncomprehending at first.

MAL
But... what...

The noise grows louder. IN SLO MO, Mal rises, the first light of day hitting his face as he scans the valley.

ANGLE: THE VALLEY

As out of the sunrise come dozens of Alliance ships, filling the sky.

ANGLE: MAL

as he sees everything lost — everything he believes, everything he fought for... In the background of the shot, we see Bendis, also looking in horror, be strafed with bullets and fall out of frame.

Mal just stares.

INT. BLOWN-OUT SHIP - NIGHT

We are in a some kind of burnt out wreck - all we see is twisted black metal, a few stars visible through breaches in the hull. It's 'night' because it's space, so it's always night. But the wreck is not empty.

From top of frame, Mal floats upside-down into a closeup. He is in a spacesuit, the light from inside his helmet glinting off the sweat on his face. He is visibly changed, older and less sickly, so the title reading

SIX YEARS LATER

should not be any surprise.

MAL
I'm gonna boil it. Give me the sticky.

WIDEN to see Zoe, also six years older, also suited up. She and Mal are in zero grav, floating by a big iron door that has buckled but not burst during whatever tore this ship apart.

Floating nearby is JAYNE: a hulking, wary mercenary who keeps watch as the other two work. His face says "thug". His face don't lie.

Zoe hands Mal a sort of glue gun looking thing. He squeezes and a clear gel comes out. In the center of the gel is a thin thread, like a wire.

Mal squeezes a circle about a foot around on the middle of the door. Zoe reaches in and snips the wire with pliers.

Since there is no sound in space, all we hear is the labored breathing of three very tense people.

Mal pulls out a small device, looks almost like electric nosehair clippers, and clamps it onto the end of the wire.

He hits a switch on the device and a charge runs through the wire, causing a reaction in the gel that turns it incredibly acidic — it starts melting through the metal in a circle.

Mal moves away from the door, holds onto something near Zoe.

ANGLE: THE GEL

as it eats through the door, further and further...

INT. BRIDGE - CONTINUING

This (as we will learn in detail later) is the bridge of SERENITY, a small transport ship. The bridge itself is small and cluttered, more like someone's car than a pristine futuristic space vessel. In the pilot's seat sits WASH, a slightly shlumpy, unassuming fellow. He's concentrating intensely.

WASH
Everything looks good from here...
(beat)
Yes. Yes, this is a fertile land, and we will thrive.

It is at this point that we realize he's playing with little plastic dinosaurs. He holds a Stegosaurus and a T-rex (or whatever the hell they call 'em these days). The dinosaurs look out over his dash/console, toward the window.

WASH (cont'd)
(as Steg)
We will rule over all this land, and we will call it... This Land.
(as T-rex)
I think we should call it... your grave!
(Steg)
Curse your sudden but inevitable betrayal!
(T-rex)
Ha HA! Mine is an evil laugh! Now die!

He makes them fight. As he does, a light near him flashes red.

He stops fighting, looks, then looks at a sort of radar screen.

ANGLE: THE RADAR SCREEN

has got three other dinosaurs on it. He sweeps them off as a blip appears in the upper right quadrant, closing fast.

WASH (cont'd)
Oh, motherless son of a b —

FWOOSH! The circle of door shoots out toward us, as we're back in:

INT. BLOWN-OUT SHIP - CONTINUING

The piece of door flies across the room, bouncing off the wall right by Jayne — he catches it as it's ricochetting. What looks like steam pours out through the hole for a few moments.

ZOE
Full pressure. The goods should be intact.

MAL
Assuming they're still there.

He's floating to the door — sticks his hand in the hole and shoves, the door slides aside and Jayne shines a flashlight in there.

ANGLE: INSIDE THE CHAMBER

WASH'S DINOSAURS

Prop master Randy Eriksen: "I bought Wash's dinosaurs in the downtown LA toy district. I repainted them. They were made in China and were pretty cheap."

Three crates, roughly the size of haybales, sit in the dark.

MAL (cont'd)
Okay. Looking good.

A voice sounds simultaneously in all three headsets: Wash.

WASH (O.S.)
We have incoming! Alliance Cruiser, bearing right down on us!

MAL
<Ta ma de.> [Dammit.]
(continuing)
Have they spotted us?

WASH
I can't tell if —

MAL
Have they hailed us?

JAYNE
If they're here for the salvage, we're humped.

ZOE
This ship's been derelict for months. Why would they —

MAL
<Bizui.> [Shut up.]
(continuing)
Shut it down, Wash. Everything but the air.

INT. BRIDGE - CONTINUING

WASH
Shutting down.

He is flipping switches, we hear engines running down, lights go off — he hits the com:

WASH (cont'd)
Kaylee! KAYLEE!

INT. ENGINE ROOM - CONTINUING

KAYLEE rolls into frame from underneath a huge engine part, ups and runs to the com. She is young, zaftig — as cheery as she is sexy. She and her jumpsuit are, as usual, speckled with grease.

WASH
Kaylee! Go to black out! We're being buzzed!

She hits the com —

KAYLEE
<Shi> [Affirmative],
(continuing)
going dark —

and keeps moving, hitting switches — climbing atop the engine to pull the last lever. Everything goes pretty damn black.

KAYLEE (cont'd)
Okay. Now I can't get down.

INT. BLOWN-OUT SHIP - CONTINUING

Jayne, Zoe and Mal all hold their positions, tense.

MAL
(softly)
Wash. Where's the Crybaby?

INTERCUT WITH:

INT. BRIDGE - CONTINUING

WASH
Right where we left her. You want her to cry?

MAL
Not yet. They slowing down?

WASH
That's a neg. Don't think they're interested in us. We should be eating wake in a minute or two.

MAL
All right. They do a heat probe, you holler.

WASH
<Shi.> [Affirmative.]

Mal looks at the other two. They wait.

EXT. SPACE - CONTINUING

And we see it, in all its glory: An Alliance Cruiser. Sleek, huge, antiseptic. The AngloSino flag painted above the name, I.A.V. DORTMUNDER.

CAPTAIN (O.S.)
What am I looking at?

INT. DORTMUNDER BRIDGE - CONTINUING

Hey, it's big. And clean, and everything a spaceship is supposed to be. The CAPTAIN speaks with an ENSIGN. They are rigid, formal, their clothes somewhat Trekkian, with a more militaristic edge to it. They're Cops, Army, Ambassadors — they're the Man.

ENSIGN
It's a carrier, blew out a few months back. No survivors, but it was only run by a skeleton crew anyway.

Now we see their view: a huge window, in which the twisted wreck of a ship is a tiny speck, and a computerized window within in which it's magnified, a rotating 3D image.

CAPTAIN
Damn shame. No point in checking for survivors...?

ENSIGN
Locals swept it right after.

A moment, and the Captain takes off his hat. The Ensign follows suit as the Captain hits the com, his voice booming out around the ship:

CAPTAIN
Crew, a moment of respect, if you please. Passing a graveyard.

The other men in the ship respond by pulling off their hats and slightly bowing their heads, a couple looking out at the approaching ghostship.

INT. BLOWN-OUT SHIP - CONTINUING

Mal waits as through a piece of ripped out wall behind him, the ship, impossibly huge and dangerously close, passes by.

ANGLE: MAL'S FACE

is set with grim dislike, as the reflection of the passing ship plays across his faceplate.

He is silent. So are the others.

EXT. BLOWN-OUT SHIP - CONTINUING

As the Cruiser passes by, leaving the ship behind, all clear...

INT. DORTMUNDER BRIDGE - CONTINUING

A MAN seated at a screen suddenly brow-furrows.

MAN
Sir, there is a reading on that thing. Some residual heat...

CAPTAIN
Do a sweep.

INT. BRIDGE - CONTINUING

An alarm sound, lights blink.

WASH
<Aiya! Huaile.> [Something's wrong.]
(continuing)
Captain! We're humped!

INT. BLOWN-OUT SHIP - CONTINUING

MAL
Fire it up. Now!
(to the others)
We move these in, double-time!

They float to the crates, start dragging them (not hard in zero g).

INT. ENGINE ROOM - CONTINUING

It's still pitch black in here.

WASH (O.S.)
Fire it up! Kaylee!

KAYLEE
I'm all over it! I just gotta find the damn...

She hits the switch that gives her light. But in the action, topples off the engine she was perched on and out of frame.

KAYLEE (cont'd)
Wahh!

EXT. BLOWN-OUT SHIP

Mal, Jayne and Zoe move straight up through twisted metal, pushing their crates. Jayne is first, reaching the top and then proceeding forward, pushing off with crate in hand before him.

INT. BLOWN-OUT SHIP/AIRLOCK OF SERENITY - CONTINUING

Mal, Zoe and Jayne all float their crates past the twisted wreckage and into the airlock. Mal hits the button and the airlock door shuts. Hits another and gravity hits, the three of them landing on their feet, crates dropping, as air rushes in.

Mal hits the com.

MAL
Wash! We're on! Go!

EXT. BLOWN-OUT SHIP - CONTINUING

The Cruiser is a good ways away as part of the black, twisted shadow begins to disengage itself, and we see for the first time that Serenity was anchored to the wreck, hidden almost in her bowels.

Serenity is a small, buglike ship, patched together, rusted in parts — everything the Dortmunder is not. And teeny in comparison. It somewhat unfolds itself as it gets free.

INT. DORTMUNDER BRIDGE - CONTINUING

The Captain is watching on his screen.

CAPTAIN
What the hell?

INT. BRIDGE - CONTINUING

Wash is seated, all business now.

WASH
Hang on, travelers...

INT. AIRLOCK - CONTINUING

Everyone grabs something, as Jayne pulls off his helmet.

JAYNE
Let's moon 'em.

EXT. SERENITY - CONTINUING

As the ship turns away from us, the back lights up — the entire bulbous back end glowing beneath a metal grid.

The ship fires away from us.

INT. AIRLOCK - CONTINUING

Mal hits the com:

MAL
Cry, baby, cry.

WASH (O.S.)
Make your mother sigh. Engaging the Crybaby.

EXT. SPACE - CONTINUING

Behind some little moon, we see a tiny jet-propelled satellite-looking thing, beeping out its distress signal. It's roughly the size of a thermos, and has written on a piece of tape: "Crybaby #6".

INT. DORTMUNDER BRIDGE - CONTINUING

The Captain and Ensign are near the screen. The Captain's face goes cold with disgust.

MAN
It's a transport ship. Firefly class.

ENSIGN
They still make those?

CAPTAIN
Illegal salvage. Lowlife vultures picking the flesh off the dead.

ENSIGN
Should we deploy gunships, bring her in?

CAPTAIN
Do it.

MAN
Captain, I am picking up a distress signal thirteen clicks ahead... From a... it sounds like a personnel carrier...

EXT. DORTMUNDER - CONTINUING

We move from a front shot of the bridge below

the Dortmunder, to see gunships preparing to launch.

EXT. SPACE - CONTINUING

The Crybaby beeps.

INT. DORTMUNDER BRIDGE - CONTINUING

MAN
Definitely a big ship, sir, and she is without power.

CAPTAIN
(considering)
Gunships'd never get back to us in time... all right. Let's go help those people.
(to the Ensign)
Put a bulletin out on the Cortex, and flag Interpol: a Firefly with possible stolen goods aboard.
(almost to himself)
Maybe someone'll step on those roaches...

INT. CARGO HOLD - CONTINUING

The airlock feeds right into the cargo hold. It's a cavernous space with a great deal of junk cluttering it. The airlock door opens and Mal and the other two step out, clearly a bit tense. They all pull off their helmets.

WASH (O.S.)
We look shiny, Captain. They are not repeat not coming about.

ZOE
Close one.

JAYNE
Any one you walk away from, right? Long as those crates aren't empty, I call this a win.

MAL
Right.

He looks away, darkness in his gaze.

MAL (cont'd)
We win.

END OF TEASER

ACT ONE

INT. CARGO HOLD - LATER

A crate is jimmied open. It is Jayne with the crowbar, Mal who pulls the top off, looking in. Zoe, Wash and Kaylee are also about. Zoe, Jayne and Mal are already dressed in their regular clothes. [Add shot from inside hidden compartment.]

MAL
Well. There we are.

ANGLE: IN THE CRATE are bars that look a lot like gold.

KAYLEE
(excited)
They're awfully pretty...

WASH
I'd say worth a little risk.

JAYNE
Yeah, that was some pretty risky sitting you did there.

WASH
That's right, of course, 'cause they wouldn't arrest *me* if we got boarded, I'm just the pilot. I can always say I was flying the ship by accident.

MAL
(harshly)
<Bizui.> [Shut up.]

He has a bar in his hand, is looking at it up close.

ZOE
Problem, sir?

Clearly, there is. But Mal tries to cover — just a bit of tension creeping into his voice.

MAL
(after a moment)
Couldn't say.
(tosses the bar back)
But we'd best be rid of these 'fore we run into another Alliance patrol.

JAYNE
What the hell they doing this far out, anyhow?

KAYLEE
Shining the light of civilization.

JAYNE
Doesn't do us any good...

KAYLEE
Well, we're uncivilized.

As they talk, Mal approaches Wash, talking over them.

MAL
How long til we reach Persephone?

WASH
Three or four hours.

MAL
Can we shave that?

WASH
(shakes his head)
We're down to the wire on fuel cells. We run hot, we might not even make it.

MAL
Play it as close as you can. This catch is burning a hole in my hull.

ZOE
You think that Cruiser could've I.D.'d us?

MAL
Gotta hope not. Contact Badger, tell him the job's done. Don't go to mentioning the Cruiser, though. Keep it simple.

ZOE
Sir, we're sure there's nothing wrong with the carg —

MAL
It's fine. I just wanna get paid.

They head up the ladder as Mal turns his attention to:

MAL (cont'd)
Jayne, Kaylee, let's get these crates stowed. I don't want any tourists stumbling over them.

KAYLEE
We're taking on passengers at Persephone?

ANGLE - POV FROM HIDDEN COMPARTMENT

MAL
That's the notion. We could use a little respectability on the way to Boros. Not to mention the money.

JAYNE
I hate tourists...

INT. UPPER CORRIDOR/BRIDGE - CONTINUING

As Wash and Zoe crest the ladder and head to their positions, talking.

ZOE
I know something's not right.

WASH
Sweetie, we're crooks. If everything was right we'd be in jail.

ZOE
It's just, the Captain's so tense...

WASH
Man needs a break. In fact...

He pulls her towards him.

WASH (cont'd)
We could all use a couple days leave.

ZOE
We still gotta drop the goods —

WASH
And when we do, we'll fly off to Boros rich and prosperous. Well, less poor. But with enough to find some sweet little getaway...

ZOE
(loosening up)
Wouldn't mind a real bath...

WASH
And a meal that included some form of food... Just a couple of days, lying around... you with the bathing, me with the watching you bathe...

They're so close...

ZOE
If the Captain says it's all right...

Wrong. Wash shuts his eyes a moment, rests his head on hers, quietly pissed. He breaks apart.

WASH
What if we just told Mal we needed a few days, 'stead of asking him?

ZOE
He's the Captain, Wash.

WASH
Right. I'm just the husband.

He lands in his seat. She still stands.

ZOE
Look, I'll ask him.

WASH
Don't forget to call him "sir". He likes that.

MAL
Who likes what?

Instinctively, Zoe's demeanor changes as Mal enters, her bearing more erect, military.

ZOE
It's nothing, sir.

Wash looks at her excitedly, mouths, "good!" and gives the thumbs up. She looks away.

MAL
Has the Ambassador checked in?

WASH
Nah, I think she had a pretty full docket.

MAL
Well, after you talk to Badger, let her know we may be leaving Persephone in a hurry.

ZOE
Inara knows our timetable, she should be checking in.

WASH
I can tell her to cut it short, meet us at the docks.

MAL
No, no. Don't wanna get in her way if we don't have to.
(leaving)
Someone on this boat has to make an honest living.

INT. INARA'S CHAMBER - NIGHT

We are close on INARA's face. She is being made love to by an eager, inexperienced but quite pleasingly shaped YOUNG MAN. She is beneath him, drawing him to his climax with languorous intensity. His face buried in her neck.

INARA
Oh... Oh... Oh my god...

He tightens, relaxes, becomes still. She runs her hand through his hair and he pulls from her neck, looks at her with sweaty insecurity.

PERSEPHONE

She smiles, a worldly, almost motherly sweetness in her expression. He rests his head on her breast, still breathing hard.

INARA (cont'd)
(softly)
Oh my boy...

INT. SAME - LATER

They are seated on cushions, close to each other with their legs entwined, sipping tea from small cups. She has a robe on.

INARA
Sihnon isn't that different from this planet. More crowded, obviously, and I guess more complicated. The great city itself is... pictures can't capture it. It's like an ocean of light.

THE YOUNG MAN
Is that where you studied? To be a Companion?

INARA
(nodding)
I was born there.

THE YOUNG MAN
I can't imagine ever leaving.

There is but half truth in her reply, and a hint of weariness.

INARA
Well, I wanted to see the universe.

THE YOUNG MAN
My cousin hopes to become a Companion. But I don't think the Academy will take her unless her scores come up.

INARA
It was the languages I struggled with. And music, at first.

THE YOUNG MAN
You play beautifully.

INARA
Thank you.

He looks down at his cup a moment.

THE YOUNG MAN
Do you really have to leave? I mean... I, my father is very influential, we could... I could arrange for you to be with...

She smiles that knowing smile again, just a tinge of sadness in it. He doesn't continue.

INT. SAME - LATER

He is dressed and exiting, his manner slightly more diffident.

THE YOUNG MAN
A very — it was very good. Thank you.

INARA
The time went too quickly.

THE YOUNG MAN
Your clock's probably rigged to speed up and cheat us out of our fun.

The smile vanishes from her face. He looks guilty, then ducks out of the chamber, shutting the door behind him.

She takes a moment, then hits a button by the door, locking it and sealing it. She moves across the room and pulls aside a tapestry that conceals the cockpit of what we now see to be a small shuttle. Gets in the pilot's seat and hits a switch (and continues hitting them as she talks).

INARA
Serenity, this is Shuttle One, what's your ETA?

WASH (O.S.)
Inara, hey. We're touching down at the Eavesdown docks in about ten minutes.

INARA
I'll join you there, thanks.

WASH (O.S.)
Looking forward. We missed you out here.

INARA
(softly)
Yeah. Me too.

She punches a few buttons, rides the joystick, and the cockpit begins to shake slightly as we CUT TO:

EXT. CITY - DAY

The outside of the shuttle, which rises slowly into the air. As it does we see it is perched atop a skyscraper in a fairly big and ritzy city. It flies off.

INT. COCKPIT - DAY

Wash deftly pilots Serenity, light shifting across his face as the ship descends into atmo.

EXT. DOCKS - DAY

We see Serenity as she touches down at the Eavesdown docks. It's a bustling bazaar, ships lined up next to each other, each one advertising passage or selling goods. The place is filled with people of all races, modes and languages. It's chaos; trade, theft and outright violence all happening amidst the jumble of humanity.

This district is clearly poorer than the gleaming city in the distance, and every ship parked looks a tad haphazard — though Serenity does seem particularly small and ratty next to the ships it docks between.

The airlock opens, the ramp coming down and our gang piling out.

MAL
(to Kaylee)
This shouldn't take long. Put us down for departure in about three hours.
(to Wash)
Fuel her up, and grab any supplies we're low on.

Kaylee moves to a computerized placard in front of their 'parking space', starts entering data. We arm up to see it reads: DESTINATION: and that BOROS appears below that. The rest is filled in thus:

CAPACITY: TWELVE

DEPARTURE TIME: 1500

KAYLEE
I'd sure love to find a brand new compression coil for the steamer.

MAL
And I'd like to be king of all Londinum and wear a shiny hat. Just get us some passengers. Them as can pay, all right?

KAYLEE
Compression coil busts, we're drifting...

MAL
Best not bust, then.

Zoe, Jayne and Mal start off.

WASH
Zoe.
(then)
<Zhu yi.> [Watch your back.]

ZOE
We will.

He watches her move through the crowd.

EXT. EAVESDOWN DOCKS - DAY

We're in the middle of the hubbub. We see a sign that advertises: Good DOGS! Arm down to see a pen of scrawny, listless dogs of various breeds. Arm further down to see a griddle, with some suspicious looking cuts of meat sizzling on it. A man works the griddle.

We see, passing through frame, Shepherd BOOK. He's about sixty, weathered and worldly, with a quiet kindness in his eyes. Farmer stock, not a trace of bullshit and a workingman's hands. He drags a few boxes and suitcases on a sort of wheeled papoose, carries another suitcase in his hand. His clothes are plain and instantly identify him as some kind of protestant minister. As he moves on, looking about him, he is approached by a MAN, who's in his face a bit.

MAN
You going on a trip, grandpa? Need safe passage? We're cheap, we're cheap and clean, The BRUTUS is the best ship in the 'verse. What's your des, grandpa, we're hitting the outer rings —

BOOK
I never married.

MAN #2
What?

BOOK
I'm not a grandpa.

The guy just looks at him like he's crazy, lets him move on past the next barker, MAN #2. This guy is fancy, with people gathered around — his ship is clearly high class.

MAN #2
— three berths left, junior suites, we are not interested in Asian or Catholic passengers, thank you, we will be bidding for the last three berths —

Book moves on. Comes to the third dock in the row. It's Serenity's. Kaylee sits outside it in a lawn chair. He looks at it, never stopping, til Kaylee says, smiling:

KAYLEE
You're gonna come with us.

BOOK
Excuse me?

KAYLEE
You like ships. Don't seem to be looking at the destinations. What you care about is the ships and mine is the nicest.

She's completely innocuous. It's hard not to be

charmed by her. He does stop, gives the ship a look-over.

ANGLE: THE BRIDGE sticking out above them, SERENITY painted on the side.

BOOK
She don't look like much.

KAYLEE
She'll fool ya'. Ever sailed in a Firefly?

BOOK
Long before you were crawling. Not an aught three, though. Didn't have the extenders, tended to shake.

KAYLEE
You wanna shake, sail the PARAGON there. Guarantee you'll barf before you break atmo.

Book looks over at the fancy ship he just passed, clearly agreeing.

BOOK
They can dress her up pretty, but a Gurtlser engine's always gonna get twitchy on ya.
(re: Serenity)
The aught three still use the trace compression block?

KAYLEE
Til they make something better.

Now she pretty much thinks he's the cool fool too. There is a moment between them.

KAYLEE (cont'd)
So how come you don't care where you're going?

BOOK
'Cause how you get there is the worthier part.

KAYLEE
You a missionary?

BOOK
I guess... I'm a Shepherd, from the Southdown Abbey. Book, I'm called Book. Been out of the world for a spell. Like to walk it a while, maybe bring the word to them as need it told.

KAYLEE
I'm Kaylee. This is Serenity, and she's the smoothest ride from here to Boros for anyone can pay.
(beat, worried)
Can you pay?

BOOK
Not what they're charging on the Paragon. But I expect we could come to terms. I've got a little cash, and, uh...

He approaches her, with a small wooden box. Shows her the contents. She goes a little bit wide eyed, eyeing the contents lustfully.

KAYLEE
Oh, Grampa...

BOOK
I never married.

KAYLEE'S COSTUMES

Costume designer Shawna Trpcic: "At first, I thought that she was going to be Asian, so I got a bunch of books on Chinese and Japanese youths and girls — one book in particular was called *Fruit*. I was also inspired by the World War Two figure Rosie the Riveter and Chinese Communist posters, with Chairman Mao and everybody smiling. We blended all these ideas together.

"I loved it when Kaylee wore her little flirty dress [in 'The Message'] — I loved it when I got to break out of the army green or metric yellow jumpsuit. I also found some fabric downtown in a remnant store, and we just made a bunch of t-shirts from it, because that was kind of her uniform. The frilly little dress I made out of actual antique Japanese kimono fabric, from the pattern of a 1970s flower girl dress."

INT. - HALLWAY - DAY

Mal, Zoe, and Jayne walk down a hallway, past a row of gunmen.

INT. UNDERGROUND 'OFFICE' - DAY

This is BADGER's place. It's not too large, and kind of dingy. The ceiling has what looks like subway grates over it — we can hear the traffic above, and every now and then the bright white of a flying vehicle pours through the grate. On one side are stairs leading up to ground level and a door beside, at the other end an oversized, beat up desk and a way into the back through a curtain.

Badger is a petty thug with pretensions to Kingpinery. He has bad facial hair, bad teeth, a crushed derby and he wears a woolly three piece and tie, though he has only a wifebeater beneath.

We find him in the room with three thugs in the corners. A fourth, an old man, is holding the arm of a clearly frightened but slightly hopeful young woman. Badger inspects her.

BADGER
Let me see your teeth.

She gives him a big smile. He pulls her lip up, the other one down.

BADGER (cont'd)
Yes.

She looks apprehensively pleased as she is shuttled behind the curtain. As she is, yet another thug leads Mal, Zoe and Jayne down the stairs. Badger doesn't look at them, heading for his desk.

BADGER (cont'd)
You're late.

MAL
You're lying.

Everybody tenses as Badger turns.

BADGER
What did you just say to me?

MAL
You're well aware we landed two hours 'fore we planned to, with all the goods you sent us after intact and ready to roll. So your decision to get tetchy and say we're late means you're looking to put us on the defensive right up front. Which means something's gone wrong and it didn't go wrong at our end so why don't we start again with you telling us what's up?

A beat. A mean little smile from Badger.

BADGER
You're later than I'd like.

MAL
Well I am sorry to hear that.

Badger sits. Briefly holds up what appears to be digital paper: a clear, pliable piece of plastic with words and images running across it, constantly changing.

BADGER
If you'd gotten here sooner, you might've beaten the bulletin that came up saying a rogue vessel, classification "Firefly", was spotted pulling illegal salvage on a derelict transport.

MAL
They didn't ID us. Doesn't lead to you.

As he speaks he sticks an apple on a rusty old peeler, slowly turns it.

BADGER
No, it doesn't. But the government stamp on every molecule of the cargo just maybe might.

Zoe looks at Mal — that's what he didn't say when he examined the bars.

BADGER'S APPLE PEELER

Prop master Randy Eriksen: "Another great prop was the hand-cranked apple peeler in Badger's place. I think it was Joss Whedon's. It looked really cool."

BADGER (cont'd)
Oh, you noticed that. You were gonna hand over imprinted goods and just let me twist, is that the case?

MAL
We didn't pick the cargo.

BADGER
And I didn't flash my ass at the gorramn law. There's no deal.

ZOE
That ain't fair.

BADGER
Crime and politics, little girl: the situation is always fluid.

JAYNE
Only fluid I see here is the puddle of piss refusing to pay us our wage.

Guns are raised, cocked.

Mal shoots Jayne a look that shuts him right up.

Mal steps forward and Badger rises — but Mal is reasonable of tone.

MAL
Doesn't have to go this way. You know you can still unload those goods. So I can't help thinking there's something else at work here.

As he talks, two more girls are hustled in. They are nudged, and both smile at Badger.

BADGER
(re: one)
Yes.
(re: other)
No.
(to Mal)
I don't like you.

He makes a face, reconsidering —

BADGER (cont'd)
(to his thug, re: other)
Dyeahh... yes.

The girl is pushed through the curtain after the first one. Badger calls after them:

BADGER (cont'd)
But keep her in the back, yeah?

MAL
I'm not asking you to like me —

BADGER
(overlapping)
What were you in the war? That big war you failed to win — you were a sergeant? Yeah, Sergeant Malcolm Reynolds, Balls and Bayonets Brigade, big tough veteran, now you got yourself a ship and you're a captain! Only I think you're still a sergeant, see. Still a soldier, man of honor in a den of thieves.
(in his face)
Well it's my gorramn den and I don't like the way you look down on me. I'm above you. Better than. I'm a businessman, yeah? Roots in the community. You're just a scavenger.

MAL
Maybe I'm not a fancy gentleman like you with your... very fine hat... but I do business. We're here for business.

BADGER
Try one of the border planets — they're a lot more desperate there. Of course they might kill you, but you stay here and I just know the Alliance'll track you down. I have that feeling.

MAL

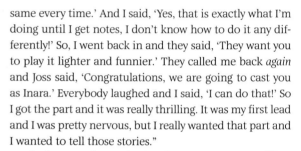

"We've done the impossible, and that makes us mighty."

For anyone confused about what *Firefly* is really about, all one needs to do is look past the spaceships and Western attire. Ignore the rag-tag heists and wacky, ethnically fused colloquialisms. Bypass the terrifying Reavers and omnipotent Alliance to get to the actual heart of the series, which is the story of a dark, world-weary man with an unshakeable love and loyalty for his adopted family. That man is Captain Malcolm Reynolds and it's on his shoulders that *Firefly* firmly rests. Suffice to say, only the right actor could bring Mal's particular mix of pathos, humor and strength to life in perfect harmony and Joss Whedon found his casting zen with actor Nathan Fillion. Equal parts handsome, rugged, goofy and tragic, Fillion inhabited the character from the moment he stepped on set and made Malcolm his own.

The actor still remembers landing the part with enthusiasm. "I walked into [casting director] Amy Britt's office to have a meeting with Joss," Fillion says. "It was dimly lit and warm and cozy in there. I knew of Joss Whedon but had never met him, nor did I know what he looked like. There was this scroungy-looking fella in the corner. He had a purple sweater on with a hole in it on the left side on his chest and I thought, 'Who's this guy and when do I meet Joss?' Halfway through the meeting, it dawned on me who *he* was," the actor laughs. "Joss told me a great

deal about the show. I had so many questions and Joss had the answers. For whatever I asked, he had an entire universe planned. I was enthralled. We talked about the show, personal experiences, work ethics, how to keep things smooth on sets and it became apparent that we had similar sensibilities. He said, 'Why don't you come back and audition for Malcolm Reynolds?' I said, 'Great', and did just that. I remember I auditioned and they had me come back and do it again. I left and they had me come back and do it *again*. Joss then came out and said, 'They think you are doing it the same every time.' And I said, 'Yes, that is exactly what I'm doing until I get notes, I don't know how to do it any differently!' So, I went back in and they said, 'They want you to play it lighter and funnier.' They called me back *again* and Joss said, 'Congratulations, we are going to cast you as Inara.' Everybody laughed and I said, 'I can do that!' So I got the part and it was really thrilling. It was my first lead and I was pretty nervous, but I really wanted that part and I wanted to tell those stories."

The key to Mal's motivations became clear once Fillion figured out what his Serenity family truly represented. "I always imagined that since he's had so much taken away from him that he had such a fear of losing anything else, especially something that might make him happy, and that's sad. Somebody asked me why he so zealously guards over the safety of his crew and I look at it that Mal gathers to him that which he no longer has within himself. In Wash, he has a lust for life and a sense of humor he's lost. In Jayne, he has selfishness. In Book, he has spirituality. In Kaylee, he has innocence. Everybody represents a facet of himself that he has lost and that's why he keeps them close and safe, and yet at arm's length."

The cast in reality brought just as much to Fillion too. "It was very much a family. They all knew exactly what they were doing and I credit Joss with that. He found not only talented actors, not only people who understood the kind of lilt to the language or the personas for their characters, but everybody brought so much to the table that it made my job so incredibly easy. People are looking at me like I'm the Captain, like I might be dangerous, like I'm their friend — everybody did my work for me. I also credit Joss with having created a family. I don't know how you do that but he did it and I am a richer man for it. The quality of my life has improved because of *Firefly*, not just because of the employment and things it did for me, but because of the people. It sounds corny and hokey, but I loved being Mal Reynolds. I really, really did. I loved having all the adventures, riding horses, flying spaceships, shooting guns. I had a great time being cool, being funny, the awesome coat and the wicked gun, but I walked away from that with close friends. I'm a lucky man."

Long beat. Mal is inches from starting a firefight — Jayne is less than inches. Zoe merely waits to back Mal's play.

But Mal turns to go. As he's leaving, he says:

MAL
Wheel never stops turning, Badger.

BADGER
That only matters to the people on the rim.

EXT. EAVESDOWN DOCKS - LATER

OPEN ON: The clash of wooden swords as two kabuki actors fight on a raised dais for the crowd. Whip pan off this action to track quickly in front of Mal, Zoe and Jayne as they head back to the ship.

JAYNE
I don't understand why we didn't leave that sumbitch in a pool of his own blood.

MAL
We'd be dead. Can't get paid if you're dead.

JAYNE
Can't get paid if you crawl away like a bitty little bug, neither. I got a share in this job, and ten percent of nothing, uh — hold on. Let me do the math here... nothing into nothing... carry the nothing...

ZOE
(overlapping him)
We'll just find a buyer on Boros. There's gotta be —

MAL
Boros is too big. It's crawling with Alliance, they could just be waiting for us.

ZOE
You really think Badger'd sell us out to the feds?

Mal looks over at:

ANGLE: TWO COPS looking around them, as though searching for something.

MAL
If he hasn't already.

ZOE
Alliance catches us with government goods, we'll lose the ship.

MAL
That's never gonna happen.

She stops, turns to him.

ZOE
We could just dump the cargo, sir.

JAYNE
No rutting way! We ain't had a job in weeks! I didn't sign up with this crew to take in the sights, all right? We need coin!

MAL
Jayne, your mouth is talking. You might wanna look to that.

JAYNE
(belligerent)
I'm ready to stop talking whenev —

MAL
You're right, though.

This stops Jayne — didn't expect to hear that.

MAL (cont'd)
Last two jobs we had were weak tea. We got nothing saved, and taking on passengers won't help near enough. We don't get paid for this cargo, we won't have enough money to fuel the ship, let alone keep her in repair. She'll be dead in the water.

ZOE
So we do like Badger said? The border planets?

MAL
(nodding)
I'm thinking we can hit Whitefall, maybe talk to Patience.

Zoe is clearly unhappy with this notion.

ZOE
Sir, we don't wanna deal with Patience again.

MAL
Why not?

ZOE
She shot you!

MAL
Well, yeah, she did a bit. Still...

He starts walking again, the others falling into step.

ZOE
So we find someone else. Horowitz.

MAL
He can't afford it.

ZOE
The Holden boys.

MAL
They wouldn't touch it. You want me to run down the list? The Capshaws are brainblown, Gruviek's dead...

ZOE
He's dead?

MAL
Town got hit by Reavers. Burned it right down.

JAYNE
Hey, I'm not going anywhere near Reaver territory. Those people ain't human.

MAL
Whitefall is the closest and the safest. Been a long

while since Patience shot me, and that was due to a perfectly legitimate conflict of interest. I got no grudge. She owns half that damn moon now, she can afford what we got and she might just need it.

ZOE
I still say the old lady's not —

MAL
(turns to her)
There's only one thing that matters.

She looks at him, then up past him, as he turns as well to look at:

ANGLE: SERENITY. They have reached her.

MAL (cont'd)
I'm not saying it won't be tricky. But we got no kind of choice.

MAL'S POV: still looking at Serenity, he sees Kaylee welcoming another passenger, introducing himself as:

DOBSON
Dobson... Thank you...

He stumbles, nearly dropping his luggage — he's just a bit bumbly and sweet. Over this we hear:

MAL
We just gotta keep our heads down and do the job. Pray there ain't no more surprises.

He is standing by the airlock ramp as he says it, looking at:

ANGLE: A BOX. Being loaded on by Wash on a dolly/truck is, among a few other things, a clearly special, futuristic-looking dark blue box with many dials and readouts.

The box clears frame to reveal SIMON, a young, clearly affluent man. He wears a dark suit and round glasses. He seems to be looking directly at Mal, then glances over to the box.

SIMON
(to Wash)
Please be careful with that.

KAYLEE
Mal, this is Simon. This is our Captain.

Both men size each other up, neither particularly anxious to make conversation.

SIMON
Captain Reynolds.

MAL
Welcome aboard.
(to Kaylee)
This all we got?

INT. CARGO BAY

Wash and Jayne are unloading stuff. We see Book and Simon unpacking — pan over to find Zoe moving to Mal, who is near the hidden compartment.

ZOE
So now we got a boatload of citizens right on top of our stolen cargo. That's a fun mix.

MAL
There's no way in the 'verse they could find that compartment, even if they were looking.

ZOE
Why not?

MAL
...'Cause.

ZOE
Yeah, this is gonna go great...

MAL
If anybody gets nosy, you just, you know... shoot 'em.

ZOE
Shoot them.

MAL
Politely.

INT. BRIDGE - DAY

Wash is prepping her for take off, sees a signal, flips a switch.

WASH
Inara. You're just in time.

INARA (O.S.)
Let me guess. We're in a hurry.

WASH
Looks like. Port hatch green for docking.

INARA (O.S.)
Locked in five. Four.

EXT. SERENITY - CONTINUING

As Inara's flying shuttle locks onto a side of the still-parked ship.

INT. INARA'S SHUTTLE - CONTINUING

As she feels the lurch of lock. She doesn't leave the pilot's seat.

INT. BRIDGE - CONTINUING

Wash turns, calls back:

WASH
The Ambassador has returned.

He is talking to Zoe, who moves to the

INT. CARGO BAY/AIRLOCK - CONTINUING

and calls down to Mal, who is stowing cargo with Jayne:

ZOE
We got a full house, Captain.

He turns to the airlock:

MAL
Kaylee. Lock it up!

EXT. AIRLOCK - CONTINUING

Kaylee looks around once...

KAYLEE
(softly)
All aboard...

ANGLE: SIMON

as he passes his box, looking at it, looking coldly at Mal.

EXT. PERSEPHONE - DAY

As Serenity shoots away from the atmosphere and into the black of space.

END OF ACT ONE

ACT TWO

EXT. SPACE - LATER

Serenity moves silently through. It is a tiny light in the black of space.

INT. PASSENGER DORM - LATER

MAL (O.S.)
Meals are taken up here in the dining area, the kitchen is pretty much self explanatory, you're welcome to eat what there is any time...

NATHAN FILLION

I put on my costume in my trailer and took one last look in the mirror. They called me to the set and I remember coming right from my trailer to inside the door of the set. When you walked into the studio, the ship was just to your left with the big open cargo bay door looking at ya. I remember walking up the cargo bay door for the first time in costume. I believe it was David Boyd, our director of photography, who turned and saw me walking up and turned back around to the crew and said, 'Captain on deck.' Some people clapped and it was kind of neat. It was a reception I will remember always.

We see Dobson hurriedly coming out of the bathroom and up the stairs from the passenger section to the upstairs

INT. DINING ROOM - CONTINUING

as Mal has already begun addressing the other two passengers. Zoe and Kaylee are there as well.

MAL
...What there is is pretty standard fare, I guess, protein in all the colors of the rainbow. We do have sit-down meals, the next being at about 1800 —

KAYLEE
(excited)
I think Shepherd Book has offered to help me prepare something.

MAL
(to Book, less excited)
You're a Shepherd.

BOOK
Thought the outfit gave it away. Is it a problem?

KAYLEE
Of course not!
(to Mal)
It's not a problem, 'cause it's not.

MAL
No.
(to the bunch)
As I said, you're welcome to visit the dining area any time. Apart from that, I have to ask you to stay in the passenger dorm while we're in the air. The bridge, the engine room and the cargo bay are off limits without an escort.

SIMON
Some of my personal effects are in the cargo bay.

MAL
I figure you all got luggage you'll need to get into. Soon as we're done here we'll be happy to fetch 'em with you. Now I have to tell you all one other thing and I apologize in advance for the inconvenience — Unfortunately, we've been ordered by the Alliance to drop some medical supplies on Whitefall. It's the fourth moon on Athens, a bit out of our way, but we should have you on Boros no more than a day off schedule. Is that gonna be all right for everyone?

BOOK
Jake by me...

SIMON
What medical supplies?

MAL
I honestly didn't ask.

ZOE
Probably plasma, insulin, whatever they ain't got enough of on the border moons.

MAL
Alliance says jump...

SIMON
All right.

These two clearly already don't trust each other. Book watches the both of them, sensing the dynamic.

DOBSON
I'm supposed to be meeting my wife's sister. I've only a few days to see her...

ZOE
I wish there was another way...

DOBSON
Oh, no, no. That woman is like a dragon. I mean, I believe she has a tail. If there's any other moons we need to visit, or if we could just fly very slowly...

The tension is broken — people smile at Dobson's disarming relief.

WASH
One last thing, sorry — Your Firefly is a solid boat, but she's older... We've been having a bit of interference with our aeronautics, the new frequencies... we need to ask you all to stay off the Cortex, at least til we get to Whitefall. We should be able to correct the problem there.

MAL
Zoe, why don't you take 'em down to the cargo bay?

ZOE
Yes sir.

As the others start leaving, Mal moves close to Wash:

MAL
You send word to Patience?

WASH
Ain't heard back. Didn't she shoot you one time?

MAL
Everyone's making a fuss...

INT. CARGO BAY - LATER

People are getting the luggage they need. Dobson is spilling clothes out of his case — he's a perpetual bumbler.

Simon is also placing things into an elegant little valise — all the while eyeing his special blue box.

Book places something wrapped in tissue into a wooden box, hands it to Kaylee, who beams at him.

ANGLE: THE SECOND SHUTTLE HATCH

opens, showing Inara's shuttle. She steps out of it, in a simple but elegant dress. The hatch opens onto a catwalk that runs above the space in an 'X', the opposite side being the entrance to the first shuttle. She descends stairs as the group notices her.

MAL
The Ambassador graces us with her presence.

Book looks up — and Inara does indeed look the part of a lady of state.

INARA
Hello, Mal. I see we have some new faces.

KAYLEE
Hey you.

INARA
Hey you.

There is sweetness between those two. Not so much with Mal, whom Inara approaches.

MAL
Ambassador, this is Shepherd Book.

INARA
I'd have to say this is the first time we've had a preacher on board.

BOOK
Well, I wasn't expecting to see a state official, either.
(takes her hand, bows slightly)
Ambassador.

Mal laughs. Inara glowers at him.

BOOK (cont'd)
I'm missing something funny.

KAYLEE
(glaring at Mal)
Not so funny.

INARA
"Ambassador" is Mal's way of —

MAL
She's a whore, Shepherd.

Book's clearly a little thrown. And disapproving.

KAYLEE
The term is "Companion".

MAL
Yeah, but the job is whore.
(to Inara)
How's business?

INARA
None of yours.

MAL
(to Book)
She is pretty much our Ambassador. There's plenty of planets won't even let you dock without a decent Companion on board. This isn't a problem for you, is it?

BOOK
Well, I... no, I certainly...

INARA
(turns to go)
It's all right. I mostly keep to myself.

(passing Mal)
When I'm not whoring.

MAL
Don't you wanna meet the rest of the bunch?

INARA
Why don't you make sure they want to meet me first.

Inara and Kaylee start out together.

KAYLEE
So how many fell madly in love with you and wanted to take you away from all this?

INARA
Just the one. I think I'm slipping.

INT. DINING ROOM - CONTINUING

Kaylee has made her way up with the box, lays it on the counter. Quietly excited, she opens it, looks in. A beat, then she pulls out a strawberry.

It's just as red and luscious as it could be. She smells it, slowly puts it in her mouth, eyes closing. Watching her savor it is not an entirely unsensual experience.

She swallows it. Smiles, broad and bright.

INT. DINING ROOM - LATER

We see a sparse but none-the-less inviting spread — Book and Kaylee have made a salad of tomatoes, and grilled up some root vegetables along with the pasta and protein/starch mush that is the usual diet of space travelers. To us, not much. To this crowd, a banquet.

People are gathering, sitting, helping themselves to things — everybody's moving and talking over each other and everyone's there save Wash and Inara.

ZOE
Oh, this is incredible.

BOOK
It's not much — I had a garden at the Abbey, thought I should bring what I could.

SIMON
It's very kind of you to share with all of us.

ZOE
I'm gonna make a plate for Wash...

BOOK
(to Simon)
Well, it won't last, and they're never the same when they're frozen.

The important thing is the spices. A man can live on packaged food from here til Judgement Day if he's got enough Marjoram.

DOBSON
(over this, to Jayne)
Can you pass me the tomatoes?

He does, after taking several slices. People settle.

BOOK
Captain, would you mind if I say grace?

MAL
Only if you say it out loud.

A beat — Mal has broken the mood. He starts eating, others follow. Book lowers his head a moment, as do Kaylee, Dobson and Jayne, then they eat as well.

SIMON
So, does it happen a lot? Government commandeering your ship, telling you where to go?

MAL
That's what governments are for. Get in a man's way.

DOBSON
But it's good, if the supplies are needed...

JAYNE
Yeah, we're just happy to be doing good works.

DOBSON
I hear a lot of the border moons are in bad shape. Plagues, and famine...

ZOE
Well, some of that's exaggerated, and some of it ain't. All those moons — just like the central planets, they're as close to Earth-That-Was as we could make 'em: atmosphere, gravity and such, but...

MAL
Once they're terraformed, they'll dump settlers on there with nothing but blankets and hatchets and maybe a herd. Some of them make it, some of them...

SIMON
Then I guess it's good we're helping.

KAYLEE
(to Simon)
You're a doctor, right?

SIMON
Oh. Uh, yes. Yes, I was a trauma surgeon on Osiris, in Capital City.

MAL
Long way from here.

KAYLEE
(to Simon)
You seem so young. To be a doctor.

SIMON
(changing the subject)
You're pretty young to be a ship's mechanic.

KAYLEE
Know how. Machines just got workings, and they talk to me.

BOOK
That's a rare gift.

KAYLEE
Not like being a doctor, helping fix people, that's important. It's kind of comforting to have a doctor on board.

JAYNE
Little Kaylee just wishes you was a gynecologist.

Kaylee, visibly humiliated, looks down.

MAL
Jayne. You'll keep a civil tongue in that mouth or I will sew it shut, is there an understanding between us?

JAYNE
(pushing)
You don't pay me to talk pretty.

MAL
Walk away from this table. Right now.

FOOD

Prop master Randy Eriksen: "I had to do all the weird food. We used Heirloom tomatoes, you know, the purple ones. We had orange ones and we used risotto and Israeli couscous. Adam ate like crazy. The crew was all sitting down eating and they make Jayne get up and leave because he was rude. He was shoveling this food into his mouth and I had to keep resetting his plate over and over. He must have eaten like five plates of this couscous. Adam is a big guy."

A beat, and Jayne goes, grabbing a bunch of food as he does. Everyone is silent a moment.

SIMON
What do you pay him for?

MAL
What?

SIMON
I was just wondering what his job is. On the ship.

Mal stares a moment.

MAL
Public relations.

INT. INARA'S CHAMBER - LATER

Inara is kneeling, robe pooled at her waist. She is sponging off — the only kind of bathing you'll find on this ship. A knock on the hatch...

INARA
<Qing jin.> [Come in.]

Book enters. She is facing mostly away from him, but she sees it's him. She continues to bathe herself, running the sponge over her breasts, more in defiance than seduction.

MORENA BACCARIN

On bathing semi-nude: "I prepared by just getting really nervous! It is basically one of those things you have to do and luckily, I had a great director who was very respectful. I can't imagine doing anything like that with somebody who doesn't give a crap. It was a great crew, everybody was quiet and silent and looking down the whole time unless they happened to be looking through a camera. Of course, they reshot it three times because Joss kept saying something about a filter — to this day, I don't believe him! However, that wasn't my most embarrassing scene, because I had my back to everyone. What was more embarrassing was when I had to orgasm. That was much worse. Hopefully, you just make noises and Joss goes 'Okay, that's enough!'"

BOOK
If I'm intruding...

INARA
Not at all. I expected you.

BOOK
Couldn't really say the same.

INARA
So. Would you like to lecture me on the wickedness of my ways?

BOOK
I brought you some supper. But if you'd prefer a lecture, I've a few very catchy ones prepped. Sin and hellfire. One has lepers.

INARA
I think I'll pass. But thank you for these.

BOOK
The Captain said you might like them. I was surprised at his concern.

INARA
For a lowly whore?

BOOK
It was unjust of him to say that.

INARA
Believe me, I've called him worse. Anyway, I suspect he has more interest in making you uncomfortable than me.

BOOK
He's not wildly interested in ingratiating himself with anyone. Yet he seems very protective of his crew. It's odd.

INARA
Why are you so fascinated by him?

BOOK
Because he's something of a mystery. Why are you?

A beat, as she decides to play cards up.

INARA
Because so few men are.

She sounds almost weary when she says it. Her feelings for him are clearly complex.

INT. MAL'S ROOM - CONTINUING

It's a tiny cell, just a bunk and a tiny fold-down desk. A ladder runs up to the hatch (the crew rooms are under the foredeck hall). The room is cluttered with junk, pictures, general mess.

Mal is in the heroic act of doing up his trousers as we find him. There is a kind of metal drawer that hinges open to knee level. It's the toilet, and Mal kicks it shut, causing a flushing sound not unlike an airplane toilet. Above it is another metal drawer. He pulls it open and it's a small sink. He runs a little water on his hands, splashes his face, when the com sounds.

WASH (O.S.)
Mal, you might wanna get up here...

Mal's up the ladder in a flash.

INT. FOREDECK HALL - CONTINUING

The hatch, set at the side of the hall at a forty-five degree angle between floor and wall, slides open and Mal climbs up. He moves through the hall to:

INT. BRIDGE - CONTINUING

Where Wash is studying a screen.

MAL
What is it?

WASH
Signal. Somebody went on the Cortex, hailed the nearest Alliance Cruiser.

❖ Above: Dobson's Astra 400 stunt pistol.

MAL
Tell me you scrambled it.

WASH
All to hell, but I don't know how much got through. Alliance got a pin in us for sure.

MAL
<Ni ta ma de. Tianxia suoyoude ren. Dou gaisi.> [Everyone under the heavens ought to die.]

WASH
We got a mole on board.

Mal's face hardens as he works it out...

INT. CARGO BAY - MOMENTS LATER

Simon is checking on his box, looking at lights and gages. The lights are low now and he is furtive and very quiet, crouching on the larger crate on which his luggage sits. He finishes and steps down.

He turns and Mal is standing before him.

MAL
Forget your toothpaste?

Mal SLUGS him, sends him sprawling. Simon feels his head, furious, as Mal shakes his hurt hand.

SIMON
Are you out of your mind?

MAL
Just about. What'd you tell them?

SIMON
(standing)
Tell who?

Mal draws his gun, puts in in Simon's face.

MAL
I have exactly no time for games. What do they know.

SIMON
You are a lunatic.

MAL
And you're a gorramn fed.

BOOK
Hate to say it, Captain, but you've got the wrong man.

Both men turn to him, Mal stunned to think the Shepherd is actually a fed. A beat, and both Mal and Simon realize Book is looking behind them. Slowly, they turn the other way, and understand Book's meaning.

Dobson holds a gun on Mal.

MAL
(defeated)
Son of a bitch.

DOBSON
Drop that firearm, Captain Reynolds.

A beat, and Mal does.

MAL
This is not my best day ever.

Dobson moves the gun to point it at Simon.

DOBSON
Simon Tam, you are bound by law to stand down.

Mal takes a moment to realize the man is after Simon. Switches gears instantly:

MAL
You — what — the Doctor? Oh!
(indignant at Simon)
Hey!
(hopeful, to Dobson)
Is there a reward?

END OF ACT TWO

ACT THREE

INT. CARGO BAY - CONTINUING

Right where we left off. Dobson is ignoring Mal, focusing on Simon. This bumbling businessman is now a very intense, tightly wound cop.

DOBSON
(to Simon)
Get on the ground. Get on the ground!

SIMON
Lawman, you're making a mistake.

MAL
I think you oughta get on the ground, son. Man seems a mite twitchy.

BOOK
I think everybody could stand to calm down a bit.

He is moving slowly towards Dobson, hoping to defuse.

DOBSON
This isn't your business, Shepherd.

BOOK
The boy's not going anywhere, Lawman. As I understand it, it's pretty cold outside.

Mal moves casually for his gun — he's of the righteous now.

MAL
Not to worry. We can hold Lord Fauntleroy in a passenger cell — won't make a peep til you hand him over to —

DOBSON
(pointing the gun at Mal again)
Get the hell away from that weapon! You think I'm a complete backbirth? You're carrying a fugitive across interplanetary borders and do you think I actually believe you're bringing medical supplies to Whitefall? As far as I care, everyone on this ship is culpable.

MAL
(icy calm)
Well now. That has an effect on the landscape.

BOOK
Please, we're very close to true stupidity here —

DOBSON
I got a Cruiser en route for intercept, so talk all you want. You got about twenty minutes.

MAL
Might have less than that.

DOBSON
Yeah, threaten me...

BOOK
(still moving)
For God's sake —

DOBSON
You think I wouldn't shoot a Shepherd? Back off!

Mal grabs Simon — and everybody's shouting —

MAL
Just take the kid!

SIMON
Get your hands off —

DOBSON
Stand the hell down —

KAYLEE
Hey, what's —

Dobson spins and FIRES.

Kaylee steps backwards, puzzled, as Jayne steps in behind her —

KAYLEE (cont'd)
Wait, why are you...

She puts her hand to her belly. Blood runs over it.

A lot of things happen. Kaylee slumps to the ground as Simon rushes to her, Mal dives for his weapon, Jayne draws his, Dobson swings to fire at Mal —

— and Book is in Dobson's face, a brutal jab in

the throat as he grabs his gun-hand whip-quick, twists and pulls the gun out, cracking Dobson across the face with it in the same motion and Dobson is down. In seconds.

INARA
Kaylee!

She is on the upper level, having come out of her shuttle at the sound of the shot. She races to Kaylee, as does Mal, seeing that Dobson is no longer a threat.

Jayne comes toward Dobson with a purpose, gun in hand, and Book turns to face him.

JAYNE
Get out of the way.

BOOK
You're not killing this man.

JAYNE
Not right away...

BOOK
He's not a threat.

JAYNE
Move.

BOOK
Not gonna happen.

JAYNE
(raising his gun)
I'm not joking with you, Preacher —

ZOE
Jayne!

She's got her gun out, pointed at Jayne.

ZOE (cont'd)
Just tie him up. Do it!

A moment, and Jayne holsters his piece, moves to get some duct tape.

ZOE (cont'd)
(to Book)
The gun, Shepherd. Please.

Book hands her Dobson's gun. A bit of blood drips off it.

ANGLE: KAYLEE AND THE OTHERS

(NOTE: much of this action will be happening simultaneously with the other.)

Simon lays Kaylee prone, keeping her head up

til the others join him.

SIMON
Lie back. How do you feel?

KAYLEE
A little odd. Why'd he... oh...

Inara and Mal join them.

SIMON
(to Inara)
Put something under her head.

Inara pulls off her robe (she is dressed beneath) and bunches it under Kaylee's head, as Simon rips open Kaylee's jumpsuit, examines the wound. It's not pretty.

MAL
(to Kaylee)
Well, that ain't hardly a mosquito bite.

He and Inara exchange a glance that means something very different.

KAYLEE
Big... mosquito...

SIMON
Can you move your feet? Kaylee. Stay with me. Can you move your feet?

KAYLEE
Are you... asking me to dance...?

Her eyes start to roll back —

SIMON
She's going into shock.

INARA
Kaylee, <xiao meimei> [little sister], you gotta focus.

Simon pushes Kaylee's stomach and she screams.

SIMON
(to Mal)
The infirmary working?

MAL
We got it stocked.

They move to pick her up —

WASH (O.S.)
(on the com)
Captain, we've been hailed by a Cruiser. Ordered to stay on course and dock for prisoner transfer.

Mal and Simon look at each other.

Simon rises, steps away from Kaylee. He is tense, but surprisingly calm.

SIMON
Change course. Run.

MAL
Hell with you. You brought this down on us, I'm dumping you with the law.

INARA
Mal...

SIMON
She's dying.

MAL
You're not gonna let her.

SIMON
Yes I am.

MAL
You can't.

Simon looks at Kaylee, helpless and sweet.

ZOE
No way the feds'll let us walk.

MAL
Then we dump him in the shuttle and leave him for them.

KAYLEE
(delirious)
Everybody's so mad...

INARA
It's okay, baby...

SIMON
You know what a stomach wound does to a person?

MAL
I surely do.

SIMON
Then you know how crucial the next few minutes are.

ZOE
(to Simon)
You let her die you'll never make it to the feds.

SIMON
She'll still be dead.

MAL
You rich kids, you think your lives are the only thing that matters. What'd you do? Kill your folks for the family fortune?

SIMON
I don't kill people.

MAL
Then do your job!

SIMON
Turn the ship around!

INARA
Enough! Mal, do it.

MAL
Don't ever tell me —

Kaylee screams again.

Mal and Simon stare at each other.

MAL (cont'd)
(eyes on Simon)
Zoe. Change course.

SIMON
Help me get her up.

Mal and Inara hoist with Simon.

INARA
It's back behind you.

ZOE
(hits the com)
Wash, change course and go for hard burn. We're running.

EXT. SPACE - CONTINUING

As the ship turns and the back lights up wicked bright — and she shoots off.

INT. INFIRMARY - MOMENTS LATER

The three of them burst in, lay Kaylee on the table. It's small and not wildly sterile here, but it is clearly functional.

SIMON
You have an extractor?

MAL
Laser saw. We can go in —

SIMON
Not good enough. In my room, the red bag.

Inara goes. Simon raids the cupboards, finds a hypo-gun and vials.

MAL
This is over, you and me are gonna have a personal chat.

SIMON
Won't that be fun.
(tosses Mal the hypo)
Dope her.

INT. INFIRMARY - CONTINUING

We see, over time, VARIOUS ANGLES of Simon operating. What's clear here is that this guy is supremely confident and good at his job. Mal and Inara assist — mostly Mal, who has the most field experience. Among the images are:

— Simon using the extractor to find and pull out the bullet shards.

— Mal holding the wound open while Simon works a laser/scope inside her. Both men with bloody hands.

— Inara holding a breathing mask over Kaylee's face, looking at instruments indicating her vitals.

— a vid image of a laser sewing up a hole in her liver.

— Inara handing over bandages as Simon sews the wound shut.

INT. INFIRMARY - LATER

Simon washes off his hands. He turns to Mal.

SIMON
I can't do any more until she stabilizes.

MAL
Will she?

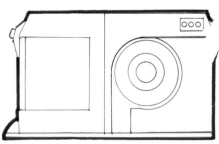

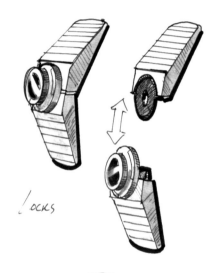

Locks

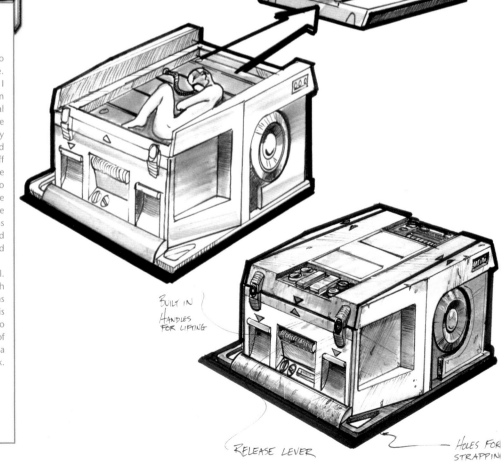

RIVER'S BLUE BOX

Prop master Randy Eriksen: "River's blue cryo box was the biggest prop we made for sure. We designed it and Neotech made it for us. I went to pick it up and it was gray. I told them it had to be this icy blue color, not gunmetal gray. We'd had to pick from color chips the size of your fingernail and maybe I was off by one color, or they were. When we repainted it, it looked great. The lid was rigged to fly off and I'd made this big aluminum handle. The first thing Nathan did when he came to rehearse is pull the handle as hard as he could! He totally wrenched it and bent the handle. It was a bad moment and he was really sorry. We sort of bent it back and nobody knew. It ended up working fine and they shot around it.

"It's one piece I wish still existed. Very cool. It was lined with this quilted material which was formed to fit around Summer's body as she lay inside. I remember I said to her, 'This is going to sound really weird, but I want you to lay down in a fetal position on this big piece of paper.' I drew around her and we used it as a pattern to cut the foam which lined the box. It fit her pretty well."

❖ Above: The finished article: River's cryo box.

❖ Left: Designs for River's cryo box.

BUILT IN HANDLES FOR LIFTING

RELEASE LEVER

HOLES FOR STRAPPING DOWN

SIMON
Can't say yet.

INARA
I wanna know what's going on here.

MAL
Well then why don't we find out?

He moves quickly from the room.

SIMON
What are you... no!

Simon follows, as do we, back into

INT. CARGO BAY - CONTINUING

Mal overturns some crates and cases to reveal Simon's big blue box, sitting atop another box.

SIMON
Stay away from that!

He moves toward Mal — but is grabbed and easily held by Jayne.

MAL
(calmly, to Jayne)
Where's the fed?

JAYNE
Secured. Shepherd's with him. Seems to think he's not safe alone with me.

Mal hops atop the first crate and pushes the blue box.

It topples off the crate and lands hard on the metal floor as Wash and Zoe enter.

Mal hops down, turns some dials on the box and pulls a release lever.

There is much flashing of lights and four latches twist automatically at the corners.

The top comes slightly up with a hydraulic whoosh, dry ice pouring out the sides.

Zoe and Mal pull at the top. Inara enters, watches as well.

MAL
Let's see what a man like you would kill for.

The top won't go.

Mal rears back and slams his heel into it.

It flies off, clattering to the floor as the smoke clears from over what's inside.

Mal steps forward, looks.

ANGLE: ABOVE THE BOX

Curled inside is a naked, unconscious seventeen-year-old girl.

The box is clearly a cryo-chamber of some

sort, perfectly conformed to her body, a sleek metallic womb.

Mal looks at the girl. At Simon. At the girl.

MAL (cont'd)
Huh.

END OF ACT THREE

ACT FOUR

INT. CARGO BAY - CONTINUING

Simon tries to wrest himself free of Jayne, who's just holding his arm now.

SIMON
I need to check her vitals.

MAL
Is that what they call it?

SIMON
She's not supposed to wake up for another week! The shock could —

MAL
The shock of what? Waking up? Finding out she's been sold to some borderworld baron? Or, I'm sorry — was this one for you? Is it true love? 'Cause you do seem —

She SCREAMS as she lurches out of the box behind Mal. He actually gives a little yelp himself as he turns, startled.

She keeps screaming, and for a moment no one does anything.

She spills out of the box, crawling backwards, breathing hard and looking around her, wild-eyed.

Simon finally pulls himself free of Jayne — who's now more interested in Naked Girl than Struggling Man — and comes to her.

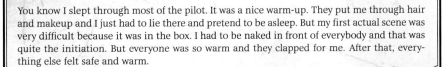

SUMMER GLAU

You know I slept through most of the pilot. It was a nice warm-up. They put me through hair and makeup and I just had to lie there and pretend to be asleep. But my first actual scene was very difficult because it was in the box. I had to be naked in front of everybody and that was quite the initiation. But everyone was so warm and they clapped for me. After that, everything else felt safe and warm.

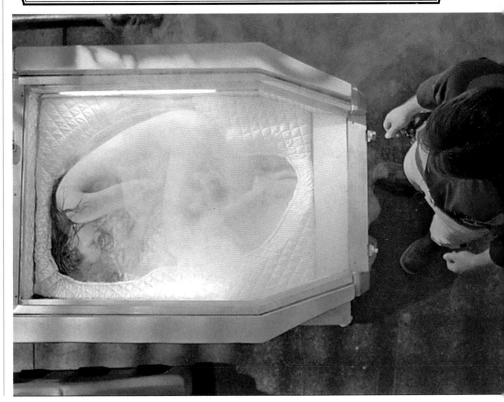

SIMON
River —

She screams at his touch — Inara instinctively moves forward — but he holds onto her, tries to get her to look in his eyes.

SIMON (cont'd)
River. It's okay. It's okay. I'm here.

Finally she looks at him, trying to focus, still breathing hard. Tears are welling in his eyes, but he just stays focused on her.

She looks about, at everyone, then back at him.

SIMON (cont'd)
River...

RIVER
Simon...?

And she realizes, begins to cry, as does he.

RIVER (cont'd)
Simon... They talk to me, they want me to... to talk...

SIMON
They're gone... they're gone and we're safe now, we're safe and I'm here.

Everyone in the room can tell this is not what Mal thought. There is a kind of respect in their silence. Well, til:

MAL
What the hell is this?

Simon pulls the weeping River to him, looks at Mal defiantly, unashamed of the tears in his eyes.

SIMON
This is my sister.

INT. DINING ROOM - LATER

Everyone is gathered, save Kaylee and River herself, to hear Simon speak. As he does, we will periodically INTERCUT to him taking care of River in the infirmary.

For a moment, they all just wait.

INT. INFIRMARY - EARLIER

River is brought — wrapped in the robe Inara used for Kaylee's pillow — into the infirmary. She sees the unconscious Kaylee, the operating room, and she freaks. Starts screaming again, struggling to get out of Simon's grip.

SIMON (O.S.)
I'm very smart.

INT. DINING ROOM - CONTINUING

SIMON
Went to the best Medacad on Osiris, top three percent of my class, finished my internship in eight months. Gifted. Is the term. So when I tell you that my little sister makes me look like an idiot child, I want you to understand my full meaning.

INT. INFIRMARY - EARLIER

Simon has calmed her down, she's sitting on the table now, looking at him with fresh tears. He prepares a hypo with a sedative. Her look of distrust at the hypo is comically grumpy — a little child's. Her eyes wander as he injects her, she mutters something to no one — this girl is gone.

INT. DINING ROOM - CONTINUING

SIMON
River was more than gifted. She was... a gift. Everything she did, music, maths, theoretical physics — even dance — there was nothing that didn't come as naturally to her as breathing does to us.
(smiles, remembering)
She could be a real brat about it, too. She used to tell me —
(losing the train)
I mean, she's a kid. You know? Like everyone else, except she *understands*. So much.

INT. INFIRMARY - EARLIER

River drifts off to sleep. We pan across to see Simon holding her hand.

INT. DINING ROOM - CONTINUING

Simon pauses a moment.

SIMON
There was a school... a, uh, government-sponsored academy, we'd never even heard of it but it had the most exciting program, the most challenging... We could have sent her anywhere, we had the money... but she wanted to go. She wanted to learn. She was fourteen.

A moment of bitter emotion, then he pulls it together.

SIMON (cont'd)
I got a few letters at first, then I didn't hear for months. Finally I got a letter that made no sense. She talked about things that never happened, jokes we never... it was code. I couldn't even figure... I talked to professors, spent a week trying to work it. It just said... "They're hurting us. Get me out."

He can't go on for a moment.

INT. INFIRMARY - EARLIER

She sleeps.

INT. DINING ROOM - CONTINUING

ZOE
How did you do it?

SIMON
Money. And luck — for two years I couldn't get near her, but I was contacted by some men, some underground movement. They said she was in danger, that the government was playing with her brain. If I funded them they could sneak her out in cryo. Get her to Boros and from there, I could take her... wherever.

MAL
How did you know it wasn't a scam?

SIMON
I didn't. Until you opened that box.

INARA
Will she be all right?

SIMON
She was supposed to reacclimate before I brought her out, she's in physical shock, but not serious. I don't know if she'll be all right. I don't know what they did to her, or why. I just have to keep her safe.
(to Mal)
You asked me what a man like me would kill for. And she's it.

There is a moment.

BOOK
That's quite a story, son.

MAL
Yeah, it's a tale of woe, very stirring but in the meantime you've heaped a world of trouble on me and mine.

SIMON
I never thought that —

MAL
No, I don't imagine you thought. In consequence of which we got a kidnapped federal officer on board, we got the Alliance hard on our trail and Kaylee...

He doesn't say it.

ZOE
(to Wash)
How much does the Alliance know?

WASH
Can't say. I killed the message pretty quick, so they might just have had our position.

MAL
Or they might have personal profiles on each and every one of us. Til that fed wakes up, we won't know.

JAYNE
What do we do?

A moment, as he thinks, looking at his crew.

At Inara.

MAL
The job. We finish the job. I got word from Patience, she's waiting for us.

Zoe looks unhappy at the prospect.

MAL (cont'd)
We circle round to Whitefall, make the deal, get out. Keep flying.

SIMON
What about us?

Mal looks at him a moment.

MAL
Kaylee comes through, you and your sister'll get off in Whitefall.

SIMON
If she doesn't come through?

MAL
Then you're getting off a mite sooner.

BOOK
That'd be murder.

MAL
Boy made a decision.

INARA
He didn't shoot her.

JAYNE
But somebody on this boat did and I'm scratching my head as to why we ain't dealt with him.

And now the room gets louder, people start talking over each other...

ZOE
Kill a fed? Can you think of a stupider thing to do?

JAYNE
He can I.D. us all.

SIMON
You wanna throw me out the airlock, fine, but River's not a part of this.

WASH
Can we maybe vote on the whole murdering people issue?

MAL
We don't vote on my ship because my ship is not the rutting town hall!

INARA
This is insanity. Mal...

WASH
I happen to think we're a ways beyond that now, sir.
(to Zoe)
Come on, we're gonna talk this through, yeah?

Zoe doesn't answer. Wash is truly pissed.

BOOK
I'll not sit by while there's killing here.

JAYNE
(smiling)
Shepherd's got a mean streak. We'd best walk soft.

Book looks down, ashamed.

MAL
<Ta ma de! Nimen de bizui!> [Everybody shut the hell up!]
(they do)
Way it is is the way it is. We got to deal with what's in front of us.

INARA
Mal, you know those two wouldn't survive a day in Whitefall anyway.

She comes close to him.

INARA (cont'd)
You throw them out, I'm leaving too.

Mal looks at her, furious at being confronted publicly, truly upset by the thought of her leaving, taking a moment to push both below the surface.

MAL
Might be best you do. You ain't a part of this business.

They stare at each other a moment. He exits towards the back.

INT. AFT HALL - CONTINUING

Simon follows him.

SIMON
What business is that, exactly?

Mal turns and gives him a murderous look, but Simon doesn't back down.

SIMON (cont'd)
I'm a dead man, I can't know? Gold? Drugs? Pirate treasure? What is it that makes you so afraid of the Alliance?

MAL
You don't wanna go down this road with me, boy.

SIMON
You're not afraid of them? I already know you'd sell me out to them for a pat on the head — Hell, you should probably be working for 'em, you certainly fit the profile —

Mal decks him. He goes tumbling. Mal looks down at him, looks back to see:

ANGLE: THE DINING ROOM

The rest are looking at him, Book and Jayne in foreground.

JAYNE
Saw that coming...

INT. INFIRMARY - LATER

The girls are asleep. Simon finishes injecting something into Kaylee, goes to return a bottle to a cabinet.

ZOE

"Big damn heroes, sir."

Whether it is as a pirate captain (Nebula in *Hercules: The Legendary Journeys*), an immortal-life-gobbling goddess (Jasmine in *Angel*), or an animal-enhanced superhero (Vixen in *Justice League*), Gina Torres has certainly made her mark on the science-fiction universe in various TV shows and films over the last twelve years. Nonetheless, it was her role as the warrior Zoe Washburne on *Firefly* which has earned the actress her most passionate fans to date. Initially, after all her genre work, it was not a role she immediately gravitated towards; however, she was won over by the quality of the source material. "I would say that even though there were several elements that were familiar, Joss had managed to create an incredibly unique world in the way that he combined and juxtaposed those elements," says Torres. "So you had these challenged characters inhabiting a challenging world and that makes for great storytelling. AND NO ALIENS!"

A former soldier in the Unification War where she served under Sergeant Malcolm Reynolds, Zoe became his loyal second-in-command on the spaceship Serenity. Despite Zoe's tough outer shell, Torres somehow managed to infuse a sense of vulnerability into her married character. Still, when it came to further fleshing out or discussing Zoe, Torres recalls, "Joss and I spoke very little actually. He said two things about her that were of great value to me: she's career military and she loves her husband. After that, it was up to me to add the flesh and bone and heart and psyche. And it was lovely to be trusted to do that."

In many ways, the characters that made up the *Firefly* crew were based on some well-known archetypes. Mal's swashbuckling heroics have been described as Han Solo-esque, while Jayne was clearly influenced by old Westerns. Similarly, Zoe's roots can be traced back. "Several different women and a couple of men went into Zoe," explains Torres. "It was important that Zoe be somewhat of a mystery, that during each episode another layer of her person be revealed, so there would be an element of surprise and maybe even shock."

On the one hand Zoe never shied away from a fight, she was never afraid to butt heads or lock and load her heavy-duty weapons. However, she was also frequently found stepping in as peacemaker on Serenity. "Her job was to get along with everybody and make sure things ran smoothly," offers Torres. "It's what Mal wasn't particularly good at. Was she perfect? Hell no!"

Besides her statuesque height and stunning looks, Zoe's costume immediately made a striking impression. In keeping with her warrior status, she opted for a rugged look with a war-torn leather vest, tight pants, and boots. "As far as the Zoe uniform goes, I thought it was pretty hot," says Torres. "I liked that it was practical and comfortable and quite appropriate. As for the necklace, I like to think it was one of the laces off the boots she wore to war."

The episode 'The Train Job' replaced the original intended pilot 'Serenity' yet still served to set up the *Firefly* world in the minds of the audience. "Having done the pilot where we got to learn so much about who these people are, setting them in motion in 'The Train Job', as an example of their everyday life, was a lot of fun," says Torres. "We were able to launch the viewers into our 'verse at about two hundred and fifty miles per hour."

The feature film *Serenity* may have blown open the secrets concerning those cannibalistic nightmares, the Reavers, but the crew came across their handiwork in the memorable episode 'Bushwhacked'. "There was a lot going on in that episode," recalls Torres. "It went from being one of our scariest to, at times, one of our most amusing. Mostly I remember Doug Savant [who played Commander Harken] not quite sure what to make of us on our set, and I mean that in the best way. We laughed a lot."

Zoe's no-nonsense attitude and combat experience made her a formidable adversary, yet Torres believes she struck a chord with viewers for another reason. "I think it was because she can be trusted," she explains. "Zoe is a great friend, in good times and bad."

Even years after *Firefly* was canceled, the actors still carry a burning torch for the series and Torres is no exception. "Ultimately, being part of something that lives on in people's memories with such affection is reward enough," she concludes. "I am still honored that Joss saw something in me that day and trusted me to bring Zoe to life." ◐

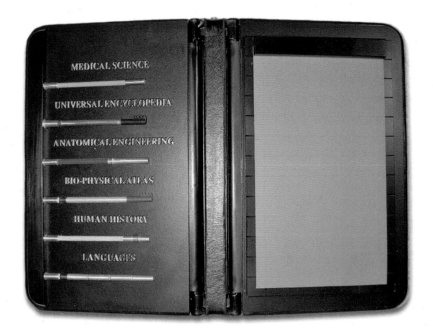

MEDICAL SCIENCE

UNIVERSAL ENCYCLOPEDIA

ANATOMICAL ENGINEERING

BIO-PHYSICAL ATLAS

HUMAN HISTORY

LANGUAGES

THE UNIVERSAL ENCYCLOPEDIA

Chris Colquhoun of Applied Effects explains why this prop seems strangely familiar: "It's a Franklin personal organizer. Randy [Eriksen] asked me to modify it. I laid it all out in Illustrator and had a design for the left side. My chemical etcher etched the brass plate away from the lettering. It was sprayed semi-flat black, as production wanted a slightly matt finish, and then I cleaned the paint off the tops of the letters, leaving the brass showing. I sealed it all with Crystal-Clear."

The organizer shell was completely gutted and the new brass face-plate installed in the left side. On the right side, a piece of Plastruct with a grid pattern was fitted. The piece of translucent material was intended as a futuristic Etcha-Sketch, a page which could be written on and erased. For shots where a data screen or animated graphic was required, it was created in postproduction.

"The data-sticks were made to fit into the pen-recess on the top. I made them from some rod, some PDA styluses and some heat shrink and I also turned some of the pieces on the lathe. They had to read on camera so we made them all different colors."

BOOK
How is she?

Startled, Simon shuts the door. Turns to the Shepherd.

SIMON
Touch and go.

BOOK
I might pray over her a bit, if you don't mind.

SIMON
Of course.

BOOK
She's a special girl. We kinda got to be friendly right away.

SIMON
That's a talent I seem to lack.

BOOK
If I can ask, what made you pick this ship?

SIMON
It looked disreputable.

Book smiles. Simon does too, though his is a bleak one.

BOOK
Well, you're not without critical judgement. Didn't happen to look at the name, I suppose?

SIMON
Um, what — "Serenity", right? That's a joke.

BOOK
I believe it's not.

SIMON
<Duibuqi?> [I'm sorry?]

BOOK
You want to get the lay of the land here, it might be what you lack isn't psychological insight. Might be it's history.

Simon looks at him.

INT. SIMON'S ROOM - LATER

Simon opens a small notebook. It's got a sheet of digital paper inside on the right, and a series of what look like little plastic pointers inserted on the left. He picks one, slides it in the spine of the notebook, and the paper lights up, reading: Universal Encyclopedia. He touches a section that says: VOICE, and says:

SIMON
Serenity.

Up comes the dictionary definition, and below that, SERENITY, BATTLE OF. He touches it and a paragraph forms with photos next to it.

SIMON (cont'd)
Read.

As the book reads, in a soft female voice, the images fill the page. Planets, banners, then images of battle and carnage, the aftermath of which we saw in the flashback.

ENCYCLOPEDIA
In the war to unite the planets, The Battle Of Serenity was among the most devastating and decisive. Located on Hera, the valley was considered a key position by both sides, and was bitterly fought over. The Independent Faction, with sixteen brigades and twenty air-tank squads, held the valley against Alliance forces for almost two months, until superior numbers and a brilliant deep-flank strategy by General Richard Wil —

ZOE
What does it say under "bloodbath"?

Simon turns off the book, seeing Zoe in his doorway.

SIMON
I was just trying to —

ZOE
We're not in there. The book, I mean. We're not generals or diplomats, we didn't turn the tide of glorious history or whatever that thing is supposed to spew.

SIMON
You know what they say: history is programmed by the winners.

ZOE
Nearly half a million people lay dead on that field at day's end, about a third of them "winners". Can you imagine that smell? Can you imagine piling up the bodies of soldiers — of friends — to build a wall 'cause you got no cover? Blood just kept pouring out of them, you'd slip in it half the time, find

out bloodbath is not just a figure of speech.

SIMON
Mal was there with you.

She enters, sits across from him.

ZOE
He was my Sergeant. In command of thirty-odd grunts — five days in, there were so many officers dead he commanded two thousand. Kept us together, kept us fighting, kept us sane. By the time the fighting was over he had maybe four hundred still intact.

SIMON
Well that's a hell of a —

ZOE
I said the fighting was over. But you see they left us there. Wounded, and sick, and near to mad as can still walk and talk. Both sides left us there while they "negotiated the peace". For a *week*. And we just kept dying. When they finally sent in Medships, he had about a hundred and fifty left, and of our original platoon, just me.

She stands.

ZOE (cont'd)
Mercy, forgiveness, trust... Those are things he left back there.

What he has now is the ship, the ship and us on it. You get Kaylee through this and I think he'll do right by you. He won't kill unless he's got no other option.

SIMON
What if he tells you to kill me?

ZOE
I kill you.

SIMON
(grim smile)
Just getting the lay of the land.

She starts to go.

SIMON (cont'd)
If that battle was so horrible, why'd he name the ship after it?

She considers the question.

ZOE
Once you've been in Serenity, you never leave. You just learn to live there.

INT. BRIDGE - CONTINUING

Mal arrives on the bridge, moving fast.

Wash is watching a screen, very apprehensive.

MAL
How the hell did they find us? I thought you said we could get around 'em.

WASH
It's not Alliance.

MAL
You're sure?

WASH
It's a smaller vessel.

MAL
Commercial?

WASH
Um, yeah, I read it as an older model, Trans-U.

MAL
I didn't think Trans-U still operated.

WASH
They don't.

MAL
Get me a visual.

WASH
They're still too far out to —

MAL
Get me something!

WASH
I'm picking up a lot of radiation... they're burning without core containment. Well, that's <kwong-juh duh> [nuts], that's suicide...

He looks at Mal, getting it.

MAL
Reavers.

Mal looks out toward a tiny speck that approaches them.

EXT. SPACE - CONTINUING

Where we see, for the first time, the ship. Once it was a commercial spaceliner, now it's a war machine. Tricked out, ornamented and painted, with giant torpedo-looking tubes jerry-rigged near the front. Everything about this vessel says "savage".

INT. BRIDGE - CONTINUING

Where Mal continues to stare ahead, and Wash repeats softly:

WASH
Oh god... oh god... oh god...

END OF ACT FOUR

ACT FIVE

INT. INFIRMARY - CONTINUING

We see the two girls laid out, unconscious. Book is quietly standing at the foot of Kaylee's bed, bible folded in his hands. Mal's voice comes over the com:

MAL (O.S.)
This is the Captain.

INT. PASSENGER DORM HALL - CONTINUING

Zoe has started out of Simon's room, has stopped to listen. He steps out of his room, listening as well.

MAL (O.S.)
We're passing another ship. Looks to be Reavers. From the size, probably a raiding party.

INT. INARA'S CHAMBER - CONTINUING

She listens, too. Gravely.

MAL (O.S.)
Could be they're headed somewhere particular, could be they've already hit someone and they're full up. So everybody stay calm.

INT. JAYNE'S ROOM - CONTINUING

Jayne pulls down a decorative blanket to reveal an arsenal on his wall. He is silent and serious.

MAL (O.S.)
We're holding course. They should pass us in a minute, we'll see what they do.

INT. BRIDGE - CONTINUING

MAL
Zoe, you come on up to the bridge.

INT. PASSENGER DORM HALL - CONTINUING

Zoe is going as Simon stops her with:

SIMON
I don't understand.

ZOE
You've never heard of Reavers?

SIMON
Campfire stories... Men gone savage at the edge of space, killing, and...

ZOE
They're not stories.

SIMON
What happens if they board us?

ZOE
If they take the ship, they'll rape us to death, eat our flesh and sew our skins into their clothing and if we're very very lucky, they'll do it in that order.

She exits. Simon moves quickly to:

INT. INFIRMARY - CONTINUING

Where he moves near River. He and Book look at each other.

EXT. SPACE - CONTINUING

We see the ships nearing each other. Slowly and silently.

INT. INARA'S CHAMBER - CONTINUING

Inara digs out a small, hidden box. She opens it. Inside is a modern syringe gun, smaller than the one Simon used on River, and a vial of black liquid. Unmarked.

She stares into the box.

INT. JAYNE'S ROOM - CONTINUING

Jayne is loading bullets the size of D batteries into a big-ass rifle. His hands are shaking slightly.

INT. DOBSON'S ROOM - CONTINUING

Bound and gagged, Dobson waits in terror.

EXT. SPACE - CONTINUING

The ships are almost upon one another. The Reaver ship is nearly twice the size of the Firefly.

INT. BRIDGE - CONTINUING

Zoe enters, says nothing. She stands behind Wash, slips her hand onto his shoulder. He covers it with his own.

Wash looks out the window at the ship, sees the

attachments on the front. Also speaks softly.

WASH
Magnetic grappler. They get ahold of us with that...

MAL
Just tell me if they alter course.

They wait.

Everybody waits.

EXT. SPACE - CONTINUING

The ships pass silently. The Reaver ship comes close enough to cast a shadow on the smaller ship.

But it passes.

EXT. BRIDGE - CONTINUING

After a few long seconds...

WASH
They're holding course.

Mal lets out a looong breath. Looks at the other two.

WASH (cont'd)
I guess they weren't hungry. Sure didn't expect to see them here...

ZOE
They're pushing out further every year, too.

MAL
Getting awful crowded in my sky.

He hits the com:

MAL (cont'd)
Jayne.

INT. DOBSON'S ROOM - LATER

Jayne and Mal are in the room with the tied and gagged cop.

MAL
I'm in a situation, I think you're aware. Got me a boatload of terribly strange folk making my life a little more interesting then I generally like. Chief among them, an Alliance mole that likes to shoot at girls when he's nervous. Now, I got to know how close the Alliance is, exactly how much you told them 'fore Wash scrambled your call. So I've given Jayne here the job of finding out.

Jayne pulls out a big-ass knife.

JAYNE
He was nonspecific as to how.

Mal says to Jayne, very quietly:

MAL
You only gotta scare him.

JAYNE
(grinning at Dobson)
Pain is scary...

MAL
Do it right.

Mal exits, shutting Jayne in with Dobson. Jayne pulls the gag out and the cop drags in ragged breaths.

DOBSON
Do you have any idea how much trouble you're in?

JAYNE
Gee, I never been in trouble with the law before...

DOBSON
Not like this you haven't. You think this is just a smuggling rap? The package that boy is carrying —

JAYNE
It's a girl. Cute, too, but I don't think she's all there.
(ugly grin)
'Course, not all of her has to be...

DOBSON
That girl is a precious commodity. They'll come after her. Long after you bury me they'll be coming.

JAYNE
I ain't gonna kill you, Dobson — what's your first name?

DOBSON
Laurence.

JAYNE
Laurence, I'm just gonna cut on ya' til you tell me how much they know.

DOBSON
They know everything. Every name, every record — they know how many nosehairs you've got.

JAYNE
(genuinely disappointed)
Oh, see — they don't know a damn thing. It's all over your face and I ain't even...
(petulant)
I was gonna get me an ear. Aren't you an officer of the law, don't they teach you how to... you know, withstand interrogation? Can't even tell a damn lie.

DOBSON
Okay. I can see you're not an idiot.

JAYNE
Wish I could say the same, Laurence, but this is disappointing as hell.

DOBSON
Let me speak a language you will understand. Money. This girl is worth a lot of money. I mean a lot. You kill me, there's nothing. But you help me out, you'll have enough to buy your own ship. A better one than this piece of crap.

JAYNE
Does helping you out mean turning on the Captain?

DOBSON
Yes it does.

Jayne thinks a moment.

JAYNE
Let's talk money, Larry.

INT. INFIRMARY - LATER

Mal is looking at River, silent.

KAYLEE
Captain...?

He turns. She has woken, is woozy and quiet.

MAL
Hey... Hey little Kaylee, what's the news?

KAYLEE
I'm shiny, Captain. A-okay. Can't feel much below my belly, though. And I'm... it's gettin' cold.

Mal moves to get her another blanket, lays it on her — all the while hiding his feelings at hearing that.

MAL
You just gotta rest. Something on this boat's gonna break down real soon, and who else I got to fix it?

KAYLEE
Don't worry none... Doc fixed me up pretty. He's nice.

MAL
Don't go working too hard on that crush, <xiao meimei> [little sister]. Doc won't be with us for long.

KAYLEE
You're nice, too.

MAL
No, I'm not. I'm a mean old man.

KAYLEE
He wasn't gonna let me die. He was just trying to... It's nobody's fault. Promise you'll remember that?

MAL
(takes her hand)
I'll keep it in mind.

KAYLEE
You are a nice man, Captain. You always look after us. But you got to... you got to have faith in people.

He says nothing, just holds her hand.

Her eyes drift to River, still sleeping.

KAYLEE (cont'd)
She is a beauty, isn't she?

She smiles... and her eyes gently close.

Her hand slips from Mal's.

INT. INARA'S CHAMBER - LATER

Simon is there, as Inara hands him a couple of packets.

SIMON
Thank you.

INARA
This is just a standard Companion immunization package. I'm not sure it'll help in this —

SIMON
It won't hurt. The supplies down there are pretty rudimentary.

INARA
Is there anything else I can do?

SIMON
I don't think so. But I appreciate it.

INARA
Kaylee's very dear. To all of us.

SIMON
I'm sorry. For my part in what happened. I've never... I don't know how to —

INARA
You're lost in the woods. We all are. Even the Captain. The only difference is, he likes it that way.

MAL
(entering)
No the difference is, the woods are the only place I can see a clear path.
(to Simon)
What's your business here?

INARA
It's my business, the usual. I gave the boy a free thrust, since he's not long for this world. What are you doing in my shuttle?

MAL
It's my shuttle. You rent it.

INARA
Then when I'm behind on the rent, you can enter unasked.

Simon elbows his way out. Mal and Inara look at each other a moment.

MAL
Thought you were leaving, anyhow.

INARA
Well I guess that depends on you.

Mal turns and goes.

INT. CARGO BAY - CONTINUOUS

Simon is walking away, but Mal stops him:

MAL
You'll ruin her, too, you know.

Simon turns.

MAL (cont'd)
This is the thing I see you're uncomprehending on. Everyone on this ship, even a "legitimate businesswoman" like her, their lives can be snatched away because of that fed. You got a solution for that? Got a way round?

SIMON
I don't.

MAL
Comes time, somebody's gonna have to deal with him. That should be you, but I don't think you have the guts. And I know you don't have the time.

SIMON
What do you mean?

MAL
Kaylee's dead.

He is steely, contained. Simon is quietly devastated.

Mal turns and walks toward the bridge. A moment, and Simon starts in a daze for the infirmary, running, unable to accept it as he enters:

INT. INFIRMARY - CONTINUING

To find Kaylee sitting up a bit, talking weakly but happily with Book. Simon turns and looks out

where Mal left, true shock in his eyes...

SIMON
The man's psychotic.

INT. BRIDGE - MOMENTS LATER

Mal, Wash, Jayne and Zoe are all laughing.

WASH
Okay, you are psychotic.

MAL
No, but you should have seen his face... ahhh... I'm a bad man.

ZOE
And Kaylee's really okay?

MAL
I'll tell you the truth, I didn't expect her to heal this quick. The Doctor knows his trade, I'll give him —

There is a noise from a console. Wash checks it out.

WASH
We're being hailed.

MAL
That'd be Patience. We're close enough for a vid, put her up.

We briefly see an image on a screen, a weathered, pioneer-looking woman of about fifty.

PATIENCE
Malcolm Reynolds.

MAL
Hello, Patience.

PATIENCE
I have to say, I didn't look to be hearing from you anytime soon.

MAL
Well, we may not have parted on the best of terms — I realize certain words were exchanged, also certain... bullets, but that's air through the engine, that's past. We're business people. 'Sides, your days of fighting over salvage rights are long behind you, what I hear. What are you, mayor, now?

PATIENCE
Just about. You telling the truth about that cargo? 'Cause your asking price is a bit too reasonable for that much treasure.

MAL
It's imprinted. Alliance. Hence the discount.

NATHAN FILLION

The first scene that we shot on the pilot was Sean Maher and myself up on the catwalk talking about how Kaylee died from her gunshot wound, which was obviously a lie. It was the very first thing we did. I won't forget that.

PATIENCE
Government goods, huh?

MAL
If it doesn't work for you, no harm. Just thought you could use —

PATIENCE
Alliance don't scare me. Just collating data, as they say. I like you being up-front about it. We can deal. I'll upload coordinates for a rendezvous point outside of town.

MAL
See you in the world.

The screen goes black — no more Patience. There is a pause. Everyone knows:

MAL (cont'd)
I believe that woman's planning to shoot me again.

JAYNE
She meant to pay you, she'd a haggled you down some.

WASH
Just a little effort to hide it would've been considerate —

Mal angrily sweeps away a pile of stuff, including a tin cup and plate, off a console and into the wall. Everybody takes a moment to let the outburst pass.

ZOE
Sir, we don't have to deal with her.

MAL
Yes we do.

JAYNE
Well, here's a little concept I been working on: why don't we shoot her first?

WASH
It IS her turn...

MAL
That doesn't get us what we need either.

ZOE
There's moons on this belt we ain't seen. We could try our luck on one of —

MAL
Our LUCK? Have you noticed anything particular about our luck, last few days? Any kind of pattern? You depend on luck you end up on the drift, no fuel, no prospects, begging for Alliance makework or being towed out to the scrapbelt. That ain't us. Not ever. Patience has the money to pay and she's going to. One way or another.

Still say there's gonna be gunplay.

MAL
Most like. And we'll be ready for that. There's obstacles in our path, we're gonna deal with them. One by one.

INT. DOBSON'S ROOM - CONTINUING

We see Dobson sawing away at his bonds with a tiny, jagged piece of metal.

MAL (O.S.)
We'll get through this. We will.

END OF ACT FIVE

ACT SIX

EXT. WHITEFALL - DAY

We see the desert planet below, as Serenity rockets down toward it.

EXT. WHITEFALL - LATER

We're on the surface now — rocks and sagebrush jutting out of low hills. Serenity touches down, the airlock door beginning to open.

EXT. DESERT - DAY

We see a small valley, dotted with brush, hills all about. Pan slowly across it to find our three looking at it.

ZOE
Nice place for an ambush.

MAL
That it is.

Jayne arrives, at a decent clip. He hands one bar from the crate to Mal.

JAYNE
I buried 'em good. Equipment's back on the boat.

He sticks an earwig in his ear.

JAYNE (cont'd)
Testing, test — Captain, can you hear me?

MAL
I'm standing right here.

JAYNE
You're coming through good and loud.

MAL
'Cause I'm standing right here.

JAYNE
Well, but the transmitter's...

He gives up. Mal steps forward, looking about him, the wheels in his head turning. After a time.

MAL
Patience is gonna figure we buried the cargo.

Which means putting us to our ease 'fore there's any action. She'll come at us from the east, talk the location of the cargo out of us. She'll have the coin to show us first. We get it, give the location, snipers hit us from...
(points)
There. And there.

JAYNE
Figure they're in place yet?

MAL
Should be. Feel like taking a walk around the park?

JAYNE
(grinning)
Sure you don't just wanna piss yourself and back down like you did with Badger?

Mal stares at him til he stops smiling.

MAL
Walk soft. I want Patience thinking they're in place. And don't kill them if you don't have to. We're here to make a deal.

Jayne takes off. Zoe and Mal look over the meeting place some more.

ZOE
I don't think it's a good spot, sir. She still has the advantage over us.

MAL
Everyone always does.
(turns back to her, smiling bleakly)
That's what makes us special.

INT. PASSENGER DORM HALL/DOBSON'S ROOM - CONTINUING

Book is there, wrestling with his conscience. He looks toward the infirmary, looks toward Dobson's room. After a moment, he heads toward the latter, stops at the door. Knocks.

BOOK
Lawman, it's Shepherd Book.

He opens the door —

BOOK (cont'd)
I believe you're in more danger than —

Dobson SLAMS his chair into the Shepherd, sending him flying back into the hall. Is on him in a second with a makeshift truncheon, hits him in the head. Book slumps, unconscious. Dobson looks out to make sure no one heard. Then, his face contorted with pent-up rage, he whips the truncheon down twice more, pure fucking spite. Starts dragging Book into his room.

EXT. DESERT - DAY

We are high and wide above Mal and Zoe, watching them walk across the valley. Them small, landscape big.

Closer in, we track with them, moving slow. They keep their eyes peeled all ways, hands near their

holsters.

A ways more, and they are nearing a rise — Over which appear:

ANGLE: PATIENCE and her crew of six — as they crest the hill on horseback — all but one, who drives a vehicle not unlike the one on Serenity. They're maybe twenty yards from our two.

Patience is in a weatherbeaten duster, grey hair flyblown about her face. Her men are a hodge-podge of old and modern clothes — not quite Road Warrior gear, but more eclectic and raggedy than even our gang is used to. One wears a shiny black top hat.

MAL
(quietly)
Jayne better come through...

PATIENCE
Mal! How you doing, boy?

MAL
Walking and talking.

PATIENCE
That Zoe? You still sailing with this old bum?

ZOE
That's an awful lot of men to haul three crates.

PATIENCE
Well, I couldn't be sure my Mal here wasn't

looking for some kind of payback. You under-stand.

MAL
We're just on the job, Patience. Not interested in surprises.

EXT. RIDGE OVERLOOKING THE MEETING PLACE - CONTINUING

A sniper is set to take a bead on Mal. Jayne drops on him like a stone, knocks him unconscious. Grabs his rifle and takes his position. He finds a mark, smiles.

ANGLE: IN HIS SIGHTS:

is Mal.

Jayne smiles, wicked-like.

INT. ANOTHER DORM ROOM - CONTINUING

As Dobson busts in, moves to his suitcase. He opens it, digs in and grabs his tiny computer, turns it on. The screen has icons on it, including CONNECT TO CENTRAL CORTEX. He hits it, waits. It comes up: INTERFERENCE. UNABLE TO CONNECT. Furious, he hurls the computer against the wall, smashing it. Reaches into the bottom of his suitcase.

He pulls out another gun. And another.

EXT. DESERT - CONTINUING

The exchange continues.

PATIENCE
I don't see my cargo anywhere...

MAL
And you're not gonna, til I'm holding two hundred in platinum.

PATIENCE
Oh, come on, Reynolds. I'm supposed to take it on faith you've got the goods?

Mal pulls out the bar from the crate. He tosses it to Patience.

MAL
It's pure, Patience.

She rips the foil off to reveal what looks like one of those awful energy bars, which, by the by, is what it is. She sniffs it.

MAL (cont'd)
Genuine A-grade foodstuffs. Protein, vitamins, immunization supplements... One of those'll feed a family for a month. Longer, if they don't like their kids too well.

She slices off a piece, chews the very end.

PATIENCE
Yeah, that's the stuff.

She pulls a small bag from her hip pocket, tosses it to Mal. He reaches in and pulls out a silvery coin.

PATIENCE (cont'd)
So where's the rest?

INT. INFIRMARY - CONTINUING

River pulls her hand from Kaylee's, sitting up. True fear is on her face.

RIVER
Simon...

KAYLEE
What's wrong, sweetie?

River doesn't answer — she moves to the door — where Dobson GRABS her, sticks a gun to her head.

DOBSON
Look at you, all woke up.

Kaylee starts to move — he pulls out the other gun, points it at her.

DOBSON (cont'd)
I'm sorry about what happened before. But make so much as a sound and the next one goes through your throat.

She looks at him with genuine terror. He pulls River back toward the dorm.

EXT. DESERT - CONTINUING

MAL
Then half a mile east, foot of the first hill. You'll

see where it's been dug.

PATIENCE
Reckon I will.

MAL
Well then.

PATIENCE
Yep.

Nobody moves.

MAL
I'd appreciate it if you all would turn around and ride out first.

PATIENCE
Yeah, well... see there's kind of a hitch.

MAL
We both made out on this deal. Don't complicate things.

PATIENCE
I have a rule. I never let go of money I don't have to. Which is maybe why I'm running this little world and you're still in that dinky old boat sniffing for scraps.

ANGLE: JAYNE'S POV, through the sights of the gun. Still on Mal, they now swing over to Patience and her gang as Mal tosses the money to her.

MAL
You got the money back. There's no need for killin'.

ZOE
We're just gonna walk away, sir?

MAL
Guess that's up to Patience here.
(to Patience)
Could be messy...

PATIENCE
Not terribly. Ah, Mal... you just ain't very bright, are you?

Mal looks at her men, notices one (with a shiny top hat) is carrying a fine looking rifle.

MAL
That's quite a rifle there. Boy must be your best shot, carry that.

PATIENCE
He's called Two-Fry. Always makes it quick and clean.

Two-Fry smiles.

MAL
Two-Fry. Nice hat.

Two-Fry is BLOWN off his horse by a shot from the unseen Jayne.

And then a lot of things happen at once.

Mal draws and nails a second man, Zoe a third (the one on the vehicle) — as the gang opens up, a fourth man blasts his shotgun, nailing Zoe right in the chest. She goes flying back — as Mal hits shotgun man, moving, diving behind some brush cover as Patience and the remaining two fire at him, their horses rearing in panic, one of them drops off his, comes up firing, Mal and he can't really find each other through the dust at this point —

INT. BRIDGE - CONTINUING

Simon and Wash are there, talking.

WASH
Should think about asking the Captain to drop you somewhere else. Whitefall ain't exactly civilization in the strictest sense...

SIMON
You don't have to worry about me.

WASH
Zoe's out on a deal, I always worry. So it's not out of my way —

Kaylee's voice comes over the com, weak and whispered...

KAYLEE
He took her...

Simon bolts out of the room. Wash is about to as well, but there is a beeping — a proximity warning.

He stops, looks at his screen.

WASH
Oh, don't... don't you dare...

INT. CARGO BAY - CONTINUING

Simon runs out, sees Dobson with River below, his grip on her loose right now as he looks around him, heading for the closed airlock —

Simon JUMPS right down on top of him — two men go tumbling, two guns go flying — and both men lie there in extreme pain, unable to get up and get the guns.

River backs into a corner, wild with terror.

EXT. DESERT - CONTINUING

ANGLE: JAYNE fires, but everything is moving too much — he misses, cursing.

JAYNE
<Hun dan!> [Damn!]

Patience dismounts, shooting from behind her horse, as Mal and the other man on the ground continue firing at each other —

The last man on his horse starts to ride away in panic —

ANGLE: ZOE

still flat on her back, Raises her gun and shoots him in the back. He falls off the still moving horse.

Now it's just Patience and the one other. He fires and clips Mal in the arm — Mal returns in kind, blasting his hip. The other guy goes down, screaming in pain.

Patience pulls out her shotgun, still with the cover of the horse.

Mal stands, no longer moving or hiding.

MAL
Zoe?

ZOE
Ahhhh... armor's dented.

MAL
Well, you were right about this being a bad idea...

ZOE
Thanks for saying, sir.

She pulls at her shirt — there is a beat up kind of superthin Kevlar underneath.

PATIENCE
Mal, don't take another step —

She doesn't really have a bead on him or she woulda shot him, but she's close, gun leveled on the back of the horse.

Mal walks toward her, shoots the horse and it collapses half onto her. He comes up to her and sticks his gun in her face.

MAL
I did a job. I got nothing but trouble since I did it, not to mention more than a few unkind words as regards to my character so let me make this abundantly clear. I do the job.

He takes the money back.

MAL (cont'd)
And then I get paid.

He moves his gun from her face.

MAL (cont'd)
Go run your little world.

Jayne runs up to him, holding out a walkie-phone.

JAYNE
Mal! It's Wash! We got a ship coming in. They followed us. The Gorramn Reavers followed us!

Everyone still alive looks scared.

EXT. SPACE - CONTINUING

As the Reaver ship whips past camera, heading towards Whitefall.

END OF ACT SIX

ACT SEVEN

INT. CARGO BAY - MOMENTS LATER

Dobson lunges for his gun — and Simon throws himself on top of him. They can both barely stand from their crash before. They struggle in an ugly fashion, until Dobson gets an elbow free and jerks it into Simon's face.

He gets free enough to crawl for the weapon, but Simon rolls around and grabs the other one, points it:

SIMON
Don't move!

WASH (O.S.)
(on the com)
REAVERS! Reavers incoming and headed straight for us. We are in the air in one minute!

INT. BRIDGE - CONTINUING

WASH
(to himself)
Guess they got hungry again.

He starts warming the ship up.

INT. CARGO BAY - CONTINUING
Inara comes out of her chamber, sees the action below.

Simon holds the gun on Dobson. His hand shakes.

❖ Above: Simon's Vektor stunt pistol.

DOBSON
You gonna do that? You gonna kill a lawman in cold blood. I know what you did for your sister and I understand. It doesn't make you a killer.

A barely conscious Book also comes to the entrance, holding onto it to stay up.

DOBSON (cont'd)
I don't wanna hurt anybody. I have a job to do. To uphold the law. That's what we're talking about here. There's nowhere you can take her that the law won't find. Nobody's gonna hurt her... unless you hurt me.

SIMON
I said don't move!

DOBSON
It's your call.

Simon doesn't know what to do. He looks over at River.

EXT. SPACE - CONTINUING

The Reaver ship breaks into atmo, headed down to the planet.

INT. BRIDGE - CONTINUING

Wash is getting more and more freaked —

WASH
Come on, come on...
(into walkie)
Where the hell are you guys!?!

EXT. DESERT - CONTINUING

As we see Mal, Zoe and Jayne RIDE into frame on horseback, moving just as fast as they can.

INT. CARGO BAY/AIRLOCK - CONTINUING

The airlock starts to open, the noise and motion distracting Simon long enough for Dobson to grab his gun and fire —

INARA
Simon!

— missing but sending Simon diving for cover as Dobson grabs River and puts himself behind her, gun to her head. Simon steps out, between him and the airlock.

DOBSON
I'm not playing anymore.

EXT. SERENITY - CONTINUING

The three pull up on their horses, jump off, Mal striding in as the others shoo the horses off.

INT. CARGO BAY/AIRLOCK - CONTINUING

Mal walks in behind Simon —

DOBSON
Anybody makes so much as a —

— and shoots Dobson in the face. He flies back, letting go of River and dead before he lands. Tilt up from him to see Book, unable to move.

MAL
Wash! We're on!

He pulls the Lawman's body up and dumps it out the closing airlock as Jayne and Zoe enter. Simon moves to River, just shocked and silent.

EXT. SERENITY - CONTINUING

The hatch is still closing as the ship takes off.

INT. BRIDGE - MOMENTS LATER

Mal and Zoe come up to Wash, Inara hanging back behind.

MAL
How close are they?

WASH
About twenty seconds from spitting distance.

JAYNE
Well lose 'em!

MAL
(to Zoe)
Give me rear vid.
She punches it up. ON THE SCREEN, we see the ship approaching from behind.

ZOE
<Ai ya. Women wanle.> [We're in big trouble.]

MAL
(to Wash)
How close do they need to be to fire the grapples?

JAYNE
Wash, you dumbass, dodge 'em!

WASH
If everybody could just be quiet a moment...

He's incredibly calm. He veers hard left, snakes through —

EXT. DESERT - CONTINUING

— the hills, where we see the ship moving fast — but the Reavers are right on them.

INT. BRIDGE/FOREDECK HALL - CONTINUING

Wash continues to pilot with serene expertise.

WASH
I need Kaylee in the engine room please.

ZOE
Can she even —

MAL
(to Jayne)
Get her in there. Now.

Jayne goes. Mal moves to Inara.

ZOE
(to Wash)
Can we lose them?

He doesn't answer. He's flying.

ANGLE: MAL and INARA.

MAL
I want you to get in your shuttle. Get the civilians and be ready to go.

INARA
We can't just leave you here.

MAL
Thought that was the plan.

INARA
Mal, don't —

MAL
We get boarded, you take off, head for town. We might be able to stop them from following.

INARA
They'll kill you.

MAL
Inara.

Just saying her name says more than he probably ever meant to. He puts his hand on the Companion's shoulder.

And pushes her gently away.

THE REAVER CHASE

Visual effects supervisor Loni Peristere: "My favorite sequence was definitely the Reaver chase. I liked it because it took spaceships that you are used to seeing in space and put them in atmospheric peril. I think for the first time on TV, and even film, you had two giant spaceships in atmosphere. Our Reaver ship was not only designed to look like a wild boar, it was painted with war paint and it was belching dirty smoke, which made it a monster coming to get you. I loved that we had a big monster trying to swallow our cute little bird, if you will. To 'shoot' the scene, we had a virtual 'chase plane', a mounted camera with a zoom lens that was not in focus all the time, smoke in the lens and lens flares blocking the view. It was all created in CGI and synthetically, but it really felt organic."

MAL (cont'd)
Go.

He turns back to the bridge. She is going as well, throws a look back, a little blown away by his caring, then continues on.

MAL (cont'd)
(to Wash)
How are we doing?

WASH
I don't want to alarm anybody... but I think... we're being followed...

EXT. DESERT - CONTINUING

The Reaver ship is hard on Serenity's heels.

INT. INFIRMARY - CONTINUING

Jayne is carrying Kaylee out as Inara enters. She speaks to Simon, River and Book:

INARA
You three. Come with me.

BOOK
I think I can help Kaylee out.
(to Simon, re: River)
Take her. Keep her safe.

Book and Inara share a glance before they go their separate ways.

INT. BRIDGE - MOMENTS LATER

Wash flies.

MAL
Can't keep this up, they get a bead, they're gonna lock us down.

WASH
(into com)
Kaylee, how're we doing?

INT. ENGINE ROOM - CONTINUING

Kaylee is propped in a corner, Jayne and Book at the ready.

KAYLEE
You want me go for full burn?

WASH (O.S.)
Not just yet, but set it up.

KAYLEE
(to Book)

You know where the press regulator is?

He looks about, heads to a part of the engine, opens a panel. Kaylee smiles.

KAYLEE (cont'd)
Head of the class.

She coughs, wincing at the pain.

INT. BRIDGE - CONTINUING

ZOE
Full burn in atmo? That won't cause a blowback? Burn us out?

MAL
Even if it doesn't, they can push just as hard, keep right on us. Wash, you gotta give me an Ivan.

WASH
See what I can do...
(into com)
Kaylee, how would you feel about pulling a Crazy Ivan?

INT. ENGINE ROOM - CONTINUING

KAYLEE
Always wanted to try one. Jayne. Open the port jet control. Cut the hydraulics.

JAYNE
Where the hell —

KAYLEE
Look. Look where I'm pointing.

He does, opens a panel near the floor.

KAYLEE (cont'd)
Okay. Now it's real simple.

ANGLE: JAYNE'S POV: A tangle mess of cables. Real simple.

EXT. DESERT - CONTINUING

The Reaver ship has Serenity locked in. The magnetic grapple warms up, latches flying off...

INT. BRIDGE - CONTINUING

MAL
They're on us...

INT. INARA'S SHUTTLE - CONTINUING

Inara moves into the pilot's seat as Simon sits River down.

INT. BRIDGE - CONTINUING

WASH
(into com)
Kaylee...?

No answer. Then:

KAYLEE (OS)
Okay!

WASH
Everybody hold on to something.
(softly, to the Reavers)
Here's something you can't do...

He SLAMS down a lever and

EXT. DESERT - CONTINUING

Serenity's port jet flips the other way and the ship LURCHES into a perfect one-eighty, spinning on a dime, the jet flips back and it's headed straight for the Reaver ship, which dodges at the last second —

INT. BRIDGE - CONTINUING

WASH
(into com)
NOW!

INT. ENGINE ROOM - CONTINUING

Book hits a big button with the heel of his hand and the room gets lighter —

EXT. DESERT - CONTINUING

As the ass-end of Serenity lights up, sending ripples of fire bursting into the atmosphere as the ship blasts out of there so fast, gradually arcing up toward space...

INT. BRIDGE - CONTINUING

Wash is pulling up at the controls with all his might. Finally he eases off, quietly pleased.

Mal and Zoe are kind of amazed.

ZOE
Ain't no way they can come around in time to follow us now.

Mal hits the com:

MAL
We're good, people.

INT. INARA'S SHUTTLE - CONTINUING

Extreme, solemn relief.

MAL (O.S.)
We're out of the woods.

INT. ENGINE ROOM - CONTINUING

Jayne whoops with delight. Even Book smiles.

Kaylee runs her hand along the hull.

KAYLEE
That's my girl... That's my good girl.

She looks at the boys and beams.

INT. BRIDGE - CONTINUING

WASH
(to Mal)
We should have just enough left in us to hit a fuel station. We'll need to do some patching up. Hope we got paid today.

MAL
We did.

Zoe exchanges a look with Wash.

ZOE
Sir? I'd like you to take the helm, please.
(re: Wash)
I need this man to tear all my clothes off.

Mal says nothing, just smiles and indicates the way out. Wash climbs out of the chair and exits with Zoe...

WASH
Work, work, work...

And Mal throws himself down into the pilot's seat. Lets out a breath he's been holding for, oh, about two days. And starts flying.

EXT. SPACE - LATER

As Serenity breaks out of atmosphere into the deep silence of space.

INT. INARA'S CHAMBER - LATER

Book sits as Inara takes a cloth from a bowl and dabs his head. He is sitting, she stands before him.

INARA
You should really have the young Doctor look at this.

BOOK
It's not so bad.

INARA
Well, I'm sure you'll be fine...

BOOK
I didn't say that.

He looks up at her and she sees how upset he is, how lost.

BOOK (cont'd)
Is this what life is, out here?

INARA
Sometimes.

BOOK
I've been out of the abbey two days, I've beaten a lawman senseless, I've fallen in with criminals... I watched the Captain shoot the man I swore to protect.
(the hard part...)
And I'm not even sure if I think he was wrong.

INARA
Shepherd...

He is shaking a bit, tearing up.

BOOK
I believe I just...
(a pained smile)
I think I'm on the wrong ship.

INARA
Maybe. Or maybe you're exactly where you ought to be.

He lowers his head. She puts her hand on it, a kind of benediction. We hold on them a moment.

INT. SIMON'S ROOM - LATER

He is tucking River into bed.

SIMON
The shot I gave you will help you sleep.

RIVER
I slept for so long...

SIMON
Just a little while. Then we'll find a place... we'll find a safe place.

He's not convinced, but he smiles at her anyway. She looks suddenly terribly sad.

RIVER
I didn't think you'd come for me.

SIMON
(welling up)
Well, you're a dummy.

He takes her in his arms, holds her tight.

JAYNE (O.S.)
The girl's a problem.

INT. BRIDGE - LATER

Mal is still at the helm as Jayne speaks to him.

JAYNE
The Lawman said they'd keep looking for her. Something about her brain being all special. Important to the Alliance brass. Sooner we dump those two, the better.

MAL
I suppose so.

Jayne gets up to leave.

MAL (cont'd)
Funny how the Lawman got out of his room. You having tied him up so well and all.

JAYNE
I didn't have nothing to do with that. Anyway it all turned out just fine. Buzzards're the only ones gonna find him...

MAL
But he did try to make a deal with you, right?

He looks at Jayne, who says nothing.

MAL (cont'd)
How come you didn't turn on me, Jayne?

JAYNE
Money wasn't good enough.

MAL
What happens when it is?

JAYNE
(smiling)
Well that'll be an interesting day.

MAL
I imagine it will.

Jayne leaves, passing Simon, who comes up next to Mal. He sees Mal's arm is a bit bloody.

SIMON
You need me to look at that?

MAL
Just a graze.

SIMON
(a beat, then:)
So where do you plan on dumping us?

MAL
There's places you might be safe. You want the truth, though, you're probably safer on the move.
(turns to him)
And we never stop moving.

SIMON
I'm confused. No wait — I think maybe you're confused.

MAL
It may have become apparent to you, the ship could use a medic. You ain't weak. I don't know how bright you are, top three percent, but you ain't weak and that's not nothing. You live by my rule, keep your sister from doing anything crazy, you could maybe find a place here. Til you find a better.

SIMON
I'm trying to put this as delicately as I can... How do I know you won't kill me in my sleep?

MAL
You don't know me, son. So let me explain this to you once: if I ever kill you, you'll be awake, you'll be facing me, and you'll be armed.

SIMON
(smiles)
Are you always this sentimental?

MAL
I had a good day.

SIMON
You had the law on you, criminals and savages... half the people on the ship have been shot or wounded including yourself, and you're harboring known fugitives.

Mal looks out at the black sky.

MAL
We're still flying.

SIMON
That's not much.

Mal answers, almost to himself...

MAL
It's enough.

A beat, then Simon goes. Mal just keeps looking ahead.

END OF SHOW.

THE TRAIN JOB

Written by Joss Whedon & Tim Minear
Directed by Joss Whedon

JOSS WHEDON

Joss Whedon says that Mal was not originally intended to have a moral crisis as early as 'The Train Job'. "Besides the action," Whedon explains, "the other adjustment the network was very firm about was Mal being more likable. And, of course, Tim and I used to joke, 'But we thought you said, "More like a bull!" Ah, this is very embarrassing...' For me, part of the show was going to be unfolding Mal to the audience and to himself. But they said, 'We want to like him up front, but he can be a little caustic if you want.' And so, yeah, him giving back the medicine in 'The Train Job' wouldn't have happened [otherwise]. This is something we did for the network. Now, it's not something that goes against the ethos of the show. This is the thing you have to remember. We scrambled to get the show on the air because we believed in it, but I've also always believed that if the show changes beyond what it should be, you walk away. The idea that Mal would return the medicine did not offend me, did not make me go, 'I've compromised and now he's kissing puppies.' Because it's something that somebody like him would do. In a harsher version, he wouldn't, because his crew was starving and he needed to get them through. Shooting the guy in *Serenity* the movie was an example of that, it was an example of, 'I'm going to make the harshest possible decision, because of the safety of my peeps.' But in this instance, assuming they're not all starving, it is something that Mal as a person is capable of doing. It's just a side of him I wasn't planning to show so much of right away."

TEASER

INT. BAR - DAY

It's a small, disreputable place, doing a brisk but low-key business. Most of the people here are probably up to something they don't want other people to know about. The dark wood and clutter suggest a Western space, but it is definitely multi-cultural: a belly dancer makes her way about the room, and everyone's mode of dress is diverse — though none is too fancy.

We follow a BELLY DANCER's undulating belly through the space, coming to a table with three people sitting at it. ZOE and JAYNE are more or less facing us, MAL has his back mostly turned. The three are concentrating on a game we can't see.

Those who look carefully will spot the belly dancer's hand as it slips Mal a piece of paper, which he slips in turn into his pocket.

JAYNE
(to Mal)
Your move.

Camera ARMS UP to see the game on the table is Chinese Checkers. Mal moves.

ZOE
That's a bold move.

MAL
I live on the edge.

Zoe makes a much better move.

JAYNE
(to Mal)
Nice work, dumbass.

MAL
I've given some thought to moving off the edge, it's not an ideal location... might get a place in the middle...

VOICEOVER (O.S.)
A toast!

The VOICE is surly, loud. Trouble waiting to happen. As it speaks, Mal turns back towards camera and we see him in closeup. Calm, assessing the danger.

ANGLE: The guy who spoke, LUND. A drunken dick, holding court at the bar.

LUND
A toast. Shut up! Quiet, I'm, I got words. I'm say, this is an asspishus day. We all know what day it is...

ANGLE: The gang. Mal is stone-faced, Zoe the same. They clearly know where this is going. Jayne has no clue.

JAYNE
Suspicious? What day is it?

LUND
A glorious day for all the proud members of the

Allied planets. Unification Day! The end of the Independent scumbags and the dawn of a new galaxy! Yeah-huh!

He downs a shot.

Mal is grabbing his empty glass, rising.

ZOE
Captain...

MAL
Just feeling the need for a drink.

JAYNE
(not paying attention)
What month is it?

Mal moves to the bar, far from Lund.

MAL
<Ching zie lie ee bay Ng-Ka-Pei?> [Can I have one more glass of Ng-Ka-Pei, please?]

Lund, naturally, sidles up to him.

LUND
You gonna drink to the Alliance with me?

Mal looks at him, looks away.

LUND (cont'd)
Six years today... The Alliance sent the brown-coats running, pissing their pants.

Mal is not biting. He gets his drink, tosses a weird looking bill on the bar.

LUND (cont'd)
Your coat's kind of a brownish color...

MAL
It was on sale.

He drinks.

LUND
You didn't toast! You know, I'm thinking you're one of them. Independents.

MAL
And I'm thinking you weren't burdened with an overabundance of schooling. So why don't we just ignore each other til we go away?

He turns back to the bar. Lund pursues.

LUND
The Independents were a bunch of inbred, cowardly pisspots shoulda been killed off a every world spinnin'.

Mal turns, ready for the fight.

MAL
Say that to my face.

LUND
I said, you're a coward and a pisspot. Now what're you gonna do about it?

Mal smiles casually.

MAL
Nothing. I just wanted you to face me so she could get behind you.

Lund spins and Zoe SWAPS him with the butt of her sawed-off. He goes down.

Mal and Zoe smile grimly at each other as she

holsters the weapon.

MAL (cont'd)
Drunks are so cute.

Suddenly, seven GUYS stand up, seeing what happened to Lund. They are not wearing colors like Mal and Zoe's.

MAL (cont'd)
<Oh, juh jen sh guh kwai luh duh jean jan...> [Oh, this is a happy development...]

Zoe turns, sees the coming fight.

ZOE
Jayne...

ANGLE: Jayne: Sits, unconcerned.

JAYNE
Hey, I didn't fight in no war. Best of luck, though...

MAL
Fine. Let's do this.

EXT - BAR - CONTINUING (AFTERNOON)

Mal goes flying through the front window — only it's not glass, rather an ionized field that CRACKLES and REFORMS after he passes through.

He rolls in the dirt, stops. Looking up, he hears the sound of fighting within — we might notice at this point that the sky contains THREE MOONS, one so close it looks like another planet on the horizon.

Mal shakes off the punch, pulls out a transmitter.

MAL
(into transmitter)
Wash, we got some local color happening... a grand entrance would not go amiss...

Zoe comes flying out the door, takes two others

with her, giving them hell.

Mal rises, helps her put them down.

MAL (cont'd)
Is Jayne even —

Three guys come backwards out of the bar, driven by the table Jayne is wielding. Another comes behind and he elbows him into dreamland without even looking back. Jayne is an incredible fighter.

Our gang ends up side by side, facing an angry bunch of at least ten guys.

We might notice our three backed up at the EDGE OF A CLIFF.

MAL (cont'd)
Well, there's just an acre of you fellows...
(to Zoe)
This is why we lost, you know: superior numbers.

ZOE
Thanks for the reenactment, sir.

Lund forces his way through the crowd and pulls his gun. This changes things. Our gang look at each other.

JAYNE
Them ain't kosherized rules...

Others pull guns (even though they feel odd about it). Our gang don't yet.

LUND
I'm thinking someone should put you down, dog. What do you think?

MAL
I'm thinking we'll rise again.

It is at this moment that SERENITY rises from behind the cliff, dwarfing our combatants.

Wind rips through everyone, the assailants starting back in fear (and grit in their eyes). An amplified voice (WASH's) comes over a loudspeaker:

WASH (O.S.)
Every man there go back inside or we will blow a new crater in this little moon.

Lund and the others back off, grumbling but cowed.

ANGLE: Behind our heroes.

The airlock door opens and our gang step onto it from the cliff face.

INT. AIRLOCK/CARGO BAY - CONTINUING

The doors shut behind them. Mal and Zoe head upstairs as Jayne wanders off, saying:

JAYNE
Damn yokels can't even tell a transport ship ain't got no guns on it.
(chuckling)
"Blow a new crater in this moon..."

INT. FOREDECK HALL/BRIDGE - MOMENTS LATER

Mal and Zoe are entering the bridge as KAYLEE is

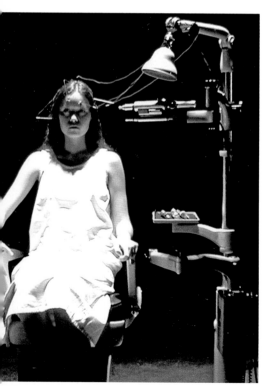

coming up the hall behind them, grease on her face and some unidentifiable ship part in her hand. She's thrilled by the drama.

MAL
(to Wash)
Nice save.

WASH
Pleasure.

MAL
How are our passengers?

KAYLEE
They're fine. What happened? Was there a terrible brawl?

ZOE
(eyeing Mal)
Oddly enough, there was.

WASH
You getting my wife into trouble?

MAL
What? I didn't start it. Just wanted a quiet drink.

ZOE
Funny, sir, how you always find yourself in some Alliance-friendly bar come U-Day, looking for a "quiet drink".

MAL
See, this is a sign of your tragic space dementia. All paranoid and crotchety, it breaks the heart.

WASH
Well, did we at least make a contact?

Mal smiles, produces the piece of paper handed to him by the belly dancer.

MAL
Ladies and menfolk, we got ourselves a job.

He hands the paper to Zoe.

MAL (cont'd)
Take us out of the world, Wash.
(looking ahead)
Got us some crime to be done.

EXT. SERENITY - CONTINUING

As it blasts past camera, heading out of the atmosphere.

END OF TEASER

ACT ONE

INT. LABORATORY

Flashes of bright lights, of people in masks approaching camera with weird-looking instruments — classic operation nightmare.

ANGLE: RIVER

strapped to a chair, with electrodes on her, needles attached to wires stuck into her head, ears, nose, blood trickling from each wound, terror in her eyes as a man's voice speaks slowly:

VOICEOVER
I'm not going to speak. I'm not going to SAY a word...

She opens her mouth to scream and —

INT. INFIRMARY

— wakes up on the operating table, freaking, scrambling off as SIMON approaches her tenderly.

SIMON
River. River. It's okay. It's me.

She says nothing.

SIMON (cont'd)
You know who I am...

RIVER
(duh)
Simon.

SIMON
Were you dreaming? Did you dream about the Academy?

RIVER
(scattered, muttering)
It's not relevant.

SIMON
If you can talk about what happened there... I know it's hard but the more I know, the faster you'll get better. I promise.

She gets up, looks around.

RIVER
This isn't home.

SIMON
No. No, we can't go home. If we go home they'll just send you back to the Academy. This is safer now.
(cheerfully)
We're on a ship.

RIVER
Midbulk transport, standard radion-accelerator core, classcode 03-K64, "Firefly".

Mal enters at that moment, saying:

MAL
Well, that's something. I can't even remember all that.

SIMON
I'm always amazed at what she knows. River, this is Captain Reynolds.

MAL
(to River)
Mal.

She curtsies with exaggerated elegance. A beat, as Mal doesn't know what to do. Then he curtsies back, somewhat awkwardly.

SIMON
(slightly amused)
You bow.

MAL
What?

SIMON
From the waist.
(he demonstrates)
The lady curtsies, the gentleman bows.

MAL
Well, I'm not overly gentle.

He makes his way to the sink, starts rinsing

his bloody knuckles.

SIMON
Need a weave on that?

MAL
It's nothing.

SIMON
I expect there's someone's face feels differently.

MAL
(smiles in reverie)
They tell you never hit a man with a closed fist, but it is on occasion hilarious.

SIMON
I suppose so. The fight didn't draw any... any attention?

MAL
No feds. Just an honest brawl between folk. Ain't none of us want the Alliance on us, Doctor. That's why you're here.

SIMON
I thought I was here because you needed a medic.

MAL
Well, not today.

He exits, River watching him. After he goes:

RIVER
Mal.
(turns to Simon)
Bad.
(looks after Mal)
In the Latin.

INT. PASSENGER DORM - CONTINUING

Mal is about to head upstairs when BOOK comes down the hall.

MAL
Shepherd Book.

BOOK
Captain. How's the girl?

They look back at the pair in the infirmary.

MAL
Still kinda whimsical in the brainpan. Seems calm enough, though.

River hurls a metal container on the ground with a great crash, starts crying as Simon tries to soothe her.

BOOK
That young man's very brave.

MAL
(whatever)
Yeah, he's my hero...

BOOK
Give up everything to free his sister from that... place... go from being a doctor on the

central planets to hiding on the fringes of the system... There's not many would do that.

MAL
Suppose not.

Mal starts up the stairs, but:

BOOK
There's not many would take him in, either.

He's going somewhere with this. Mal turns back.

BOOK (cont'd)
Why did you?

MAL
Same reason I took you on board, Shepherd. I need the fare.

He starts upstairs, the Shepherd following him.

BOOK
There's neither of us can pay a tenth of what your crew makes on one of your "jobs".

INT. UPPER AFT-HALL/ENGINE ROOM - CONTINUING

MAL
Are you referring to our perfectly legitimate business enterprises?

BOOK
I'm wondering why a man who's so anxious to fly under Alliance radar would house known fugitives. The Alliance had her in that institution for a purpose, whatever it was, and they will want her back. You're not overly fond of the boy, so why risk it?

Mal turns, with all mock seriousness.

MAL
Because it's the right thing to do.

He looks in at the engine room — which is an unholy mess of wires and patchwork and tools lying about.

MAL (cont'd)
Will you look at this? Kaylee...

BOOK
I begin to wonder if you yourself know why you're doing it.

MAL
What about you? How come you're flying about with us brigands? Shouldn't you be off bringing religiosity to the Fuzzie-Wuzzies or some such?

BOOK
Oh, I got heathens aplenty right here.

MAL
(smiling)
If I'm your mission, Shepherd, best give it up. You're welcome on my boat. God ain't.

He turns to go, grumbling to himself:

MAL (cont'd)
Where the hell is that girl...

INT. INARA'S SHUTTLE - CONTINUING

We see Kaylee in closeup, eyes closed, a dreamy smile on her (still grease-stained) face. Soft, classical music is playing.

Widen to see that she is sitting on the floor of Inara's sumptuous chamber, and that INARA herself is on the couch behind her, brushing Kaylee's hair.

INARA
Do you want me to put it up?

KAYLEE
Mmmmmm... that's okay...

INARA
You have lovely hair.
(knowingly)
I'm sure the Doctor would agree.

KAYLEE
Simon? No, he's much too... I'm just... Do you think it looks better up?

INARA
We can experiment... We might even get wild later and wash your face.

Kaylee smiles, shutting her eyes again.

KAYLEE
Do you ever do this for your clients?

INARA
Very occasionally. Not all of my clients have enough hair to get a brush through.

KAYLEE
I shouldn't much like a bald lover... some bald men have awfully furry backs.

INARA
Yes, hair often doesn't disappear so much as migrate south.

KAYLEE
Have you ever had to service a really hideous client? With boils and the like?

INARA
A Companion chooses her own clients; that's guild law. But physical appearance doesn't matter so terribly. You look for a compatibility of spirit... there's an energy about a person that's difficult to hide, you try to feel that...

MAL
(entering)
Then you try to feel the energy of their credit account. It has a sort of aura...

INARA
What did I say to you about barging into my shuttle?

MAL
That it was manly and impulsive?

INARA
Yes, precisely, only the exact phrase I used was "don't".

MAL
Well you're holding my mechanic in thrall and Kaylee what the hell is going on in the engine room? Were there monkeys, some terrifying space monkeys that maybe got loose?

KAYLEE
No monkeys, mister funny — I had to rewire the grav-thrust because somebody won't replace that crappy compression coil.

MAL
Well get the place squared away. It's dangerous in there and I ain't paying you to get your hair played at.

Kaylee rises, grumbly, and exits.

KAYLEE
<Kuh-ooh duh lao bao jurn...> [Horrible old tyrant...]

MAL
We work before we play.
(to Inara)
You're servicing crew now?

INARA
In your lonely, pathetic dreams.

MAL
How would you know what I dream about?

INARA
It never occurred to me that you did. What do you want?

MAL
We got a job.

INARA
Congratulations. This job wouldn't be on a decently civilized planet where I could screen some respectable clients, perhaps?

MAL
Respectable clients? Seems a contradiction —

INARA
Don't start.

MAL
We don't have the location yet. We're docking on a skyplex in a bit, it's run by a fellow called Niska.

INARA
Never heard of him.

MAL
Well I have, and while we're there you'll stay confined to the ship.

INARA
Is the petty criminal perchance ashamed to be riding with a Companion?

MAL
Niska has a very unlovely rep. If he's got work for me, fine, but I don't — I'm not sure you'd be safe.

INARA
Mal, if you're being a gentleman, I may die of shock.

Mal bows, slightly, and leaves. Pops his head back in:

MAL
Have you got time to do my hair?

INARA
Out.

He goes.

EXT. SPACE - LATER

We see Serenity docking on a large space station, Niska's SKYPLEX. It has docks for at least eight ships, and though somewhat dingy, it is bustling.

INT. BRIDGE - CONTINUING

As Wash settles her down.

INT. HALL/NISKA'S OFFICE - LATER

Mal, Zoe and Jayne are walked through the hall by two armed goons. The three are quiet and watchful. One of the goons knocks on a door and it is opened.

Standing behind it is CROW. He is as mean and large a tattooed motherfucker as ever stood behind a door. He stares grimly at the crew a moment, then:

NISKA (O.S.)
It's fine, Crow, they can come in.

The accent is heavily European, and the man (NISKA), when revealed by Crow stepping aside, is a slight, old, bespectacled fellow — looks more like Gepetto than the Godfather. He comes from around a desk, looks our gang up and down as they enter.

NISKA
Malcolm Reynolds is which?

MAL
I'm Captain Reynolds. My First Mate, Zoe, and this is Jayne.

NISKA
Very nice. I'm Adelai Niska, you've seen Crow, he loves to stand at the door to say "Boo!", but he is, you say it... my Good Right Hand.

MAL
We got word you might have a job for us.

NISKA
Yes, yes, an exciting job — a train! Has something I need. You've worked a train before?

MAL
We've hit a few.

NISKA
Are you going to ask me what it is I need?

MAL
As a rule, no.

NISKA
Yes, good, you have a reputation. You do the job, no complications, that's what. Malcolm Reynolds gets it done, is the talk.

MAL
Well I'm glad to hear that.

NISKA
Do you know what a reputation is? It's people talking, gossip, it's not... to hold, touch it, you can't. Not from gossip. Now I also have reputation, not so pleasant, I think you know. Crow.

Crow opens a door to another room.

ANGLE: in the room is a man hung from the ceiling, clearly dead from being hideously tortured. Crow steps in, brandishing a curved blade that is his trademark weapon.

MICHAEL FAIRMAN

Michael Fairman has been acting since 1971, with well over 100 film and television credits, but he says he's never played anyone quite like Adelai Niska, the indelible villain of 'The Train Job' and 'War Stories'. "I knew he had a Czech accent and I ran around trying to find somebody who spoke Czech, so I got a quasi-Czech accent, a sort of Czech-Russian accent," Fairman remembers. "I gleaned from the script that he was a very sadistic kind of guy, but very, very charming, very easy, not brusque or tough or loud, and I took it from there. I kept pushing the envelope on him. I tried to put a little bit of feyness into him, sort of dandyish, not gayness, but dandyish, and I started really enjoying that."

Wardrobe was important, Fairman elaborates: "I loved the glasses. I think the glasses really helped in some way that I can't really describe. They just gave me a more specific feeling about him, that maybe he was a little bit near-sighted. When an actor is given a prop, there are very subtle changes that take place physically and emotionally in terms of your point of view. Placing that retro idea in the future was kind of interesting, too. I tried to make him Old World European."

In playing Niska's attitude, Fairman explains, "I felt superior to everyone. Everybody was my underling. And, of course, I was hiring Mal — I certainly felt superior to the Captain and those guys, *deliciously* superior."

Even as a guest, Fairman said he noticed the mood on set. "It was a particularly gregarious group of leading actors welcoming me. That happens quite often, but they were particularly nice. I had worked with Gina Torres in a pilot and we got on right away. I just got very friendly with everyone. They enjoyed the character in the first episode and were very happy when they heard I was coming back!"

WASH

*"Oh, gawd! What could it beee? We're doomed!
Who's flyin' this thing?! Oh. Right. That'd
be me. Back to work."*

It's a long way from Plano, Texas to outer space, but in both his life and career, native Texan Alan Tudyk has always relished taking on roles that transport him from the ordinary to the extraordinary. He's built his career around his chameleon-like ability to play anyone convincingly, from a gay German drug addict (*28 Days*), a delusional pirate (*Dodgeball*), Lancelot à la Monty Python (*Spamalot*), to a machine with an awakening heart (*I, Robot*). Yet despite his varied résumé, Tudyk is arguably best known to his dedicated fan base as the goofy, wise-crackin', dinosaur-lovin' pilot — Hoban 'Wash' Washburne of *Firefly*. Interestingly enough, it's a role that the actor admits initially barely registered on his radar way back in the early months of 2002. "I was aware of the project and that Joss Whedon was involved," Tudyk remembers about his first audition for the pilot. He was rehearsing for a play in New York City at the time, Tudyk recalls, "I went on tape in a casting office in New York with the one scene from the original pilot, which has me playing with the dinosaurs. It was like, 'There's no script, here's a couple of lines, let's see what you can do with it.' They sketched a little paragraph that said it would be set in the future and in space, but not alien space, so there aren't prosthetics or bumpy foreheads and all that stuff. Basically, it was the outline of what we became."

After the audition, Tudyk details, "A month or so went by. I did a play and then flew out to LA to test for two other pilots. Originally, it was just one. I tested and it didn't go, so I was going back to New York and they said, 'Wait, they want you to test for this other thing.' I didn't get that one either and I was really done with LA and excited to go back home to New York. Then they said, 'Wait, they want to test you for *Firefly*.' I'm like, 'I don't even know what the hell that is. I auditioned for this, evidently?'" the actor deadpans. "They reminded me it was the Joss Whedon pilot and I said, 'Oh, wait! Cool! No, I liked that!' They got me the script and I went and auditioned.

"My first meeting with Joss was at that test. I just thought he was some guy. I remember he had a beard and I didn't think it was Joss Whedon," he laughs. "He came out to tell us all good luck and to have fun with it. So I went in and auditioned against two other guys; and they then said, 'Now, we are down to just two of you. You need to come back and we will pair you with our possible Zoes.' It was me and this guy, Carlos [Jacott] — who is Dobson in the original pilot. We were both up for Wash. We were there waiting to be paired up with the Zoes, but they didn't like any of the Zoes they had that day. They sent us both home and when I got back, I got a call saying I'd got it. I said, 'Okay, fine, great! I'm not going to argue!' And then it became the show."

Cast as Wash, the everyman, smart-ass of the crew, Tudyk says he immediately embraced the character because of their shared qualities. Full of humor with a true passion for flying and his wife Zoe, Wash became the voice of reason the audience could identify with amongst the crew. Wash was a character Tudyk says he understood and one that fit a familiar Whedon model. "*Buffy* was still on the air when we were doing the show — so I'm the space Xander," he jokes. And even if the actor is a little less Zen in reality about navigating the potholes in life, he smiles, "It's my instinct more to be... when everything is high-octane around you and moving fast, I can get caught up in it really easily. Wash reminds me that I can just relax and be calm." ◐

Our gang sees this, takes it in.

None of them pleased, but all of them silent.

Crow starts cutting down the body as Niska shuts the door, shaking his head sadly before he turns to the group.

NISKA (cont'd)
Now, for you, my reputation is not from gossip. You see this man, he does not do the job. I show you what I do with him and now, my reputation for you is fact, is... solid. You do the train job for me, then you are solid. No more gossip. That is strong relationship.

MAL
Right...

NISKA
You do not like I kill this man.

MAL
Well, I'm sure he was a... very bad person...

NISKA
My wife's nephew. At dinner I am getting an earful, there is no way out of that. So. The train job.

He moves to his desk, hits a piece of clear paper, the train schematic appears.

NISKA (cont'd)
Here in fifth car, two boxes, Alliance goods. You don't mind taking from the Alliance, I think. From your reputation.

He smiles at Mal, who doesn't really have it in him to smile back.

NISKA (cont'd)
You get on the train at Hancock, heading to Paradiso. I give you cover story in case of questions, but you are not bothered, I think. You get the boxes off before you reach Paradiso and you deliver to Crow... here.

He touches the paper again and a map appears, with a point marked a few miles from the train line (where the city, PARADISO, is also clearly marked).

NISKA (cont'd)
Half the money now, Crow gives you the other half at rendezvous point. Anything goes wrong... then your reputation is only gossip, and things between us are not so solid. Yes?

Off Mal's look...

EXT. DESERT - DAY

We see the quiet countryside — and then the train WHIPS through frame. It has an old, wrought-iron and brass feel to it, but it HOVERS above a lit track, a series of slim metal dorsal fins arching out from the undercarriage, just above the ground.

INT. TRAIN - CONTINUING

Mal and Zoe, dressed in civvies that look not terribly unlike their usual clothes, sit in the crowded car.

MAL
How long til we hit Paradiso?

ZOE
Another twenty minutes. We should be at the foothills in five.

MAL
Best get to work.

They rise, start toward the back.

ZOE
He's a psycho, you know. Niska.

MAL
He's not the first psycho to hire us, nor the last. Do you think that's a commentary on us?

ZOE
I've just got an image in my head of a guy hanging from the ceiling.

MAL
And I got an image of it not being me. Let's do the thing.

They reach the end of the car, are moving into the next one:

MAL (cont'd)
It's a simple job. And we're simple folk, so it shouldn't be a problem.

He is finishing that sentence as they enter the next car.

ANGLE: THE CAR

is entirely filled with a regiment of Alliance soldier/cops (called FEDS), all facing this way. All armed.

ANGLE: MAL AND ZOE

stop and stare.

MAL (cont'd)
Hi.

END OF ACT ONE

ACT TWO

INT. DINING ROOM - DAY

Inara enters to find Book sitting at the dining room table, reading his bible distractedly. He rises, nods to her.

INARA
Shepherd.

BOOK
Good day.

He sits again. She fusses about getting food. A beat.

BOOK (cont'd)
So, how do you think it's going?

INARA
(slightly amused)
The "caper"?
(less amused)
Mal knows what he's doing.

BOOK
How long have you known him?

INARA
I've been on the ship eight months now. I'm not certain that I'll ever actually know the Captain.

BOOK
(laughs a bit)
I'm surprised a respectable Companion would sail with this crew.

INARA
It's not always this sort of work. They take the jobs they can get. Even legitimate ones. But the further you get from the central planets, the harder things are. So this is part of it.

BOOK
I wish I could help. I mean, I don't want to help, not help help, not with the thieving, but... I do feel awfully useless.

INARA
You could always pray they make it back safely.

BOOK
I don't think the Captain would much like me praying for him.

INARA
Don't tell him.

She turns a bit, says, mostly to herself:

INARA (cont'd)
I never do.

INT. TRAINCAR - CONTINUING

Mal and Zoe are still standing in front of the feds.

There is a beat, and then the door at the other end opens, an immigrant-looking family coming through towards Mal and Zoe. They take the opportunity to move as well, heading back and passing the family. A couple of feds eyeball them, but there is no comment made.

INT. THE NEXT TRAINCAR - CONTINUING

This one is filled with poor, immigrant families. Mal and Zoe take a moment, make sure they're out of earshot.

ZOE
Sir, is there some information we might maybe be lacking? As to why there's an entire fed squad sitting on this train?

MAL
It doesn't concern us.

ZOE
It kind of concerns me...

MAL
I mean they're not protecting the goods. If they were, they wouldn't be letting people past 'em.

ZOE
You don't think it changes the situation a bit?

MAL
I surely do. Makes it more fun.

ZOE
Sir, I think you have a problem with your brain being missing.

MAL
Come on. We stick to the plan, we get the goods and we're back on Serenity before the train even reaches Paradiso. Only now we do it under the noses of twenty trained Alliance feds and that makes them look all manner of stupid. Hell, this job I would pull for free.

He starts off, she follows.

ZOE
Then can I have your share?

MAL
No.

ZOE
If you die can I have your share?

MAL
Yes.

EXT. DESERT - DAY

We are moving with the train — and we suddenly move laterally, over low hills, to find Serenity flying low at the same pace, some 300 yards away.

INT. BRIDGE - CONTINUING

Wash is piloting. Jayne is with him.

WASH
We start flying with the hatch open, keeping her steady is gonna be a job of work, so you strap in.

JAYNE
You get me killed, I'm a come back as a ghost and punch your liver out.

WASH
Well, there goes Plan A...

JAYNE
I'm not messing around. You'd best run straight or you'll get a boxing.

WASH
You sound like my father. Which is weird because you look more like my mother.

JAYNE
One of these days —

A beeping. Wash looks at his monitors.

WASH
We're close. Get down there.

JAYNE
(as he goes)
Hell, I ever call you out, you'd probably just hide behind the Mrs.

WASH
(working the panels)
Go.
(a beat. To himself:)
My liver?

INT. CARGO BAY - CONTINUING

Kaylee opens the bay doors. She drags over some cable and winches, starts attaching them to the walls.

Simon appears, tentative.

SIMON
Hey.

KAYLEE
Oh hey Doctor.

SIMON
You really should just call me Simon.

KAYLEE
I'll do that then.

He a little bit causes the shyness in her.

SIMON
So what are we doing?

KAYLEE
Oh! Crime.

SIMON
Crime, good. Okay. Crime.

KAYLEE
It's a train heist. We fly over the traincar, The Captain and Zoe sneak in, we lower Jayne onto the car, they bundle up the booty and we haul 'em all back up. Easy as lyin'.

SIMON
You've done this before?

KAYLEE
(laughing)
Oh hell no!
(serious)
But I think it's gonna work. The captain is <jen duh sh tyen tsai> [an absolute genius] when it comes to plans.

SIMON
Is there anything I can... something I should be doing?

JAYNE
(entering)
Staying the hell out of everyone's way.

We can see he's added some layers, including a hat tied around his chin and a scarf to pull over his face. Gonna be windy.

KAYLEE
No call to be snappy, Jayne.

JAYNE
(to Kaylee)
Are you about to jump onto a moving train?

She backs off. He turns back to Simon.

JAYNE (cont'd)
Captain's not around, I'm in charge.

KAYLEE
Since when?

JAYNE
(ignoring her)
Just 'cause Mal says you're a medic don't make you part of the crew. You just play at figuring what's wrong with that moon-brained sister of yours til we call for you, <dong ma> [understand]?

ANGLE: UP ON THE CATWALK

is River herself, sitting and watching the exchange. It's impossible to tell if she even understands what she's hearing. Simon stares at Jayne a beat, weighing the advantages of arguing.

SIMON
Right.

He turns and goes. Kaylee starts strapping Jayne in.

KAYLEE
You shouldn't be so rude to him.

JAYNE
Why, 'cause he's all rich and fancible?

KAYLEE
He's not rich. Alliance crashed his accounts when he snuck out his sister.

JAYNE
Yeah, well, we could all be rich, we handed her back.

KAYLEE
You're not even thinking that!

JAYNE
Mal is.

KAYLEE
That's not funny.

JAYNE
He ain't stupid. Why would he take on trouble like those two if there weren't no profit in it? Captain's got a move he ain't made yet. You'll see.

He tests his straps and such. They're good.

JAYNE (cont'd)
Time for some thrilling heroics.

INT. TRAINCAR - CONTINUING

Mal and Zoe are at the door marked: STORAGE. NO PASSENGERS. Mal pulls out a keycard.

MAL
Niska's sources better be good...

A beat, and he inserts the card.

INT. TRAINCAR WITH FEDS - CONTINUING

One of the feds gets up, stretching, and heads back to where Mal and Zoe are.

INT. TRAINCAR - CONTINUING

The panel lights on the corners of the door turn from orange to purple. We hear locks withdrawing and the door swings open.

ZOE
Shiny.

She pulls a gas canister out of Mal's bag, prepares to hurl it as Mal readies himself and whips the door open.

ANGLE: INSIDE THE CAR

there are no guards. Just a room full of various crates and baggage. They enter, pulling the door shut behind them — but leaving it slightly ajar, as Zoe fiddles with the canister and some wire at the bottom of the doorway.

Mal moves to the center of the car, pulling what looks like a wicked powerful screw gun from his bag.

MAL
Find the cargo.

He steps up on some boxes. The ceiling is separated into three corrugated iron panels, all about eight feet by four. Mal puts the gun to one of the rivets in the center panel, triggers it, and we hear a ripping/sucking sound. He pulls the gun down, rivet stuck in it. Removes it and starts on the next.

ANGLE: ZOE

is going through boxes. Rips a tarp off some and sees two big metal crates with the AngloSino flag printed on top. They are the burnished purple of the soldiers' uniforms.

ZOE
All hail the great Alliance.

EXT. DESERT - CONTINUING

We are with the train as Serenity appears right above it, keeping pace with it.

INT. AIRLOCK/CARGO BAY - CONTINUING

The doors are closing behind Jayne and Kaylee as the bomb bay door is opening, letting in daylight and a shitload of wind. When the hatch is open all the way, Jayne gets down and crawls to the edge of it, looks over. He has a cable attached to him.

ANGLE: OVER JAYNE

We see the train some twenty feet below. Everything is moving very fast.

INT. BRIDGE - CONTINUING

Wash pilots, hands tight on the wheel, ship bucking slightly.

INT. AIRLOCK - CONTINUING

Jayne gives the thumbs up to Kaylee. She hits a lever on a winch and it starts letting out cable as Jayne jumps —

EXT. DESERT - CONTINUING

— from the ramp to the car twenty feet below, cables trailing out above him. He hits hard but holds on, keeping his head down. Waits.

INT. TRAINCAR - CONTINUING

Mal pops the last rivet and he and Zoe lower the panel down as gently as they can. It makes a bit of clatter as they lower it to one side —

INT. TRAIN - CONTINUING

The fed who moved back hears the noise, starts in that direction, curious...

PARADISO

Production designer Carey Meyer: "The town we used for 'Paradiso' is very Western. It's a little gold mining area with some mineshafts and other useful locations. We stumbled on it while location scouting for 'Serenity' and almost used it; we'd always liked it and Joss remembered it and so he went back to it when we came to do 'The Train Job'. I came up with a way to connect the train to the area — have the train tracks come up along the ridge. We built one traincar, for the actors to enter and exit, out on a ramp in this built up space; the train was all CG on the other side. Once we had connected the train to the location, everything else fell into place and we could use it and dress it the way we wanted to."

❖ Above: Building the set for the interior of the train.

INT. TRAINCAR - CONTINUING

Jayne flips in through the big hole in the roof as Zoe and Mal drag the crates in a net to right under the hole. They start pulling cable off Jayne and securing it onto the corners of the net. Jayne hops on top (still with his own line on) and calls into a walkie:

JAYNE
Fifteen seconds!

ANGLE: KAYLEE

ready to reverse the winch.

ANGLE: WASH

piloting. Tense as hell.

ANGLE: THE FED

sees the door ajar, pulls his rifle off his shoulder, approaches the door. Zoe hops on the crate with Jayne, about to buckle onto his line, as Mal is finishing his end of the net —

The soldier stands by the door, rifle ready, and rips it open —

ANGLE: THE GAS CANISTER

is popped when the wire is pulled.

It shoots gas up into the Fed's face before he can see anything. He shoots blind (the sound is a series of muffled pops), Mal moving towards him as Zoe dives off the crate for cover as boxes splinter by her head from stray bullets. One hits Jayne's leg, he sags but holds on.

ZOE
(to Jayne)
Go!

JAYNE
(into walkie)
Go! Go now!

Kaylee hits the winch —

And Jayne goes up with the netted crates, out of the traincar as Mal gets to the blinded soldier, fights him in the smoke. Mal is precise and brutal, and though it's messy, the guy is unconscious in moments.

MAL
(to Zoe)
Come on!

They head out of the traincar, towards the front —

EXT. DESERT - CONTINUING

As Serenity moves away from the train, Jayne and the crates still being pulled up.

INT. TRAIN - CONTINUING

THE ALLIANCE

Costume designer Shawna Trpcic: "The classic image was Nazi Germany, and to try to avoid it just being totally German, we again went to different wars. The first sketches that we did were way too Nazi," she laughs. "You don't need to be so obvious when you're conveying a bad guy, and Joss was like, 'Okay, pull it up a little...' but we took the hat shapes and things from that World War Two time period."

❖ Above: Trpcic's costume designs for the Alliance soldiers.

❖ Right: An Alliance soldier's armor.

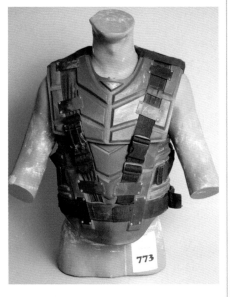

773

Mal and Zoe reach the car — full with poorer passengers — between them and the car full of soldiers. They roll out a couple of gas canisters. Gas billows up just as feds are entering from the other side. Mal and Zoe blend in with the other civilians, choking and keeping low, as the soldiers pass them.

INT. CARGO BAY - CONTINUING

Jayne climbs up, the crates pulled up by the winch. As soon as the door is shut, Kaylee unhooks herself and moves to him, finally able to speak without the rushing wind:

KAYLEE
Where are the others?

JAYNE
Shot my gorramn leg!

KAYLEE
Jayne? Are they on the train? Are they gonna be okay?

EXT. PARADISO TRAIN STATION - DAY

The train has stopped. Many passengers have climbed off, still red eyed and coughing from smoke. Mal and Zoe are among them. Behind them, though paying them no particular mind, is Sheriff BOURNE, talking to a fed.

FED
Our man didn't get a look.

BOURNE
Well, Jesus, can someone at least find out what they took?
(calls out to a deputy)
Pendy, keep these people together! And quiet 'em down!

Mal is listening, but his attention is also drawn to:

ANGLE: A group of families, mostly women and children. Clearly very sick, clearly waiting for something on that train. Someone comes to talk to them and several of the women start crying, clutching their children to them.

A deputy comes up to the sheriff, and Zoe and Mal hear very clearly.

DEPUTY
It was the medicine, sir. All the supplies.

BOURNE
They stole the gorramn medicine? We been waiting — all of it?

DEPUTY
Every ounce.

BOURNE
God help us.

Zoe looks at Mal. Mal looks stone-faced.

ANGLE ON: the crying women. The sickly children.

MAL
Son of a bitch...

END OF ACT TWO

ACT THREE

EXT. SPACE - ALLIANCE CRUISER

A giant Alliance Cruiser moves slowly through space.

INT. ALLIANCE CRUISER - CONTINUING

Big. Clean. Corporate. No bantery chit-chat to be had. The crew is dressed in the same formal Alliance attire we saw the soldiers wearing in the traincar.

An OFFICER looks over an ENSIGN's shoulder to a viewing screen.

OFFICER
What's the fuss?

ENSIGN
All network alert. Cargo theft. Medical shipment lifted off a train in the Georgia System, en route to Paradiso.

OFFICER
(eyeing screen)

Two crates of Pasceline D. Right. Get you a tidy fortune on the black market.

ENSIGN
Paradiso's a mining community, sir. Most there are afflicted with Bowden's Disease. The miners pass it on to their children.

OFFICER
(almost to himself)
And yet they insist on breeding...
(then)
Tag it received and bounce it back. Locals can deal with it.

ENSIGN
Sir, there is a regiment holding in Paradiso. They were on the train, headed to the installation.

OFFICER
Then get 'em back on that train and get it moving. Who's holding them there?

ENSIGN
Sir, the Sheriff requested we deploy a few to help him inves —

OFFICER
Those are Federal Marshals, not local narcotic hounds. They have better things to do. And so do we.

The Ensign nods as the Officer moves off.

EXT. DESERT - NIGHT - SERENITY

is parked in a canyon, away from prying eyes and spying probes.

INT. SERENITY - INFIRMARY - CONTINUING

Simon is patching up the wounded Jayne who's on an operating table. Kaylee is nearby, trying to keep him steady while Simon works. We may or may not notice River quietly sitting in the b.g. On Wash's entrance, Jayne pulls away from Simon, starts to rise.

SIMON
(re: wound)
I'm not finished.

JAYNE
(ignoring Simon, rises)
Why you got us parked here? This ain't the <go tsao de> [dog humping] rendezvous spot.

WASH
It is now.

JAYNE
Niska's people're waitin'. They're not partial to waitin'.

WASH
Let 'em read a magazine. We don't make the sale until Mal and Zoe are back on the boat.

JAYNE
These are stone killers, little man. They ain't cuddly like me.

WASH
I'm not flying anywhere without my wife.

KAYLEE
She'll be okay. She's with the Captain.

JAYNE
See there? Everybody wins. Gahh!
(to Simon)
Dammit, Doc, I need a pop to quiet this pain some.

Simon goes for the medicine, loads it onto the hypo as he talks.

SIMON
What about the authorities? We're sitting here with stolen Alliance goods.
(no one denies it)
Won't they be looking for us?

WASH
They buzz this canyon, we'll hear 'em before they ever see us. I figure we're good for a...

RIVER
Won't stop. They'll never stop.

That was unnerving. Everyone just looks at her.

RIVER (cont'd)
They'll just keep coming until they get back what you took.

She laughs softly to herself, her eyes betraying fear.

RIVER (cont'd)
Two by two, hands of blue... two by two, hands of blue...

JAYNE
(to River)
How's about you keep your crazy mouth shut? Is that a fun game?
(to the others)
Now I'm in rutting charge here and I'm telling you how it works.

Simon injects him with painkiller as he continues.

JAYNE (cont'd)
Niska doesn't get the goods on time he will make meatpies of the lot of us. I ain't walking into that.

BOOK
This Adelai Niska you're talking about?

JAYNE
Now how would a Shepherd know a name like that?

BOOK
As I've heard it, he made a deal with the Captain. If the Captain's not there to finish it — If Niska finds out he's being held and may speak as to who hired him... I think we're better off being a little late.

A beat, as Jayne takes this in.

JAYNE
Fine. We wait. For a spell. Then we make our appointment.

That's good enough for Wash, for now.

INT. POLICE STATION - NIGHT

Mal and Zoe sit stiffly next to each other.

MAL
This is a nightmare.

❖ Top: Fed badges.

❖ Above: The Sheriff's badge.

INARA

"Mal, if you're being a gentleman, I may die of shock."

As a highly respected Companion, Inara Serra is a woman noted for her calm, graceful style, but as a late and integral addition to the cast, Julliard graduate Morena Baccarin felt far from calm on her first day. "I came on set and was *petrified*," she recalls. "I had auditioned probably two days before. It all happened very quickly. I had just come to Los Angeles; it was my first time here, and my first television show, so it was a first for a lot of things. I'm glad it happened so quickly because I didn't have a chance to freak out. I was so scared, but they were so warm and so sweet. They all seemed happy to meet me and see who the new Inara was going to be. [Baccarin replaced the originally cast Rebecca Gayheart shortly after filming began.] Joss brought me down from the testing room like a proud dad, holding my hand and introducing me."

Inara defied the conventions of her profession and despite being labeled a whore several times by Mal, she never warranted that description. Rather, she defined elegance and decorum — more closely resembling a Japanese Geisha than a traditional prostitute. "It was really important to Joss that she was regal, a woman of class, high standing, and moral grounds," says Baccarin. "She's against the stereotype and the way he described her is exactly what attracted me to the character and the project. We had a lot of conversations about how she would be an ambassador and bring all these people together on the ship. And she's got pride — which is why she can't express herself with Mal.

"I also liked the fact that she was a whore, even though it was kind of scary for me. I originally got just a few pages of the script. Even before I read those, there was just a treatment that

kind of explained what she did and I thought, 'This could be bad. This could really be *not* fun to do.' Then I met Joss, and he persuaded me that it would be a really good thing.

"I don't think I was conscious of what I was doing. It just came out of the text, what I was saying, and how I was dressed. It was a combination of a lot of elements coming together. I didn't really make a decision about what I was going to sound like. I did do some research on Geisha because I thought it was important that she had a sense of tradition and ceremony; but it is really difficult to do research for a show set in a world that doesn't exist. However, it was very clear in Joss's mind, so it was easy to translate for us."

Inara's beautiful Eastern-inspired wardrobe helped to define her character. "I loved those outfits!" smiles Baccarin. "Every day coming to work, I used to wonder, 'What am I going to be wearing today?' Shawna [Trpcic] did such a great job designing the costumes that I felt like a princess all the time. All the girls were like, 'You are so lucky. We're in grease and overalls all day long.' Although it could get kind of old after twelve hours of being in some of those corsets. You can't breathe. They were designed not to be too tight, but you wear anything like that for over ten hours and it's going to be uncomfortable. There was always something sticking into me. I was always the one standing while everyone was sitting. Some of that stuff I just wanted to rip off, so I could put on sweat pants! It's funny — Inara might be 'the stylish one', but any time we do conventions, I'm the one in the jeans and sneakers."

Baccarin really valued being directed by Joss Whedon: "It was a dream. He's great to work with because he's very specific and knows what he wants, but he'll let you put in your two cents. If you are wrong, he'll tell you; but for the most part, he will let you try stuff. It feels like a collaboration, which makes all the difference sometimes."

Although *Firefly* was a casualty in the ratings war, it inspired a legion of loyal fans. "It is one of those things people identify with," she offers. "It's a fantasy world, but so tangible. A part of you is in almost every one of the characters. People are really drawn to that, to stories that are like myths but teach you life lessons."

ZOE
Nothing points to us yet, sir.

MAL
That ain't what I'm talking about.

WIDER - we see they're currently sitting alone. About them the place is a hive of activity. Hill-Street-Blues-meets-Rio-Bravo-by-way-of-Blade-Runner. The understaffed constabulary is working its way through questioning the train passengers.

And more of the sick women and children are near Mal and Zoe, a constant reminder of their crime.

The SHERIFF, no-nonsense, tired, finishes questioning A COUPLE that we might recognize from the train. He thanks them perfunctorily. They take their luggage, exit.

MAL (cont'd)
Whatever happens, remember I love you.

ZOE
(shocked)
Sir?

MAL
(you idiot)
Because you're my wife.

ZOE
Right. Sir. Honey.

The Sheriff confers with a deputy, who checks a list, points to Mal and Zoe. Sheriff crosses to them. Has the train manifest.

BOURNE
Car three, row twelve. Mister and Missus... Raymond.

Mal is suddenly the protective young husband.

MAL
Can you tell us what's going on? We've been here for so long. Did someone on the train get killed?

BOURNE
No, no. Nothing like that. I see here your fares were purchased by a third party...

MAL
My uncle. A wedding gift.

BOURNE
(it's unheard of)
Wedding gift... You spending your honeymoon in Paradiso?

ZOE
Actually we're here looking for work.

BOURNE
That right?

MAL
My uncle said he knew a Joey Bloggs out here. Said he might have an opening. Thought we'd try our luck.

BOURNE
You a miner by trade, either of you?

MAL
Not really.

BOURNE
Haven't seen many folk choose this life weren't born to it.

ZOE
Well, work's real scarce for a couple just starting out.

MAL
How come there's so many sick here?

BOURNE
Bowden's Malady. You know what that is?

ZOE
Affliction of the bone and muscle. Degenerative.

BOURNE
Very. Every planet that's been terraformed for human life has its own little quirks. Turns out the air down underground, mixed up with the ore processors, it's a perfect recipe for Bowden's. Everybody gets it: minors, dumpers — hell, I got it and I ain't ever set foot in a mine. It's worst on the kids, of course.

ZOE
But it's treatable.

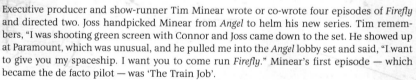

TIM MINEAR

Executive producer and show-runner Tim Minear wrote or co-wrote four episodes of *Firefly* and directed two. Joss handpicked Minear from *Angel* to helm his new series. Tim remembers, "I was shooting green screen with Connor and Joss came down to the set. He showed up at Paramount, which was unusual, and he pulled me into the *Angel* lobby set and said, "I want to give you my spaceship. I want you to come run *Firefly*." Minear's first episode — which became the de facto pilot — was 'The Train Job'.

"It was all there story-wise to be aired instead of the pilot, but always, always, *always* with our hope that we would eventually be able to talk the network into airing the pilot first. Joss and I wrote the episode in forty-eight hours, and that included coming up with it, breaking it and writing it. We put it all up on a board and then broke it into pieces. He refigured it in his office and I refigured it in mine until we finished. He wrote the teaser and the first two acts and I wrote acts three and four.

"We knew we wanted action and humor and something really simple that went to the heart of the most basic elements of the concept, which is that these are outlaws on the fringe who take jobs that are not altogether legal, *but* they have their own code. That's why we did a story of a basic heist, but then when they realized that real human people were going to suffer because of this job, they ended up doing the only thing they could do morally, which was give the medicine back to the people of Paradiso and try to square ethically with the person who hired them to do this thing. What we tried to do was look for points in the story where we could say something essential about each character.

"I like 'The Train Job'. It is what it is. It was there to service a very particular thing. We approached it a little bit more from the head as opposed to the gut. There are things in it I really like: Jayne is doped up and he shoots a guy while half paralyzed. I like pretty much anything with Jayne."

BOURNE
There's medicine, Pasceline — works on the symptoms. Person could live like a person, they get it regular. But our shipment got stole right off that train you was ridin' in. Which is why you won't be seeing a parade in town today.

MAL
(feigned shock)
Stolen? Didn't we see an entire regiment of fine young Alliance Federals on the train?

BOURNE
You did. The same regiment that let the medicine get swiped from under their noses and then took off for their camp without so much as a whoopsie daisy.

MAL
That sounds like the Alliance. Unite the planets under one rule so everyone can be interfered with or ignored equally.

BOURNE
Alliance ain't much use to us on the border planets. But they ain't the ones stole that medicine. I find those people, they'll never see the inside of a jail. I'll just toss 'em in the mine, let 'em breathe deep for the rest of their lives.

MAL
Can't argue with that.

BOURNE
Mind telling me when it was you last spoke to Joey Bloggs?

Mal tenses, senses the trap.

MAL
Never did myself.

BOURNE
Right. Your uncle. And it was indicated to you that Joey had an opening?

MAL
Any job would do...

BOURNE
Funny your uncle never went to mentioning the Bowden's problem. Or that Joey Bloggs ate his own gun 'bout eight months back.

MAL
Did he.

BOURNE
Yep. Blew the back of his head right off.

MAL
(a long beat)
So... would his job be open?

The Sheriff gives a wan smile. The game's afoot and they both know it, neither one about to be so rude as to say so openly.

BOURNE
Say, I don't suppose you folks would mind if we took a retinal scan? We're doin' it with all the folks we don't know by sight. Just to make sure

ADAM BALDWIN

On improvising a drugged up and delusional Jayne during 'The Train Job': "I came up with that part about reaching out for the pixie dust, the little fairies, the shining lights... There were a few things Joss didn't write that would get added in. I would always try to busy it up because Jayne wasn't speechifying all over the place so I had to try and find things to do. I would work closely with the prop master and find doings with straps, belts, buckles, guns, gloves and wristbands. So Joss allowed me to play around. We did a few takes and I did a couple of takes just reaching for it. Then for whatever reason — Summer blew her line or something. You know, she was the set scapegoat. Anytime any of us would screw up a line or the camera would get out of focus, we'd all be 'Summer! Goddamit! Get your lines right!' The most innocent of us all! Anyway, Joss came up to me and said 'Why didn't you reach for the little fairies? Where were they?' I was like 'Oh, you like that huh?' And he's like 'Yeah, keep that. Okay good.'"

they are who they say.

INT. SERENITY - BRIDGE - NIGHT

Jayne comes barging into the bridge. Wash is there, with Kaylee. Wash stands up, knowing this will be unpleasant. Simon follows Jayne.

JAYNE
That's it. We waited long enough. Get this bird in the air.

WASH
No rutting way.

SIMON
(to Jayne)
You really should sit down...

KAYLEE
We can't just leave the Captain and Zoe here.

JAYNE
They ain't coming! We can't walk in there and get 'em so they're done.

Jayne shoves Wash back toward the controls.

JAYNE (cont'd)
Now fire it up.

Wash flares. He'll get trounced, but he's ready to fight. Inara and Book appear in the doorway.

INARA
What's going on?

JAYNE
(without looking at her)
Strap in. We're takin' off.

WASH
We're not.

JAYNE
Captain'd do the same if it were one of us —

KAYLEE
Not in a million years —

JAYNE
Shut it!

His intensity shuts them down. Wash is quiet but firm:

WASH
Listen to me —

JAYNE
Do you know what the chain of command is? It's the chain I go get and beat you with til you understand who's in rutting command here!

Wash is truly scared, but not backing down.

JAYNE (cont'd)
Now we're finishing this deal and then maybe — MAYBE we'll come back for those... morons... got themselves caught and you can't change that just by gettin' all bendy...

WASH
All what?

JAYNE
(drifting)
You got the light, from the console to keep you, to lift you up... they shine like little angels.

He topples forward, hits the floor hard, chin leading. Out like a two ton light. Everyone just blinks. Except for Simon.

WASH
Did he just go crazy and fall asleep?

SIMON
I told him to sit down...

KAYLEE
You doped him!

SIMON
It was supposed to kick in a good deal sooner. I just didn't feel comfortable with him in charge. I hope that's all right.

The look on everyone's faces tells him it is.

BOOK
So how do we get the others?

WASH
Jayne was right about them not making contact. Chances are they got pinched getting off that train.

KAYLEE
And we can't just waltz in and pull 'em out...

BOOK
Someone respectable enough might be able to.

WASH
A Shepherd can't just demand they hand over —

BOOK
I know. I wasn't talking about me.

INT. POLICE STATION - NIGHT

Mal and Zoe still cooling their heels. The Sheriff in the near distance conferring. Eyeballing them.

ZOE
You figure Serenity's still waitin' for us?

MAL
If they are, everyone's fired.

ZOE
And if they're not?

MAL
Everyone's fired.

ZOE
So how you wanna play this?

There is a buzz of activity. A deputy moves to the Sheriff with some news. He reacts with surprise.

Mal and Zoe watch, curious. Commotion as someone pushes through the deputies —

INARA - appears, the bearing of a monarch. Mal reacts to the sight. So does Zoe. Inara strides magnificently over to Mal. He opens his mouth to speak —

MAL
What the h—

SMACK -

she slaps him hard across the face.

INARA
Don't you dare speak to me.

A deputy has given the Sheriff Inara's official papers. He peruses them as he crosses to her.

INARA (cont'd)
Sheriff, I want this man bound by law at once. That's assuming he hasn't been already...

BOURNE
No one's been bound. Not yet.

INARA
Well thank god you stopped them.
(to Mal)
Did you honestly think you could access my accounts and I wouldn't find you?
(sadly, to Zoe)
And Zoe... what would your husband say if he knew you were here?

ZOE
I was weak.

BOURNE
(not surprised)
So I take it they ain't newlyweds?

INARA
Hardly. Malcolm's my indentured man. With three years left on his debt. I imagine we'll have to add another six months after this little adventure.

The deputies stare in awe and whisper amongst themselves, as they have been since her entrance. Inara glances to them. Gathers herself with tremendous dignity.

BOURNE
You'll have to pardon them. Don't think a one of em's ever seen a Registered Companion before. Fancy lady such as yourself don't pass through here everyday.

INARA
I apologize for my manner.

BOURNE
Not a bit.

INARA
(to Mal and Zoe)
Though I've half a mind to leave you both here. If your debt weren't so large, I would.
(then)
Should I contact my ship? Will you need to hold them very much longer?

BOURNE
Looks to me like we're done. We're having some unrelated trouble. And his story had kind of an odor to it...

INARA
Yes. It's not the only thing about him that does.

Mal refuses to show that it burns him how much fun she's having.

INARA (cont'd)
Thank you very much, Sheriff.
(to Mal and Zoe)
Come along.

Mal and Zoe rise, follow her out.

The Sheriff watches them go. Something not sitting just right with him.

BOURNE
(to the deputy)
That's a hell of a lady. Her files were all in order?

DEPUTY
Ran 'em twice.

BOURNE
(lets out a breath)
Let's get started with the rest, then.

INT. CARGO BAY - LATER

Mal, Zoe and Inara all step off the shuttle. Kaylee and Wash are there to greet them. Zoe and Wash hug, make with smoochies.

KAYLEE
How'd it go?

MAL
She hit me.

He starts downstairs, they all follow.

They all react now to see Jayne sprawled out/propped against the stairs/catwalk. He's sort of in and out of consciousness. A floppy puppy. They have to step over him. Mal does a take.

KAYLEE
(approaching)
We tried to get him to the infirmary. He's just heavy.

Mal doesn't even ask.

WASH
Kept the engine running. We're good to go.

MAL
We're not going.

WASH
Not what? Not why?

MAL
We're bringing the cargo back.

Astounded looks from all save Zoe. Jayne moans in his full-body-novocaine stupor.

JAYNE
(slurred)
What? Whaddya mean back? I waited for you!

ZOE
Let's get this on the Mule.

WASH
What're you talking about? What about Niska? Won't that put him more or less in a killing mood?

Mal hits a button and the cargo bay ramp starts to lower.

MAL
There's others need this more.

INARA
My shuttle is faster —

MAL
You risked enough flying in there once. And I don't wanna get slapped around no more.
(to Wash)
Far as Niska goes, we'll just have to explain the job went south on us when we return the money.

Jayne groans.

WASH
You wanna explain, now's your chance...

He's seeing something that Mal doesn't. Mal turns, following Wash's gaze to see —

ANGLE - CARGO BAY RAMP

At the bottom of the ramp, just outside the ship are CROW and THREE MEN. Every man large, every man pissed.

END OF ACT THREE

ACT FOUR

INT. CARGO BAY/AIRLOCK - CONTINUOUS

Mal looks down on Crow and his men. They start to walk up the ramp. Mal takes a step forward.

CROW
You didn't make the rendezvous.

MAL
Ran into a few complications.

❖ Above and Below: Inara's official Companion papers and book.

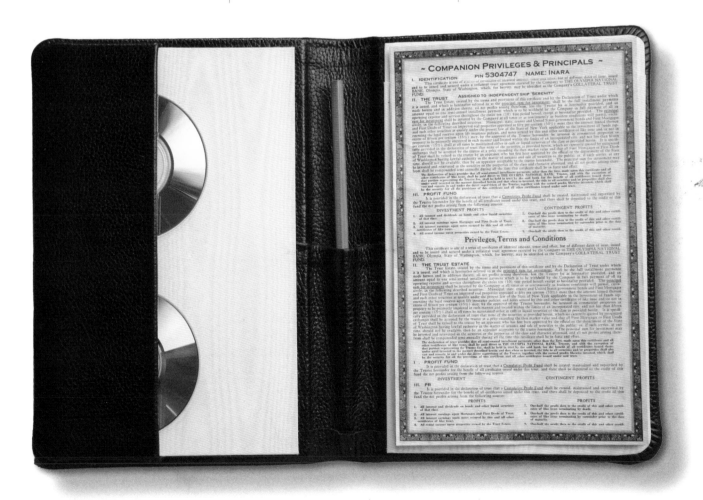

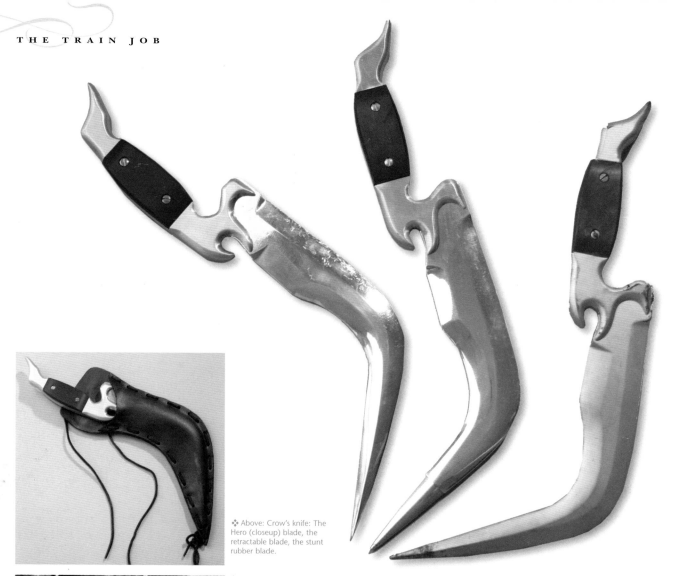

❖ Above: Crow's knife: The Hero (closeup) blade, the retractable blade, the stunt rubber blade.

CROW
You were thinking of taking Mister Niska's money and his property, maybe?

MAL
Interestingly — neither.

Crow furrows his brow.

CROW
I don't understand...

MAL
Yeah. Look. Here's what it is: deal's off.

Still with the brow furrowing from Crow.

MAL (cont'd)
We changed our minds.

CROW
You entered into an arrangement with Mister Niska. There is no mind-changing.

MAL
'Fraid that's where you're wrong. We just, we can't take this job. So you just relax, and we'll get you the money Niska paid us up front, you return it to him and call it even.

CROW
And there is no "even".

MAL
Is that right?

During all this...

MAL'S HAND

has been drifting toward his gun, as —

CROW

whip quick, releases his curved knife — buries it in Mal's right shoulder. Mal rears back, big pain.

And all hell, as they say, breaks loose —

Zoe is pulling her weapon, as...

Crow's men storm the cargo bay, guns out and firing...

MAL

Suddenly Crow is there, pulling out the knife, then slamming his fist into the wound. Mal fights back.

ZOE

Zoe has her gun out, takes out one of the guys right off, then lunges at Kaylee, pulling her down behind some cover as she avoids getting hit by the return fire. She looks over to make sure Wash is okay.

He is, nods to her from behind some crates, as...

CROW AND MAL

Crow just fucking wails on Mal, driving him staggering back up the ramp with each bone jarring blow.

Mal's pretty much only good with his left at this

point, and manages to get in a few good hits, but Crow's punishment is taking its toll on him.

Crow is distracted suddenly, as —

A ROAR

The MULE comes bouncing up over the top of the ramp, sending the other thugs scattering. Wash is driving it.

Mal presses his advantage. Gets in a few good licks. But Crow comes back strong. Sweeps up his fallen knife, is about to bury it in Mal's skull, when

A SHOT RINGS OUT

Crow goes down, screaming pain, a big hole in the back of his leg. Mal looks up, astonished to see —

JAYNE

still propped in the same spot, but with his gun out, sort of lazily aimed in that general direction. He still looks like a stroke victim, desperately trying to keep his eyes open.

MAL
Nice shot.

JAYNE
(slurred)
I was aimin' for his head.

EXT. JUST OUTSIDE TOWN - NIGHT

Mal and Zoe are on the Mule, Zoe driving, Mal on top of the crates, with a better view. The town becomes visible in the distance and he taps her shoulder. She cuts the engines and they get off, start untying the crates.

MAL
We're gonna have to drag 'em from here. We can leave 'em just off the street, notify the Sheriff once we're in deep deep space.

BOURNE
Why don't you tell him in person?

They draw — but SIX MEN with rifles appear from the brush. Mal and Zoe slowly holster their guns.

BOURNE (cont'd)
We got word of a ship not far out, came looking. Didn't expect to find you coming back.

MAL
Didn't expect to be coming.

The deputy from Act Two comes over as they speak, opens the crates.

DEPUTY
Nothin' missing.

Mal and the Sheriff stare at each other. Clearly an understanding, as he addresses the pair of them:

BOURNE
You were truthful back in town. These are tough times. Hard to find yourself work. A man can get a job, he might not look too close at what that job is.
(to Mal)
But a man learns all the details of a situation like ours, well then he has a choice.

MAL
I don't believe he does.

There is a moment then. The Sheriff slightly smiles.

BOURNE
(to his men)
Let's get these crates back to town. Make ourselves useful.

Two men each take a crate and haul them off. The Sheriff walks off with the rest of them, not saying anther word.

After a beat, Zoe climbs back onto the Mule and starts to turn it around.

EXT. SERENITY - NIGHT

Crow goes down in a heap onto his knees. He is on the ramp, the huge jet engine behind him just starting to whir to life, wind kicking up as the ship prepares to take off.

Mal stands before him, holding a wad of bills.

MAL
Now this is all the money Niska gave us in advance. You give it back to him, tell him the job didn't work out. We're not thieves — well, we are thieves, but — the point is, we're not taking what's his. We'll stay out of his way as best we can from here on in. You'll explain that's best for everyone, okay?

Crow rises. He towers over Mal, hatred on his face.

CROW
Keep the money. Use it to buy a funeral. It doesn't matter where you go, how far you fly — I will hunt you down and the last thing you see will be my blade.

MAL (sighs)
Darn.

He kicks Crow back — and the huge fellow is

❖ Above: The transparency of River produced by the Blue-Gloved Men.

instantly SUCKED into the engine of the ship. It's very sudden, but the resultant crunching noise goes on for a bit. A beat, and Zoe shoves one of Crow's henchmen in front of Mal.

MAL (cont'd)
Now. This is all the money Niska —

HENCHMAN
Oh I get it. I'm good. Best for everyone, I'm right there with you.

Mal smiles, puts the money in the man's breast pocket and pats it.

EXT. SPACE - NIGHT

As the ship leaves the planet behind.

INT. INFIRMARY/PASSENGER DORM/RIVER'S ROOM - NIGHT

Mal is being stitched up by Simon.

SIMON
You should have let me do this sooner.

MAL
I've had plenty worse. This is just a OWWW!

SIMON
Sorry.

MAL
Just be careful.
(a beat)

That was pretty fast thinking, dopin' up Jayne. Can't say you've made a lifetime friend...

SIMON
I'll deal with him.

MAL
I'm not too worried about you. How's your sister?

We begin drifting away from them as they speak, heading toward River's room as Simon's voice becomes a voiceover...

SIMON
The same. One moment she seems perfectly cogent, the next... she speaks nonsense. Like a child. It's so difficult to diagnose; I still don't know what the government was trying to do with her. So I have no idea if they succeeded.

and we land on River, sitting up in her bed and worrying the sheet with her hands, repeating to herself:

RIVER
Two by two, hands of blue, two by two, hands of blue...

over and over and

INT. ALLIANCE CRUISER - CONTINUING

The officer we saw before steps into a starkly lit room.

OFFICER
I'm sorry to keep you waiting. There's always one crisis or —

MAN
We're not interested.

OTHER MAN
We're here about a theft.

OFFICER
The medicine? On that planet... Word came up that was returned.

MAN
We didn't fly eighty-six million miles to track down a box of band-aids, Colonel.

The officer is increasingly uneasy. We finally

REVERSE ANGLE to see TWO MEN sitting at the table. They reek of government. Whatever the CIA is in the future, it's these guys. They are blank as slate.

OTHER MAN
We're looking for a girl. This girl.

As he says it the first man slides a folder forward, with a picture atop it. The picture is of River. The hand sliding it forward has, incongruously, a skin-tight latex glove on it. Blue.

Tilt back up to the men to see they are both wearing blue gloves.

They stare, impassively.

BLACKOUT.

END OF SHOW

RANDY ERIKSEN

I did a lot of the graphics on the show's props myself. I remember the money. I think I got a bunch of different foreign currency, including some Thai money, and Photoshopped and manipulated the colors and stuff and printed it. I got some parchment and some hand-made paper from the art store and printed and cut it in my office. The Hero money was printed on some translucent paper, like tracing paper but with sparkly bits in it. That way I only needed to print the bills one side and the design would show through to the other. Of course the sound guy hated the crackly paper I used!

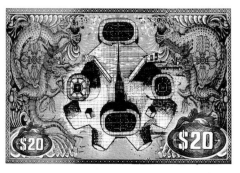

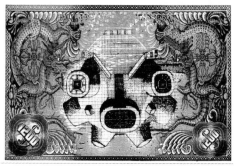

"I'M THINKING YOU'RE ONE OF THEM INDEPENDENTS"

Mal's Pistol & Browncoat

❖ Above left: The Taurus 85. Mal's pistol prop was built around this real revolver.

❖ Above right: Mal's pistol with the dummy ammo clip removed, and the side shroud taken off, to reveal the Taurus 85 beneath.

Courtesy of Applied Effects.

❖ Opposite page: "The name's Reynolds, Mal Reynolds…"

Once in a while, a prop comes along which is perfect for its purpose.

Television and film both need for us to suspend our disbelief if they're to tell the story, but never more so than in science fiction. The carefully contrived framework of a fictional universe is a fragile one. In the *Firefly* universe, everyone is armed as a matter of course. The Black is a dangerous place. Altercations with the Alliance, Reavers and disgruntled traders are all too common.

The pistol Mal carries is rather special. Its design captures both the antique romance of the Old West and the extravagant flair of golden-age science fiction. It has a timeless quality and would seem as at home strapped to the hip of H.G. Wells' time traveler, as it would on the Outlaw Josey Wales. Its robust but elegant lines evoke *Wild Wild West* retro-tech. It conjures brass robots, Disney's *Nautilus* and the fancifully spindly, almost organic look of black powder weapons like the Colt 1860 Army and 1851 Navy and, like the Navy, it has an octagonal barrel.

The sweeping, gracefully flared steel grip frame and wood grips announce it as the weapon of a gunfighter, born to be worn on the thigh. Its heavy, bullish barrel is offset by two intriguing thumbscrews which counter the blocky weight of the business end, adding a touch of delicacy and technical refinement. There's an almost whimsical scrolled fin on the base of the ammunition clip, which is mirrored by that of the lanyard attachment,

at the grip's base. Though artful and interesting, it means business. Its owner may not start the fight, but he is certainly equipped to finish it.

Applied Effects, an LA prop shop, were tasked with creating this key prop for *Firefly*. Regina Pancake, Applied's co-founder, remembers it well. "Randy Eriksen showed up at the shop. And it was a big rush job. All of a sudden we had to deal with this gun. It was Mal's Hero [closeup] gun and you can imagine how much of a priority it was. I think Randy had a week and a half or something to get it done. It was a panic. But, even with all the hypertension of getting the pistols done in time, he was way mellow. He's a very mellow guy, he's like Bing Crosby. He even wears a hat like Bing Crosby, with a little feather in it."

The production called Applied and told them that they had the base guns for the prop. It was decided to build the prop on an existing, live-firing revolver. In sequences where Nathan Fillion had to actually fire the weapon, the blanks used would produce a realistic muzzle flash and the report would be a cue for the sound designer. (Actual gunfire is far too loud to be accurately recorded live. When gunfire is heard in a film it's invariably a sound effect, added in postproduction.) The two base guns were supplied by Gibbons Ltd, the show's armorer, and delivered to Applied's workshop. Randy Eriksen also provided a foamcore conceptual mock-up of the pistol, made by *Firefly*'s art department.

The foamcore model was laid on a desk next to one of the base guns, a five-shot .38 caliber Taurus model 85

❖ Above and opposite: Profiles of the Hero prop, photographed before it was fully weathered.

Courtesy of Applied Effects.

revolver, and they got to work. The main objective was to hide the shape and size of the Taurus. After much discussion it was decided that a set of investment-cast bronze dressing shrouds would do the job. They'd be hollow metal shells which still allowed operation of the revolver's mechanism, but which changed the lines of the gun radically, leaving only the Taurus' trigger, trigger guard and the bottom of the frame visible. Mal's pistol comprises the Taurus revolver with the original grip frame chopped off, a new custom-made steel grip frame, two wooden grips, a hollow octagonal barrel shroud, a front sight, two front shrouds, two middle shrouds and two rear shrouds, plus a slim top-strap which is the base of the rear sight. There is also a removable ammunition clip which slips into a recess just forward of the Taurus' trigger guard. The ammo clip is a dummy; the firing blanks are contained in the Taurus' original cylinder.

The first stage in the production process was to design and produce the bronze castings. Eric Haraldsted, Applied's co-founder and resident gun expert, designed the cast pieces using a CAD (computer aided design) program. Various versions were drawn up in different sizes. One problem was that they had no idea what the shrinkage ratio would be when the pieces were finally cast. To be certain they could produce the pistol within the time frame, it was decided to cast pieces in different sizes and test fit

RANDY ERIKSEN

Prop master Randy Eriksen: "Of course Mal's pistol was manufactured. We went through the design process, several drawings to get a look. We did a lot of research on the Civil War revolvers and kind of manipulating them and stretching them a little bit. To have it look like brass or bronze. Applied Effects did great work for me on that gun."

them on the Taurus. Wax models were produced on a 3D wax printer and bronze castings were made by a jeweler. Finally they had a set just the right size, and another was made for the second pistol.

The Taurus' original grip was very small as the revolver is designed as a concealment sidearm. It wasn't at all in keeping with the large and robust captain's pistol. The original grip frame was chopped and discarded. A new frame was designed in CAD and produced from steel stock which was cut to shape with a high-pressure water jet. The witness marks from the cutting jet are visible on the side of the frame. To allow the revolver to operate, the Taurus' mainspring was reseated in the new frame. The grip panels themselves are carved from American Walnut wood and stained to a rich, reddish brown color. The final finish on the polished bronze shrouds is Plum Brown Barrel Finish, a chemical surface treatment. This was applied and left to weather naturally with use and handling, giving the prop the look of a weapon which isn't new and has probably spent a lot of time in its holster.

To load Mal's pistol, simply undo the thumb-screw on the pistol's left side, as held. As the screw retracts, the middle shroud will be released. The Taurus revolver is then visible inside the casing. The cylinder release catch is still present and functional on the revolver, but the bulky thumb-tab has been replaced by a low-profile brass piece. Push the cylinder release forward and the cylinder will swing out on its crane, through the gap where the side shroud was. Empty and reload as normal. Swing the cylinder back in and replace the shroud plate, tighten the thumbscrew and you're ready to defend some honor.

In the hand, the pistol initially feels a bit nose-heavy. The Colt single-action revolvers feel this way too, to start with. Like the Colt revolvers, the pistol does have that rare quality in a handgun — pointability. It seems to point naturally at the target. It isn't a light prop, the steel revolver and brass casings all add up to a hefty 1.48 kg (3.26 lbs), but it doesn't feel clumsy or awkward in any way. Holding it makes you want to do something just and reckless. Something brave but misguided. Like a Big Damn Hero.

MAL'S HOLSTER

It's a great Western tradition to wear a sidearm proudly on display on the gunfighter's leg. Not only is this an essential show of force to ward off the more casual would-be aggressor, but it's also a purely practical arrangement. The hand hangs naturally at mid-thigh, the ideal location for the gun. The holster must be secure so the weapon doesn't fall out, it must allow an easy and fast draw (as the owner's life may depend on it) and it must be well made to stand up to the rigors of the trail.

Brennan Byers, of GBB Custom Gunleather in Los Angeles, has been handcrafting leather since he was ten. When Mal needed a gun rig, he was the logical choice to make it. "I went to the studio and met with Nathan to measure him, and I remember it seemed like he'd just got the call. He was beaming and very excited about the part. The first thing I said was 'Congratulations'. To be honest, sometimes when you hear an actor has landed a plum job, you think uncharitable things because maybe that actor is so unpleasant. With Nathan, I just felt really happy for him. He was on cloud nine and you were right there with him — what a nice guy."

The holster itself was constructed using traditional methods. Oak-tanned, five to six ounce (weight per square foot) carving leather, with no bug-bites or scars, was used for the exterior, and a soft 'Kip' leather for the lining. "I knew the show was set in space, but with Western influences too. I decided to hide any modern-looking hardware by lining the holster." Recalls Byers. "I only had Nathan for one initial fitting, so I made the holster adjustable for three hanging positions. The adjustment snaps were set in the leather first and then the back of the fittings covered by the lining. The lining also protects the gun from being scratched when drawn or being carried in the holster."

The pistol is retained in the holster by means of a 'thumb-break'. This is a strap which fits over the hammer of the pistol when in the holster. When the pistol is drawn, the natural action of gripping the weapon causes the thumb to pop the snap open on the strap, freeing the piece. The snap is positioned between the holster and the body so it is hidden from view when the holster is secure.

"I called the studio to tell them when the holster was done and they asked me if I thought it needed anything else. I said a leg-tie would be a good idea." A leg-tie is a simple leather thong, attached to the barrel end of the holster. It's tied around the wearer's leg and its job is to keep the holster down when the gun is drawn.

"I think they made a few changes after it was delivered. They put a strap and buckle around the middle, and it looks like they armed someone with some sandpaper! I appreciate the need for this; the holster has to look like it's been around."

❖ Below: Nathan Fillion wears the 'Number 1' Browncoat, one of three made for the series.

❖ Right top: The drawn on 'bullethole' on the Number 1 Browncoat.

❖ Right middle: The 'Hero' coat has a more detailed cut and sewn bullethole.

❖ Right bottom: Buckle detail.

The symbol of 'Browncoats' the world over, Mal's coat came about as the result of a collaboration between costume designer Shawna Trpcic and leather artist Jonathan A. Logan. Shawna and Jonathan are old friends and they've worked together on many TV shows. Shawna contacted Jonathan about making some garments for *Firefly* and took her conceptual sketches to show him.

When expensive material like deerskin is used for a garment, an initial conceptual proof is made in the shape of a cloth mock-up. The design is tweaked until it is approved. Leather samples are carefully selected and the right material for the job is chosen; in this case, domestic-farmed deerskin, dyed a deep mahogany. The closures were custom made in antique-finished brass. The oval clasps have a concealed spring-clip underneath to keep them securely closed. The sleeves of the coat appear to be leather trimmed but are, in fact, the very long sleeves themselves folded back to show the inside of the deerskin – a feature of Oriental robes where the sleeves are often lined with silk of a different color.

The coat embodies the very spirit of the production design of *Firefly*: East meets West. Although steeped in the traditions of Western, Victorian and Civil War garments, it still manages to evoke its oriental influences with flair. In all, three coats were made for Mal. They were sent to the studio in pristine condition and then dirtied-down by Shawna herself, to give them a lived-in look. Unlined, it's not the coat of a rich man or core-planet dandy.

Jonathan describes it: "I do love that coat, a warrior's coat, kind of like a kimono. Three-quarter length is great for heroes' coats, I think. It looks rugged and tough and it could give a very masculine presence to the person who wears it. It automatically looks like you're standing in the wind."

❖ Top: Front and back views of the Hero Browncoat.

❖ Above left: The Number 1 Browncoat.

❖ Above right: Shawna Trpcic's original design.

BUSHWHACKED

Written & Directed by Tim Minear

TIM MINEAR

"I felt really confident after 'Bushwhacked'," says Tim Minear. Detailing how the episode was developed, he adds, "Early on, I don't know that there really was a writers' room per se. Joss and I were still pretty much doing it ourselves, while we were looking for writers and hiring people. I do remember that 'Bushwhacked', being as close to 'The Train Job' as it was, was still servicing certain things because we didn't have the pilot aired and also because we were still trying to get the network on board. The network really, *really* hated the Western element, so my feeling on this episode was to try to keep it all in spaceships so it wouldn't have the onus of sage and tumbleweed. I think with 'Bushwhacked', at least the things I was attempting to do made sense for a second or third episode. If you look at it, every scene is a little piece of exposition. You want to reiterate the concept for the first few episodes, particularly when it's such a complicated concept; you kind of have to do it.

"So we wanted to make something scary because we had just done something funny ['The Train Job']. Plus, I was still trying to set up two things: the universe and the characters. I set up the universe by exploring the two extremes — the Reavers and the Alliance. The first half of the episode is about the Reavers and the second half is about the Alliance. In the first half they come upon this ship, and it's about homesteaders and regular people trying to get by. It's about the savagery of being too far away from civilization. The second half was about civilization being *so* civilized that it becomes this collectivist, bureaucratic behemoth that can't get anything done, and it's trying to control you too much. Really the story is about how our people inhabit a space in between those two extremes. The other thing I was trying to do was, once again, establish who everyone was. The centerpiece of that episode is the interrogation. I needed some device in order to have these people talk explicitly about who they were. The whole interrogation scene, all the way to the reveal of Simon and River outside of the ship, it's like a movement of music. The inter-cutting of everyone being interrogated, building to, 'If those kids are on that ship, we will find them', and then pulling out from the dining room and then all the way out to Serenity, that's my favorite thing in the episode.

"I was trying to explain the world, the concept, the universe, and the characters. It's almost like a pencil sketch of what the show is. I don't think the episode gets under the skin of anything emotionally and it's not intended to do that. We hadn't earned anyone's allegiance to any of these characters in order to persuade them to identify with anybody emotionally. When you step back from it, like a painting, really what you see are the extremes of savagery and bureaucracy. It looks like they have no rules and it's just chaos, which is the metaphor of the whole Calvinball game at the beginning, they really do know what the rules are, even though to Simon it looks like there are none.

"It was the first one I directed and it was so much fun. There were three spaceships and it was just great, huge, giant fun. We found this great spaceship for the derelict on a stage in the San Fernando Valley. I think it was the set they used on *Power Rangers* or some kids show. It was a really cheesy spaceship set, but it worked perfectly. We took a piece of the airlock with us to the Valley so it looks like they are actually walking off of a giant hangar in Serenity into the airlock that is directly on this other ship."

TEASER

INT. SERENITY - CARGO BAY

BANG! MAL lands hard against a wall. Ouch. He's sweaty, out of breath. We're in the middle of some violence. Now a winded ZOE appears, coming to his aid.

MAL
We're dead.

ZOE
I believe we still have a shot, sir.

MAL
Haven't really learned a terrible lot about losing — have you, Zoe?

ZOE
Only since I've been under your command, sir.

MAL
Fair.

She pulls him back into the fray of a BASKETBALL GAME. Or some raucous, post-modern version of one, anyway. BOOK joins them as they head back into it —

BOOK
I think we've got 'em on the run now!

MAL
Our cunning strategy of getting our asses plainly whooped must be starting to confound 'em.

The teams are: MAL, ZOE, BOOK versus JAYNE, KAYLEE, WASH. It's a messy free-for-all, with everyone pretty much all over the place. Kaylee has the ball, gets past Mal, passes over to Wash. Wash shoots to a sideways hoop which hangs high, connected to the hoist chain. Scores!

Mal goes after the ball, but Jayne barrels through, steals it, drives past Book, past Zoe, passes the ball back to Wash. Wash dribbles, looks for an opening.

WASH
Somebody cover my wife.

JAYNE
(has appeared at his side)
Everytime you ain't lookin'.

Jayne moves off. Wash to Kaylee:

WASH
He's dampening my team spirit.

Kaylee has noticed —

— SIMON appears on the uppermost catwalk level with RIVER. Here to watch. Kaylee sees him, grins. Simon smiles.

KAYLEE
Gimme the ball.

He does. She drives forward, Mal tries to intercept, but she sidesteps him.

He goes sprawling. Kaylee, intensely aware of the handsome Doctor watching, shoots — scores!

MAL
(aside to Zoe)
Don't s'pose I could threaten to put her off the boat, she does that again?

ZOE
You could, sir. But she's the only one who knows how anything works.

MAL
There's a point.

The bash and crash of the game resumes. Jayne gets the ball, passes it, but Zoe intercepts. It's keep-away time.

INARA emerges from her shuttle. Smiles at the camaraderie.

Wash scoops up the ball. Zoe is hot on him. Kaylee clatters to an upper level. Wash passes over Zoe's head, Kaylee catches the ball. Mal tears off after her, coming up the steps, gonna get her from behind.

KAYLEE
Ah! Jayne!

Jayne runs up, gets under Kaylee and she climbs up on his shoulders. She just escapes Mal. As she rides Jayne toward the hoop, she sees —

— Inara is moving along the catwalk, over to:

SIMON
Hello.

Kaylee shoots. Misses. Badly. The rest of the players dive in. The chaos is on again, as above...

Inara stands next to Simon. They both watch

the game.

INARA
Who's winning?

SIMON
I can't really tell... they don't seem to be playing by any civilized rules that I know.

INARA
Well, we're pretty far from civilization.

She glances over at River who seems delighted with the game unfolding below her, but we can just see that her mouth is moving, muttering to herself...

INARA (cont'd)
How is she?

SIMON
She's... good. Better. She has her days.

INARA
Don't we all.

SIMON
There're even moments when she seems like the little sister I used to know... but then it passes. She still won't talk about what it was they did to her at the Academy.

INARA
Perhaps she's not sure herself.

SIMON
She dreams about it. I know that much. Nightmares. I can't begin to imagine what the government...
(then)
You know I supported Unification?

INARA
So did I.

SIMON
I believed everything they told us. How the Alliance would solve our problems. Right the wrongs. I wanted to be a part of that.

INARA
Things are better for a great many.

SIMON
It would have been unthinkable, three years ago, that I'd be on a ship like this, with people like that.

INARA
They're good people.

SIMON
Yes. And I'm grateful. Very grateful that Captain Reynolds has allowed us to remain on board. I just... I don't know if I'll be able to help her here. And I need to help her.

INARA
Simon. You are. I think your sister understands what you risked to rescue her from that place... leaving your whole world behind. That was incredibly selfless.

SIMON
I "selflessly" turned us both into wanted fugitives.

INARA
(a wistful smile)
Well. We're all running from something, I suppose.

He looks at her, curious. She doesn't expound. But her wise smile hints at something. The moment is interrupted by an ELECTRONIC BEEP-ING, an alert.

The game is halted as everyone reacts to the BEEPING.

ZOE
Proximity alert. Must be comin' up on somethin'...

WASH
Oh, gawd! What could it beee? We're dooomed! Who's flyin' this thing?
(then, deadpan)
Oh. Right. That'd be me. Back to work.

He tosses the ball to the others, heads off.

KAYLEE
Hey, guess that leaves us a man short, don't it?

JAYNE
Little Kaylee's always a "man short".

Kaylee slugs Jayne in the arm as she calls up to:

KAYLEE
Say, Doc? Why don't you come on down, play for our side. Inara won't mind.

INT. SERENITY - BRIDGE

Wash arrives on the bridge, the proximity alert still beeping. Through the cockpit window —

A DERELICT SHIP

A vessel about the size of Serenity, eerily

rolling in space.

Wash slides into the pilot's seat, absently switches off the alert, leans forward peering through the window to get a better look at the... DEAD BODY that lolls into view, directly in front of him. Eyes just black staring sockets in a pruned-up purple face, mouth stretched back in a grimace. Wash recoils with a start, instinctively grabs the controls and banks the ship hard.

INT. SERENITY - CARGO BAY

Simon is coming down the metal steps as the ship lurches. Simon grabs hold of the rail, manages not to take a tumble. Everyone reacts to the sudden shift —

INT. SERENITY - BRIDGE

The entire gang, Mal leading, appears.

MAL
Wash, you have a stroke or something?

WASH
Near enough.

ZOE
What happened...?

She trails off as they all now see the derelict ship.

JAYNE
<Wuh de ma.> [Mother of god.]

MAL
Anyone home?

WASH
Been hailing her. But if whoever's there's as healthy as the guy we just ran over, can't imagine they'll be pickin' up.

MAL
Bring us in a little closer.

WASH
Get you close enough to ring the doorbell.

SIMON
What is it?

Everyone craning to get a good look now at the dead ship just rolling, rolling... We move past this discussion to find...

...River who has pressed herself tight against the wall in the foredeck hall, just outside the cockpit. From where she is she can't see the ship, and still she says to herself:

RIVER
Ghosts.

Off that —

BLACK OUT.

END OF TEASER

ACT ONE

INT. SERENITY - BRIDGE

Where we left off. Everyone eyeing the derelict ship silently spinning in the distance.

MAL
So what do we figure? Transport ship?

WASH
(nods)
Converted cargo hauler or short range scow, maybe.

KAYLEE
You can see she don't wanna be parked like that. Port thrust's gone, which is makin' her spin like she is.

SIMON
A short range vessel? This far out into space?

WASH
Retrofitted to carry passengers.

ZOE
Travelers pick 'em up cheap at government auction. A few modifications and they serve well enough for a one-way push to the outer planets.

BOOK
(realizing)
Settlers.

WASH
Probably squeeze fifteen, maybe twenty families on a boat that size, you pack 'em tight enough.

INARA
Families...

JAYNE
Tell you what I think. I figure that fella we ran into did everyone on board, killed 'em all, then decided to go for a swim, see how fast his blood'd boil out his ears.

WASH
You're a very "up" person.

BOOK
Shouldn't we report this?

MAL
To who? Alliance? Right, 'cause they're gonna run right out here lickety-split, make sure these taxpayers are okay.

BOOK
Then we'll have to.

JAYNE
Rudderless boat this far out, probably canned fish by now.

KAYLEE
You can't know that for sure.

JAYNE
If there's folks in need of help, why ain't they beaming no distress call?

ZOE
(to Mal)
It's true. There's no beacon.

MAL
(taking her meaning)
Which means it's likely nobody's looking to find 'er.

BOOK
All the more reason for us to do the right thing.

JAYNE
How 'bout you just say a prayer while we slide on by? That oughta do it.

BOOK
Shall I remind you of the story of the Good Samaritan?

MAL
Rather you didn't.
(then)
But we will check it out.

JAYNE
So we a search and rescue tug now?

MAL
No. But the Shepherd's not wrong. Could be survivors. And if not, well — then no one's gonna mind if we take a look around, see if there's not something of value they might've left behind.

JAYNE
(hadn't thought of that)
Right. Yeah... No. Someone could be hurt.

MAL
(as he goes)
Wash, hook us up.

EXT. SPACE

Serenity is piloted in close, locks into the spin-cycle of the derelict ship. Ka-chunk — Serenity's airlock latches onto the other ship's standard matching bulkhead.

As it does, WE SEE a web of insect like electronic tentacles attach themselves at the seam. RED LIGHTS within this weird network start blinking...

INT. SERENITY - CARGO BAY

Simon appears, entering. He's carrying his portable med-kit. He slows and stops as he sees —

SIMON'S POV

over near the airlock, Mal and Zoe suiting up (there are several spacesuits hanging there), going through the checklist as they prepare to board the derelict.

JAYNE (O.S.)
Where you think you're headed?

Jayne is there, stepping up behind Simon. We see he's loading Zoe's shotgun, prepping weapons.

SIMON
I thought I'd offer my services, in case anyone on board required medical attention.

JAYNE
Yeah, well, Cap and Zoe are going in first. We'll holler if we need ya.

Simon's not looking at Jayne, a bit spellbound, watching as Mal and Zoe pull on their helmets. Jayne reads Simon's discomfort at the suits, smiles.

JAYNE (cont'd)
Somethin' wrong?

SIMON
Hmmm? Oh. No. I... I suppose it's just the thought of a little mylar and glass being the only thing separating a person from... nothing.

JAYNE
Impressive what "nothing" can do to a man. Like that feller we bumped into. Yeah. He's likely stuck up under our belly about now. That's what space trash does, ya know. Kinda latches onto the first big somethin' stops long enough. Hey — now that'd be a bit like you and your sister, wouldn't it?

Jayne works the pump action on the shotgun. Cha-chunk. He crosses off, toward Mal and Zoe. Off Simon —

INT. SERENITY - CARGO BAY/AIRLOCK

Mal's gloved hand hits the airlock control button. WHOOSH. The door opens. Mal and Zoe, fully suited and armed, step into the airlock. The door closes behind them.

INT. SERENITY - AIRLOCK

Mal speaks to Wash through the com-link in his suit.

MAL
Okay, Wash. Ask Serenity to knock for us.

WASH (O.S.)
Just as nice as you please...

A light on the derelict's airlock door goes from RED to GREEN. WHOOSH. It opens. A beat. Mal and Zoe fire up their flashlights, enter into —

INT. DERELICT

They take a few steps and — THUNK. The airlock door shuts automatically behind them. The ship is running on emergency power only. Footlights marking the way. Mal and Zoe move with caution, their weapons at the ready. As they go:

MAL
Emergency power's up. Dashboard light.

We move with them as they step carefully down the dark passageways. They pass an abandoned child's TRICYCLE. Share a look, keep moving, to

INT. DERELICT - MESS HALL

Mal and Zoe enter. They both stop, look to —

— cafeteria style. Several tables set up. A high chair here and there. Slop counter with sneeze guard. And here's what's weird — plates of food in various states of being consumed. Big ladles still buried in (gnarly old looking) grub in the tins behind the slop counter. Evidence that folks were in line with trays.

MAL
Whatever happened here happened quick.

Zoe nods. Mal starts moving again. Zoe follows, to —

INT. DERELICT - BRIDGE - CONTINUOUS

They enter the bridge — more of the same,

basically: a book is open, coffee cup, some board game in mid-play, etc. More personal detail which suggests habitation. But no people. Zoe looks at the controls, computers, etc.

ZOE
Everything was left on... Ship powered down on its own.
(continues looking)
No sign of struggle. Just —

MAL
— gone.

As Zoe moves to the control panels:

ZOE
(seeing something)
Sir.

He moves to her.

ZOE (cont'd)
Personal log. Someone was in the middle of an entry —

Her look says "shall I?" Mal nods. Zoe hits the log button — and the screen BURSTS with EAR PIERCING STATIC.

INT. SERENITY - RIVER'S QUARTERS

River sits up INTO FRAME, sweaty and freaked — GASPS.

Simon pushes into her room, never far from her. He moves to her bed, kneels down.

SIMON
Shhh. It's okay. I'm here. Bad dreams again?

RIVER
(shakes her head "no")
No. Can't sleep. Too much screaming.

He looks at her, his sadness for her state right there on his face. Gently:

SIMON
River. There is no screaming.

She looks at him, utterly lucid, and says, darkly:

RIVER
There was.

He holds her look for a beat. He starts a bit at —

JAYNE
Grab your med-kit and let's hoof it. Mal wants us both over there on the double.

Jayne is at the door, loading (yet another) weapon.

SIMON
They've found survivors?

JAYNE
(shrugs)
Didn't say.

SIMON
Right.
(torn)
I'll ask Inara to look in on River.

JAYNE
Yeah, whatever. I ain't waiting.
(as he goes)
Meet you over there. But don't take forever. Still gotta get suited up.

And he exits. Off Simon —

INT. DERELICT

The airlock door opens revealing... SIMON. All packed into one of the suits. He loathes this. He looks into the dark, creepy derelict. Hesitates. Finally he steps across the threshold.

WHOMP. The door shuts behind him. His breathing becomes more rapid.

As he moves, we play a lot of this from his point of view... through the faceplate of the helmet... that thin, transparent sliver of life. The building rhythm of his BREATHING practically scoring this sequence.

INT. DERELICT - MESS HALL

As Simon continues his tense passage.

INT. DERELICT - BRIDGE - CONTINUOUS

Simon comes around a corner, sees —

Mal, Zoe, Jayne and Kaylee. All of them spacesuit-and-helmet-less, having a conversation he can't hear. Simon reacts. So do the others. Bemused, Simon clutches at his helmet. It's not coming off. Kaylee runs to him, helps him with it. He's gasping for breath. Before Simon can ask anything —

MAL
What are you doing here?
(also)
And what's with the suit?

Simon glances over to Jayne who's trying to stifle his gales of laughter. Simon's furious, humiliated.

SIMON
(glaring at Jayne)
Oh, you're hilarious. Sadist.

MAL
(forces back his own smile)
All right. That's enough. We ain't got time for games.
(to Simon)
Long as you're here, you might as well lend a hand. You can run with Kaylee.

He tosses Simon a canvas loot bag. (Mal and the others also have their portable salvage kits with them now.)

MAL (cont'd)
Let's do this quick, people. Coupla loads each. No need to be greedy.

SIMON
Where are all the people?

MAL
Ship says the lifeboat launched more'n a week ago. We're gonna assume everyone got off okay. Anyway, we're just here to pick the bones. You two start in the engine room. Jayne, take the galley.

They head off. As they go:

KAYLEE
(re: helmet)
You had this on wrong.

That's kind of a horrible thought. Simon blanches. Makes Jayne laugh all the harder. Once Mal and Zoe are alone:

ZOE
Sir... I count sixteen families signed on. Lifeboat wouldn't hold a third of that.

MAL
I know.
(into transmitter)
Wash? Any luck?

INTERCUT WITH:

INT. SERENITY - BRIDGE - CONTINUOUS

Up on the screen, ship schematics. Wash scrolls through.

WASH
Think I found something pretty well matches that class. Layout looks about right. Seems to me any valuables, if there are any, likely be stored somewhere in C-deck, aft.

MAL (O.S.)
Good work. Keep the motor running. Won't be long.

Wash signs off, leans back/swivels in his chair. Sees Book standing in the doorway behind him.

BOOK
Can't say I much care for this business.

WASH
It's abandoned, Shepherd.

BOOK
And if that's the result of some violence? What if that ship's a crime scene?

WASH
Well — if it wasn't before, it certainly is now.

Book smiles unhappily at the attitude.

INT. SERENITY - PASSAGEWAYS

Inara approaches River's quarters with a tray of food. Knocks. No answer.

INARA
River? It's Inara. Are you hungry, sweetie?

She pushes the door open...

INARA (cont'd)
I brought you a little...

Inara reacts. The room is empty.

INARA (cont'd)
River?

Off the empty room —

INT. DERELICT - AIRLOCK

The door opens with a WHOOSH, revealing River. The gust from the door gently blowing her hair. She seems to be in an almost trance-like state. Barefoot, she pads onto the derelict ship.

INT. DERELICT - PASSAGEWAYS

Mal and Zoe arrive at a storage door.

MAL
This'd be it.

ZOE
(tries it)
Locked.

MAL
Well — now I'd say that's like to be a very good sign.

He brings up a mini-blowtorch. Sparks it.

INT. DERELICT - ENGINE ROOM

Kaylee and Simon going through the engine room. Kaylee examines the machinery.

SIMON
Aren't you the least bit curious?

KAYLEE
'Bout what?

SIMON
Well — what happened here. Why would anyone abandon their ship in the middle of nowhere like this?

KAYLEE
Oh, all sorts of reasons...
(as she realizes)
Just... not mechanical...

SIMON
What?

KAYLEE
(a little surprised)
Well.. there ain't nothing wrong with this. Not that I can see, anyhow. Some of this's like new.

SIMON
Well, that makes it even more...

KAYLEE
(brightening)
Oooh, here's a good'n!
(as she pries away)

Hold the bag open.

She starts tossing pieces in, as —

INT. DERELICT - MESS HALL

Jayne tears the place apart, loading up, and snacking. He pauses, thinks he senses something. Takes out his gun... moves to the door. Nothing. He resumes his work, as —

INT. DERELICT - PASSAGEWAYS

River haunts this place like a ghost herself, drifting along, drawn by something —

INT. DERELICT - STORAGE ROOM

THUNK. The blowtorched door falls forward. Mal and Zoe enter. Very dim light in here. They use their flashlights.

Zoe whips a tarp off some crates, cracks one open. Within, family photo albums, heirlooms, like that. She runs her light along the front of the other crates — various FAMILY NAMES emblazoned there. All personal stuff.

MAL
Here —

Zoe joins him. Their FLASHLIGHT BEAMS illuminate stacks of government issue terraforming supplement materials. They are emblazoned with the AngloSino insignia of the Alliance.

MAL (cont'd)
Gen-seed, protein, crop supplements. Everything a growing family needs for a fresh start on a new world.

ZOE
Hard subsidies for fourteen plus families... that's...

MAL
...about a fortune.
(rising)
We forget the rest and just take this stuff. We'll need a hand hauling it out of here.

ZOE
Sir... even on a lifeboat. You'd think those who escaped would have found room for some of this.

MAL
(looking past her)
No one escaped...

ZOE
Sir?

MAL
I'm feelin' like nobody left this boat. Nobody...

She turns to see what he's looking at... Standing in the storage room doorway is...

RIVER. She seems to not even notice the two of them, her attention is directed above them. Mal turns, aims his flashlight upward, way up, into an overhead shaft. Zoe reacts with disgust...

THE BODIES

are strung up from the ceiling. Three clumps of twisted flesh. The skin pale, almost luminescent (the bits of it we do see).

ZOE
There's no blood. Not a drop anywhere...

MAL
<Jen dao mei!> [Just our luck!]
(pulls transmitter)
I know what did this.

River starts to wander in.

MAL (cont'd)
(re: River)
Keep her out of here.

Zoe moves to do that, as —

MAL (cont'd)
(into transmitter)
Jayne —

INT. DERELICT - MESS HALL

Jayne gorges and gathers — Mal's voice from his transmitter.

MAL (O.S.)
Jayne — drop what you're doing and get to the engine room. I want you to take Kaylee and the Doctor off this boat.

Jayne reaches for it, his mouth is full. He swallows, puts the transmitter to his mouth — but that's when the attack comes. The THING that ATTACKS him from behind is a BLUR. It comes so fast, so violently, he never had a chance to respond at all. Off his fallen transmitter and Mal's voice:

MAL (cont'd; O.S.)
Jayne? Jayne, do you read? Jayne?!

BLACK OUT.

END OF ACT ONE

ACT TWO

EXT. SPACE

Serenity still attached to the rotating derelict, as —

INT. SERENITY - BRIDGE

Wash sits up straight in his chair as he hears MUFFLED GUNFIRE over the two-way. He pounds on the mic —

WASH
Captain? Captain?
(then)
Zoe?

More GUNFIRE.

INT. DERELICT - PASSAGEWAYS

Mal and Zoe, who is steering River by the shoulders, emerge. Mal has his gun out. So does Zoe.

ZOE
Came from above, sir.

MAL
Galley —

They start to move but nearly collide with —

SIMON AND KAYLEE

coming around the corner, reacting to the

gunfire. Kaylee gasps, realizes it's Mal.

KAYLEE
We heard shootin' —

SIMON
River...? What are you...

RIVER
I followed the voices.

SIMON
(moves to her)
Don't ever leave the ship. Not ever.

MAL
(on the alert, to Simon, re: River)
Handle her, will you, son?

WASH (O.S.)
What the <tyen shiao duh> [name of all that's sacred] is going on in there?!

ZOE
(into transmitter, quickly and professionally)
Not now, dear.

She clicks him off. Nods to Mal that she's ready to roll. Together they move off, guns leading the way...

INT. DERELICT - MESS HALL

Tense beat as Mal enters the mess hall, his gun leading. Evidence of violence, upturned table, gross food on the floor. A noise — Mal whips around with his gun... and finds himself drawing down on...

JAYNE

who has his gun pointed right back at Mal. They both relax. Jayne is a bit mussed, but not really hurt.

MAL
What'd you see?

JAYNE
Didn't. Came at me from behind. Big, though. Strong. Think I mighta hit him.

Simon has entered with Kaylee and River.

SIMON
You did...

Simon points to tell-tale blood droplets. Mal moves to him, notes that the blood droplets lead to a grate in the wall. Mal eases Simon out of the way. Indicates to Zoe to hand him her shotgun. He pushes the grate up with the nose of it.

WALL GRATE

Mal's face appears. He squints at —

A YOUNG MAN

cowering in the shadows. He's feral, fearful, drawing himself as small as he can.

SURVIVOR
(muttering)
Mercy... mercy... no. Mercy.

MAL
Easy, now. Nobody's gonna hurt you.
(noticing gunshot wound in arm)
Anymore than we already did...

SURVIVOR
No mercy...

MAL
Oh, we got mercy. We got lots and lots of —

WHAM!, suddenly Mal comes up and gives the poor bastard the butt of the shotgun right in the kisser.

MESS HALL

As Mal pulls the unconscious guy out through the hole and lets him drop to the floor, a heap. Not big at all, just average. Practically a kid.

SIMON
(to Jayne)
Oh, yes. He's a real beast. It's a wonder you're still alive.

JAYNE
(confounded)
Looked bigger when I couldn't see him.

MAL
(grim)
Let's get him out of here.

INT. SERENITY - OUTSIDE INFIRMARY

In the common area are Inara, Kaylee, Jayne, Zoe, Wash. Book is there, too, sitting, clutching his bible. Kaylee and Inara are watching as inside the infirmary Simon can be seen tending to the Survivor, Mal over his shoulder.

INARA
I wonder how long he'd been living like that?

KAYLEE
Dunno. Must be real brave, though. Surviving like that when no one else did.

JAYNE
Yeah, a real hero. Killin' all them people.

KAYLEE
What? No. We don't believe that.
(turns toward Zoe)
We don't, do we?

ZOE
Captain wouldn't have brought him on board were that the case.

But she doesn't sound as convinced as she might.

INT. SERENITY - INFIRMARY

Simon has patched up the arm wound. The patient mutters in his delirium.

SIMON
Pulse is rapid, blood pressure's high side of normal. To be expected.

SURVIVOR
Weak. They were all weak.

SIMON
Other than the bullet wound, there doesn't appear to be any exterior trauma. Though that crack to the head you gave him probably didn't do him any good.

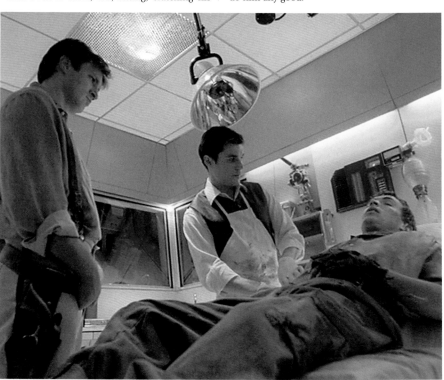

The patient rises up a bit, tries to focus on the faces outside the glass. This isn't lost on Mal.

SURVIVOR
Cattle. Cattle for the slaughter.

MAL
Dope him.

SIMON MAL
I don't think that's — Just do it.

Simon moves to load a syringe. Mal eyes the muttery patient.

SURVIVOR
No mercy... No resistance...

Simon leans over him. The man's hand grabs Simon's wrist.

SURVIVOR (cont'd)
Open up. See what's inside.

Simon gives him a shot. Pulls away from the man's weak grip.

MAL
Let's chat.

Mal moves to the door. Simon glances at his patient, who is slipping into semi-consciousness. He follows to —

INT. SERENITY - OUTSIDE INFIRMARY DOOR

As Simon appears here, he looks to Inara.

SIMON
River?

INARA
Resting in my shuttle. Not to disparage the other accommodations on this ship, but I think she'll find it more comfortable. And the door locks.

SIMON
Thank you.

KAYLEE
So? How's our patient?

SIMON
Aside from borderline malnutrition, he's in remarkably good health.

BOOK
(some relief)
So he'll live, then?

SIMON
Yes.

MAL
Which, to my mind, is unfortunate.

The others react, surprised.

BOOK
Not a very charitable attitude, Captain.

MAL
Charity'd be putting a bullet in his brainpan.

INARA
Mal!

MAL
Only save him the suffering.

Mal shuts the infirmary door, bolts it from the outside.

MAL (cont'd)
Nobody goes in there. Nothing more we can do for him now. Not after what he's seen.

SIMON
What do you mean?

MAL
That ship was hit by Reavers.

Mal turns, heads off. The others don't follow right away as the horror hits them.

JAYNE
(fear)
Reavers...

Wash looks to Zoe who doesn't deny it — she knows it, too.

WASH
<Tzao gao.> [Crap.]

Inara glances back into the infirmary, where the man is writhing in his delirium. She knows what this means.

INT. SERENITY - DINING ROOM - CONTINUOUS

Mal's pouring himself some coffee as the others follow him in.

INARA
Mal, how can you know?

JAYNE
He don't, that's how. No way.

Mal sips his coffee. Whatever you say.

JAYNE (cont'd)
It was that other fella. The one we run into. It's like I said before — he went stir crazy, killed the rest, took a walk into space.

KAYLEE
A second ago you were saying —

JAYNE
Don't matter what I said.

MAL
One of 'em was just lucky enough to get out, that's all.

WASH
He was the lucky one?

MAL
Luckier'n the rest.

JAYNE
Couldn't be Reavers. Wasn't Reavers. Reavers don't leave no survivors.

MAL
Strictly speaking — wouldn't say they did.

BOOK
What are you suggesting?

MAL
Don't matter we took him off that boat, Shepherd. It's the place he's gonna live from now on.

BOOK
I don't accept that. Whatever horror he witnessed, whatever acts of barbarism, it was done by men. Nothing more.

JAYNE
Reavers ain't men.

BOOK
Of course they are. Too long removed from civilization, perhaps — but men. And I believe there's a power greater than men. A power that heals.

MAL
Reavers might take issue with that philosophy. If they had a philosophy. And if they weren't too busy gnawing on your insides.
(then)
Jayne's right. Reavers ain't men. Or they forgot how to be. Now they're just... nothing. They got out to the edge of the galaxy, to that place of nothing. And that's what they became.

JAYNE
Why we still sittin' here? If it was Reavers, shouldn't we be gone?

WASH
Have to say I was kinda wondering that myself.

MAL
Work ain't done. Substantial money value still sitting over there.

JAYNE
Pffft. I ain't going back in there with them bodies. No rutting way. Not if Reavers messed with 'em.

ZOE
(stop your blubbering)
Jayne. You'll scare the women.

SIMON
I'll go.

They all look at him.

SIMON (cont'd)
I've dealt with bodies. They don't worry me.

BOOK
I'd like to go with him. Maybe see what I can do about putting those folks to rest.

MAL
They're already "resting" pretty good, Shepherd. Reavers saw to that.

BOOK
How we treat our dead is part of what makes us different than those did the slaughtering.

MAL
(considers)
All right. You go say your words.
(then)
Jayne, you'll help the Doctor and Shepherd Book cut down those people. Then you'll load up the cargo.

JAYNE
I don't believe this. Now we're gonna sit put for a funeral?

MAL
Yes, Jayne. That's exactly what we're going to do. I won't have these people lookin' over my shoulder once we're gone. Now I ain't sayin' there is any peace to be had. But on the off chance there is — then those folks deserve a little of it.

JAYNE
<Fong luh.> [Loopy in the head.] All of you.

He storms off. Simon follows. Book takes a beat,

might say something, decides against it then goes. Kaylee's beaming at her Captain. Inara now moves to Mal.

INARA
And just when I think I've got you figured out.

She holds the look. Might kiss him. Doesn't. Instead she moves off. He watches her go.

KAYLEE
That was real pretty, Captain. What you said.

WASH
Didn't think you were one for rituals and such.

MAL
I'm not. But I figure it'll keep the others busy for awhile. No reason to concern them with what's to be done.

ZOE
Sir?

CUT TO:

INT. SERENITY - BRIDGE

Mal pulls a visual up on a screen. The tendril like booby trap connected where the two airlocks joined.

MAL
It's a real burden being right so often.

Wash, Zoe and Kaylee at his side, looking at the screen.

WASH
What is it?

MAL
Booby trap. Reavers sometimes leave 'em behind for the rescue ships. We triggered it when we latched on.

WASH
And when we detach —

MAL
— it blows.

WASH
Okay — so we don't detach. We just, I don't know, sit tight until...

ZOE
What? Reavers come back?

Kaylee's been studying the image on the vid screen.

KAYLEE
Looks like they've jerry-rigged it with a pressure catch. Only thing that'd work with all these spare parts. Could pro'lly bypass that easy, we get to the DC line.

MAL
You tell me now, little Kaylee — you really think you can do this?

KAYLEE
Sure. Yeah. Think so. 'Sides, if I mess up, it's not like you'll be able to yell at me.

EXT. SPACE

Serenity and the derelict, locked together in a death grip. And under the soundlessness of space, MUSIC, carrying us through...

INT. DERELICT - STORAGE

Simon, Jayne and Book all have paper dust masks on as they lower down the bodies. This is done in an elliptical way, more a suggestion of the carnage than a strict depiction.

INT. SERENITY - CARGO BAY

The bomb bay doors are pulled open by Mal. Kaylee climbs in first, then Wash. Mal and Zoe stand topside, nervous.

INT. SERENITY - INFIRMARY

The tortured delirium of the survivor in his fever sleep. Somehow his distress seems to be affecting...

INT. SERENITY - INARA'S SHUTTLE

River, who is sleeping in Inara's bed. Her sleep becomes more and more fitful. Nearby, Inara reads a book, not yet noticing River's sleep become more and more agitated, as...

INT. SERENITY - INNARDS

Kaylee has to squeeze in tight to the confined space. She's looking at the seam where the two airlocks meet. The tendrils of the booby trap are visible, flashing RED.

WASH is in the pit, a bit above her, with a box full of tools. He hands her some wrench-like gadget. She blows a strand of hair out of her eyes, goes to work on the device.

INT. DERELICT - STORAGE

Jayne dragging crates, slamming them onto a dolly, looking over with some disdain, to —

Book reads from his bible, saying a few words for the dead. Simon shows respect, bowing his head.

INT. SERENITY - INARA'S SHUTTLE

Inara reacts now as she sees River's state, growing ever more agitated, as

INT. SERENITY - INFIRMARY

the patient's eyes SNAP OPEN.

INT. SERENITY - CARGO BAY

Kaylee working on the booby trap.

— Wash handing her down more tools.

— Mal and Zoe waiting helplessly, nervously, topside.

— Kaylee takes a stab at the booby trap. We see her recoil, nervous. Still here. She really concentrates, goes back at it. Cuts into some of the tubing and a dark OOZE drips out.

INT. SERENITY - INARA'S SHUTTLE

River's really thrashing now. Inara goes to her, gathers her in her arms, holds her close, tries to soothe her. River starts to calm, but GASPS with a START as...

INT. SERENITY - INFIRMARY

a drawer of SURGICAL TOOLS hits the floor, and with it returns the SYNCH SOUND. A HAND reaches in, picks up one of the more evocative- and lethal-looking surgical tools.

INT. SERENITY - CARGO BAY

WHOOSH — the airlock door opens and Jayne rolls in the dolly with the cargo. He reacts as he sees —

— CLANG. As the bomb bay doors are dropped shut. Mal, Kaylee, Wash and Zoe look over at him.

JAYNE
What's going on?

MAL
Not a thing.
(looks to Kaylee)
Right?

She nods her little greased smudged face.

KAYLEE
Not a gorramn thing.

Mal looks to Wash. Nods. Wash nods back, heads off.

JAYNE
Looks like a thing to me.

Book and Simon enter from the airlock. Mal hits the controls, closing it behind them:

MAL
Thought we might have had a situation, but it looks to be taken care of. Let's get that stuff stored.

Jayne, still not convinced, moves to the smuggling compartments, pops a panel.

MAL (cont'd)
(into transmitter)
Everybody's home, Wash. Let's go.

We HEAR the start of the detaching process.

EXT. SERENITY

As the two ships come apart, harmless remnants of the booby trap tearing away.

INT. SERENITY - CARGO BAY

Mal looks to Zoe and Kaylee. Now they can really breathe. In the b.g., Simon and Book move to Jayne.

Suddenly — that familiar PROXIMITY WARNING BEEPING. Everyone who was on pins and needles before is right back there — and Jayne freaks:

JEWEL STAITE

Jewel Staite on crawling in the vent: "It was built up on a platform, and it was a tiny, tiny little tunnel; there really wasn't much to crawl through. All the wires were filled with either water or this really weird oily substance. Tim Minear said, 'Just start fiddling around and then make a decision to cut one,' and I said, 'Which one should I cut?' and he said, 'Oh, whichever one you feel like cutting.' So the first take, I cut one and it was water, and that was fine. Then they reset the shot and I cut this other one and this weird oil came spurting out. It got me in the face, and it was gross and stank. I don't think they used that one, because I was sort of pissed off. I was like, 'Why didn't you tell me which one to cut?'" she laughs.

JAYNE

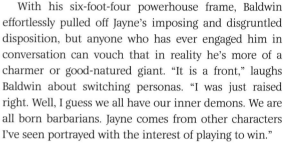

"Time for some thrilling heroics."

Every crew has one: that trigger-happy loose cannon who could explode at any given moment; the mercenary-for-hire whose top priorities are making a quick buck and bedding the ladies; the muscle who, even with his numerous faults, is invaluable in a scrap. On *Firefly*, that tough scruff is the man called Jayne Cobb, a character actor Adam Baldwin immediately latched on to. "Well, *Firefly* is a Western and I grew up watching Westerns like *The Magnificent Seven*, *The Wild Bunch*, *Once Upon A Time in the West*, *The Good, The Bad, and the Ugly*, movies like that," he explains. "I felt very comfortable slipping into such a role. I figured [adapting Jayne's drawl] 'Hell, I'll just try talking like this and see how far Joss lets me go.' I connected right away with the character and it fit at a time in my life where I was comfortable enough to stand there and just go broad. It can be a risky endeavor to go as broad as I did in some instances with Jayne, but Joss Whedon let me to a certain degree. That was sort of my deal with Joss: 'I'm gonna go as broad as I can in rehearsals and the first couple of takes and it is up to you to dial me back.' Once we had that communication established, you can find some things. You are not fearful of looking bad."

Despite carrying an extensive arsenal of guns including Jayne's beloved Vera, his other weapon of choice was a sharp wit and wounding sense of humor. "I forget the exact wording Joss used to describe Jayne but he was basically the guy who said what was on everybody's minds," says Baldwin. "It's like 'Cut to the chase guys! Quit your pussyfooting around and all your existential musings about the goodness of this existence. Let's go kill them!' I always thought of Jayne as this practical guy, a hands on problem solver — but selfish."

In fact with dialogue such as "Do you know what the chain of command is? It's the chain I go get and beat you with until you understand who's in rutting command here!" Jayne spouted some of the best lines of the series. "It's just the way I deliver them," chuckles Baldwin. "Everyone else had good lines too. I just said them better," he laughs. "I can say that now that I'm not on the show!"

With his six-foot-four powerhouse frame, Baldwin effortlessly pulled off Jayne's imposing and disgruntled disposition, but anyone who has ever engaged him in conversation can vouch that in reality he's more of a charmer or good-natured giant. "It is a front," laughs Baldwin about switching personas. "I was just raised right. Well, I guess we all have our inner demons. We are all born barbarians. Jayne comes from other characters I've seen portrayed with the interest of playing to win."

In 'The Message', viewers were treated to a glimpse of Jayne's family life when he received a letter and a knitted pompom hat from his dear old mom. "We kind of fantasized that Jayne was a middle-class cretin, not unlike the children of the late sixties, seventies, and eighties whose parents were a little bit too busy for them," offers Baldwin. "They got to the point where it was 'Screw this! I'm heading off to the Black! I want some adventure!' I think he had a good connection with his mom, and his dad not so much — but all this isn't Joss. He hadn't fleshed all that out because we only got to do half a season."

Captain Malcolm Reynolds recruited Jayne under strained circumstances and at times, the two experienced a volcanic relationship, although there was also respect and a warped loyalty there. "Jayne considers himself as a co-equal subservient," states Baldwin. "He considers himself a hired hand to Mal. His loyalty is as far as the money goes, although Mal's honor among thieves attitude had been growing on him. I think he was learning to respect that more. So they were sort of like brothers-in-arms."

However, their relationship was really put to the test when Jayne delivered Simon and River into the hands of the Alliance. "In 'Ariel', Mal knocks Jayne on the head with a wrench, throws him out the airlock and was going to space him," explains Baldwin. "Then Mal honors Jayne's last request to not tell the rest of the crew why he was dead. That was a turning point."

Joss is famous for killing off his characters but even at death's door, Baldwin wasn't worried about Jayne. "No, by then I was the favorite character on the show," he laughs. "Had that been the first episode, I'd have been worried. By then, I think my position was pretty secure." ◑

JAYNE
No, no. Do not say that — it's the Reavers! Gorramn Reavers come back!

MAL
(already on the move)
Get that stuff stored.

JAYNE
Like it's gonna matter.

MAL
Just do it!

He's running, now. Zoe right behind him.

INT. SERENITY - BRIDGE

Wash just sits staring straight ahead, hasn't switched off the alert.

Mal and Zoe come running up the foredeck hall.

MAL
Reavers?

Wash absently shakes his head "no". A GREEN GLOW starts to overtake the cockpit. They all react as they see —

THROUGH THE COCKPIT WINDOW — outer space pretty well blotted out by the green glow of an enormous ALLIANCE CRUISER... Over the radio:

MALE VOICE (V.O.)
Firefly Class Transport, you are ordered to release control of your helm. Prepare to dock and be boarded.

MAL
Looks like civilization's finally caught up with us...

EXT. SPACE

Serenity dwarfed by the looming Alliance Cruiser.

And coming off the Alliance ship: several smaller GUNSHIPS, swarming around Serenity —

BLACK OUT.

END OF ACT TWO

ACT THREE

INT. ALLIANCE CRUISER

COMMANDER HARKEN watches from the bridge as Serenity moves toward us. An ENSIGN approaches. Harken points to Serenity.

HARKEN
No mandatory registration markings on the bow. Make sure we cite them for that. What is it, Ensign?

ENSIGN
Sir, we've identified the transport ship they were attached to. It was licensed to a group of families out of Bernadette. They were due to touch down in Newhall three weeks ago. Never made it. We've

DESIGNING THE 'VERSE

Prop master Randy Eriksen: "It was mixed technology from the brain of Joss Whedon. Starting with the whole look of the ship and the characters, it was very much influenced by the American Civil War. Especially the hand guns and the rifle. It really wasn't very 'spacey', we made a choice between Buck Rogers and the Old West, and this is like the Old West with some kind of technological twist in there. The Alliance was always glass and chrome and crisp and clean and bright, and everything else was all dingy and dirty and rusty and crappy. The Alliance look is what you classically think of as science fiction."

been hailing the vessel, get no response. It appears to be derelict.

HARKEN
Continue hailing. Once we secure these vultures, we'll send a team over. Check it out.

A RADIO OPERATOR sits at a communications station speaks:

RADIO OPERATOR
Didn't we have a flag a while back on a Firefly?

HARKEN
Check.

RADIO OPERATOR
Here it is. Alert issued for unidentified Firefly Class, believed to be carrying two fugitives. A brother and sister.

HARKEN
What are they wanted for?

RADIO OPERATOR
Not available. It's classified.

HARKEN
Forty thousand of these old wrecks in the air and that's all they give us? Well, I won't have any

surprises on a routine stop. We run into these two, we shoot first. Brass can sort it out later.

INT. SERENITY - CARGO BAY

Simon helps Jayne and Book finish loading the cargo into the smuggling hold. Mal appears, walking fast, entering the cargo bay. The three look over —

JAYNE
What was it? Was it Reavers?

MAL
Open the stash, pull out the goods.

JAYNE
What? Just got done putting it all in —

MAL
Yeah, and now I'm telling you to take it all out again.

JAYNE
Why for?

MAL
I got no notion to argue this. In about two minutes time this boat's gonna be crawling with Alliance.

SIMON
No...

Zoe, Wash and Kaylee appear. Kaylee hangs back, Zoe and Wash head further in, toward the others. Zoe and Wash help Book and Jayne with the goods. Simon's in a bit of shock.

SIMON (cont'd)
We've gotta run...

MAL
Can't run. They're pulling us in.

SIMON
If they find us they'll send River back to that place. To be tortured. I'd never see her again.

MAL
(to Jayne et al)
Stack everything right here in plain sight. Wouldn't want it to seem as if we're hiding anything. Might give them Alliance boys the wrong impression.

WASH
Or the right one.

MAL
That, too.

JOSS WHEDON

Obviously, 'Bushwhacked' had the basketball scene and a set with rotting food on it. Why they bothered to show rotting food, I don't know, but, man, that set was hard to be on. I think it is also an underrated episode. It was really an attempt to show just how creepy it could get out there, just how bad it was. And to show exactly where they were in the universe — caught between the most terrifying savages and the most antiseptic and annoying bureaucracy, and not really caring for either.

(turns to Simon)
Now run fetch your sister.

A beat. Simon suddenly becomes suspicious.

SIMON
What? Why? Are you going to put her in "plain sight", too?

MAL
Don't get tetchy. Just do as I say.

SIMON
Is that why you let us stay? So you could use us as bargaining chips?

JAYNE
I knew there was a reason!

SIMON
They're not taking her... and you're not giving her to them.

BOOK
(steps forward)
Don't be a fool, son. Do as the man says.

EXT. SPACE

As Serenity attaches to the bottom of the Alliance Cruiser, just a little bump now on the big ship.

INT. SERENITY - CARGO BAY

WHOOSH — the airlock doors open and a compliment of ALLIANCE SOLDIERS streams onto Serenity, their boots clicking on the hard cargo bay floor. Harken appears, looks at —

— Mal, Zoe, Jayne, Wash, Kaylee, Inara, Book, lined up. No sign of Simon or River. (We may or may not notice the smuggling compartments have been closed up again.)

Harken gives the signal to his lead man. Soldiers move in, start relieving our gang of any weapons.

MAL
Well now, ain't this a whole lotta fuss. I didn't know better, might think we were dangerous.

HARKEN
Is this your vessel?

MAL
It is. Bought and paid for. I'm Captain Malcolm Reynolds.

HARKEN
And is this everyone, Captain?

MAL
By way of crew, it is. Though you're gonna find in our infirmary a fella we rescued from that derelict. Saved him, guess you could say.

Harken nods to a couple of his guys, they head off.

MAL (cont'd)
(calling back)
Straight back, next to the common area.

HARKEN
(re: the goods)
And these items — I take it you "rescued" them as well?

INT. SERENITY - INFIRMARY

The two Alliance Soldiers force open the infirmary door. The operating table is empty. The place is a wreck. They look over, see something that WE DON'T. One of them turns away, loses his lunch right there. The other one reacts with similar, though less colorful, disgust. Off that —

INT. SERENITY - CARGO BAY

Harken eyes the "line up".

HARKEN
Looks to me like an illegal salvage operation.

MAL
Does it? That's discouraging.

HARKEN
Alliance property, too. You could lose your ship, Captain. But that's a wrist slap compared to the penalty for harboring fugitives. A brother and sister. When I search this vessel, I won't find them, will I?

MAL
No children on this boat.

HARKEN
I didn't say "children". Siblings. Adult siblings.

MAL
I misunderstood.

HARKEN
No chance they could have stowed-away? No one would blame you for that, Captain. I know how these older Firefly models often have those troublesome little nooks.

MAL
Do they?

HARKEN
Smugglers and the like tend to favor them for just that reason.

Now the two Alliance Soldiers return. The not-nauseated one approaches Harken. Whispers something to him. Harken eyes Mal, Mal looks back, wondering what's happened.

HARKEN (cont'd)
We'll continue this conversation in a more official capacity.

Harken motions to one of his men. Instantly some of the Alliance Men start to hustle our guys toward the door. Harken continues with the order-giving:

HARKEN (cont'd)
Every inch of this junker gets tossed.

KAYLEE
(as they go)
Junker?!

MAL
Settle down, Kaylee.

KAYLEE
But, Cap'n! You hear what that purple belly called Serenity?

MAL
Shut up.

INT. SERENITY - PASSAGEWAYS/VARIOUS

A MED TEAM wheels a gurney out with the survivor on it. We don't really get a good look at his current state, under an oxygen mask and sheet and the Med Team members mostly concealing him from us. They're moving fast, we follow them, passing SEARCHING SOLDIERS, and they take us to...

INT. SERENITY - CARGO BAY

...MUCH ACTIVITY. DOZENS of SOLDIERS searching Serenity — tossing it. We PICK UP a particular SOLDIER who moves into...

INT. SERENITY - INARA'S SHUTTLE

...Inara's shuttle. Reacting to the lavish difference.

HARKEN (O.S.)
You're a Companion.

INARA (O.S.)
Yes.

INT. ALLIANCE CRUISER - INTERROGATION ROOM

Inara sits in the sterile surroundings. Harken will be doing the grilling. (We'll be INTERCUTTING between INTERROGATIONS and THE SEARCH quite liberally throughout the following.)

HARKEN
You were based for several years on Sihnon. It's only been in the last year that you've been shipping out with the crew of The Serenity.

INARA
It's just "Serenity", and that's correct. In a few weeks it will be a year. Why is this important?

HARKEN
Just trying to put the pieces together. It's a curiosity. A woman of stature such as yourself falling in with these... types.

INARA
Not in the least. It's a mutually beneficial business arrangement. I rent the shuttle from Captain Reynolds, which allows me to expand my client base, and the Captain finds that having a Companion on board opens certain doors that might otherwise be closed to him.

HARKEN
And do you love him?

TIME CUT TO:

INT. ALLIANCE CRUISER - INTERROGATION ROOM

Zoe sitting rigidly in the interrogation room.

ZOE
I don't see how that's relevant.

ALLIANCE SHIPS

Production designer Carey Meyer: "We wanted to contrast the Alliance with the Outer Planets and our spaceship, Serenity. We wanted a very clean, sterile environment, and that's exactly what we ended up with. Unfortunately we never were able to explore that world enough. All we really created was the bridge, which connected to a massive CG exterior, which really did give you the flavor of what that environment was all about — extremely high-tech and powerful and completely devoid of any character."

HARKEN
Well, he is your husband.

ZOE
Yes.

INT. SERENITY - ZOE AND WASH'S ROOM

SOLDIERS moving in here, examining the evidence of Wash and Zoe's private life together...

HARKEN (V.O.)
You two met through Captain Reynolds?

ZOE (V.O.)
Captain was looking for a pilot, I found a husband. Seemed to work out.

INT. ALLIANCE CRUISER - INTERROGATION ROOM

HARKEN
You fought with Captain Reynolds in the war.

ZOE
Fought with a lot of people in the war.

HARKEN
And your husband?

ZOE
Fight with him sometimes, too.

HARKEN
Is there any particular reason you don't wish to discuss your marriage?

ZOE
Don't see that it's any of your business, is all. We're very private people.

TIME CUT TO:

INT. ALLIANCE CRUISER - INTERROGATION ROOM

Wash looking much more relaxed in the interrogation.

WASH
The legs. Oh, yeah. Definitely have to say it was her legs. You can put that down.

INT. SERENITY - VARIOUS

The search continues, moving into the engine room...

INT. ALLIANCE CRUISER - INTERROGATION ROOM

Still indignant.

KAYLEE
...six Gurstlers crammed right under every cooling drive so that you strain your primary artery function and end up having to recycle secondary exhaust through a bypass system just so's you don't end up pumping it into the main atmo feed and asphyxiating your crew. What [genius] thought up that lame design? Now that's "junk".

TIME CUT TO:

INT. ALLIANCE CRUISER - INTERROGATION ROOM

JAYNE just sits there, closed mouthed. Arms crossed. We play the silence for a moment, then —

INT. SERENITY - JAYNE'S ROOM

Knives. Guns. Girly magazine (with Chinese markings). Another knife.

INT. ALLIANCE CRUISER - INTERROGATION ROOM

Jayne sits silently. Not a word. More shifting. More silence.

INT. ALLIANCE CRUISER - INTERROGATION ROOM

KAYLEE
She ain't "junk".

INT. SERENITY - BOOK'S ROOM

As the Soldiers toss Book's room: bible, a cross, etc.

HARKEN (V.O.)
Pirates with their own Chaplain. There's an oddity.

INT. ALLIANCE CRUISER - INTERROGATION ROOM

BOOK
Not the only oddity this end of space, Commander. Way of things not always so plain as on the central planets. Rules can be a mite fuzzier.

HARKEN
Not for me. Our rules are written down. In books.

BOOK
I take my rules from a book, too. But just the one.

HARKEN
(smiles)
Southdown Abbey. Home to a fairly pious order. How long were you in residence there, Shepherd?

BOOK
Don't right recall. Didn't tend to keep track of the days there. Seemed like long enough, though.

HARKEN
You met up with Captain Reynolds and his crew on Persephone.

BOOK
That's true.

HARKEN
These fugitives we're looking for, the brother and sister... they were last seen on Persephone.

INT. SERENITY - VARIOUS

The swarm of the search team continues. One of the Soldiers looks at the panels of the stash. Moves to it...

BOOK (V.O.)
That a fact?

HARKEN (V.O.)
They also left port aboard a Firefly class transport. Just about the time you shipped out with Serenity.

He presses — a panel opens. He calls some others over. They rip the panels up — empty.

INT. ALLIANCE CRUISER - INTERROGATION ROOM

BOOK
Well, Persephone's a big place.

HARKEN
Yes. But that Firefly isn't. And if there is anyone hiding anywhere on it — we will find them.

INT. SERENITY - DINING ROOM

The Soldiers are starting to pack up, file out. As the swarm begins to disperse... CAMERA pulls back and up, out past the overhead windows, moving to —

EXT. SERENITY

— the outside of the ship. Where WE FIND SIMON and RIVER both in spacesuits, clinging to the side of the ship.

Simon is just freaking out, his gloved hands the only thing keeping his sweaty palms from losing purchase on the side of the ship. He touches the seam of his helmet, making sure it's connected properly. He looks to River, worried. But he reacts —

River stares off into the limitless void of space, seemingly taking a kind of deep comfort from the vastness of it. She's doing something that we haven't really seen her do... she's smiling. Off Simon, continually amazed by his sister...

INT. ALLIANCE CRUISER - INTERROGATION ROOM

Mal sits alone in the room. Presently, the door opens. Harken enters, carrying a thick folder. Harken moves to the chair opposite Mal. Harken studies his documents. Won't look at Mal. A calculated move to put Mal on edge. Mal breaks the silence:

MAL
I figure by now you been over to that derelict. Seen for yourself.

HARKEN
Yes. Terrible thing.

MAL
You want my advice, you won't tow it back. Just fire the whole gorramn thing from space. Be done with it.

HARKEN
That ship is evidence. I'm not in the habit of destroying evidence.

MAL
'Course not. Be against the rules. I'm gonna make a leap and figure this is your first tour out here on the border.

Harken finally looks at Mal.

HARKEN
That's a very loyal crew you have there. But then I see by your record you tend to inspire that quality in people — Sergeant.

SERENITY CREW SPACESUITS

Chris Gilman's company, Global Effects, has produced high-end spacesuits and armor for countless movies and TV shows from *Bram Stoker's Dracula* to *Armageddon*. Chris recalls the origins of the suits used in *Firefly*. "They were originally created for Kurt Russell's movie *Soldier*. The movie's costume designer asked us to come up with some sort of 'soldier spacesuits'. I thought it was a perfect job for us as it combined two areas I'm really interested in: armor and spacesuits. The suits are a variant of the S10 high altitude flight suit."

Originally the *Firefly* production team rented the *Soldier* suits unmodified, but Shawna Trpcic asked Chris if they could create a new look for our crew when outside the ship in space. "We came up with a custom designed helmet for use on the *Soldier* suits. We wanted to give the impression that the helmet could retract back over your head, so we incorporated pleats of the suit material up on the back of the helmet so it would look collapsible. The helmet is basically in two parts, there's the front shell and faceplate, and the pleated back section which is on a plastic cap. The texture of the shell surface is in the molding and the finish is a drab olive, golden green color to match the suits. There's a dry-brush effect over the top to make the helmets look used and armored. A fan system in the backpack forces air up the helmet hose and over the inside of the faceplate. All of our helmets have fans as they would fog up without this and create a big problem. They saw some pieces we did for *Armageddon* and liked the vents on them, so we sculpted some smaller ones for the helmets. The light tubes on the side were rigged by our guy on set, at the request of the production. They're a couple of flashlights and some tubing we usually use for air hose."

Jayne's yellow spacesuit is somewhat different. There were only two of the *Soldier* suits available for rent, so Jayne's suit is an exact replica of an SR-71/10-30 suit, originally made for Dolph Lundgren, who's a similar size to Adam Baldwin. The helmet is the same launch/entry model as those worn by current shuttle crews and is a basic grey color with a black stipple effect. The neck seal ring is a replica of that on an Apollo suit. "Replica spacesuits are surprisingly complicated to make. The *Firefly* suit has about 300 to 400 components. Our replica Shuttle EMU suits have over 1,200, but the real EMU has over 19,000."

Costume designer Shawna Trpcic: "We couldn't afford to make our own spacesuits. Joss said, 'Well, they're scavengers anyway, so just scavenge them from a couple of different shows.' I designed my own helmets to go with the suits, so that at least they would look a little different from the original. We tried to make them look like they'd been through a lot."

❖ Below right: The spacesuits as they originally appeared in the movie *Soldier*.

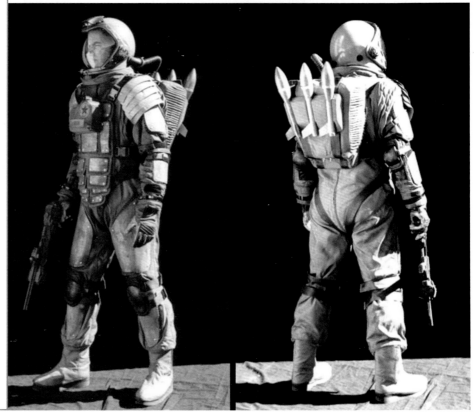

MAL
It's not "Sergeant". Not no more. War's over.

HARKEN
For some the war'll never be over. I notice your
ship's called "Serenity". You were stationed on
Hera at the end of the war. Battle of Serenity
Valley took place there, if I recall.

MAL
(now let me think)
You know, I believe you may be right.

HARKEN
Independents suffered a pretty crushing defeat
there. Some say after Serenity, the Browncoats
were through. That the war really ended in that
valley.

MAL
Hmmm.

HARKEN
Seems odd you'd name your ship after a battle you
were on the wrong side of.

MAL
May have been the losing side. Still not convinced
it was the wrong one.

HARKEN
Is that why you attacked that transport?

MAL
What — ?

HARKEN
You're still fighting the same battle, Sergeant.
Only these weren't soldiers you murdered. They
were civilians. Families. Citizens loyal to the
Alliance, trying to make a new life for themselves.
And you just can't stand that, can you?

MAL
So we attacked that ship then brought the only
living witness back to our infirmary? That what
we did?

HARKEN
I'd ask him... but I imagine he'll have some trouble speaking with his tongue split down the
middle.

MAL
(realizing)
<Wuh de tyen, ah.> [Dear God in heaven.]

HARKEN
I haven't seen that kind of torture since... well,
since the war.

Mal's stunned into silence for a beat, going inter-
nal as the full weight of his realization hits him.

MAL
(to himself)
Shoulda known... shoulda seen this comin'...

HARKEN
You and your crew will be bound by law. Formal
charges will be transmitted to central authority —

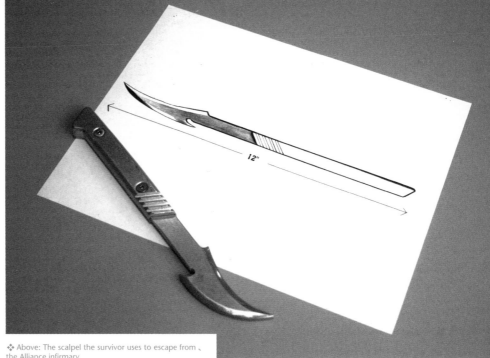

❖ Above: The scalpel the survivor uses to escape from
the Alliance infirmary.

MAL
Commander, I am not what you need to be concerning yourself with right now. Things go the
way they are — there's gonna be blood.

Off that —

INT. ALLIANCE SHIP - INFIRMARY

Again, we're only seeing bits and pieces of what's
become of the survivor. Think Hannibal Lecter
being worked on in the ambulance. His body
lurches and convulses. Team of Alliance medics
working to save him.

So involved in their good work are they, that
they don't see his hand slip off the side of the
operating table, dangling there, clutching the
sharp, shining surgical tool that comes up now
— slashing.

BLACK OUT.

END OF ACT THREE

ACT FOUR

**INT. ALLIANCE CRUISER - INTERROGATION
ROOM**

Harken stares at Mal. Harken's unimpressed as he
says:

HARKEN
Reavers?

MAL
That's what I said.

HARKEN
Can't imagine how many times men in my position hear that excuse. "Reavers did it."

MAL
It's the truth.

HARKEN
You saw them, did you?

MAL
Wouldn't be sitting here talking to you if I had.

HARKEN
No. Of course not.

MAL
But I'll tell you who did — that poor bastard you
took off my ship. He looked right into the face of
it. Was made to stare.

HARKEN
"It?"

MAL
The darkness. Kinda darkness you can't even
imagine. Blacker than the space it moves in.

HARKEN
Very poetic.

MAL
They made him watch. He probably tried to turn
away — they wouldn't let him. You call him a "survivor"? He's not. A man comes up against that
kind of will, only way to deal with it, I suspect... is
to become it. He's following the only course that's
left to him. First he'll try to make himself look like
one... cut on himself, desecrate his own flesh...
then he'll start acting like one.

Harken seems to be considering that for a
moment, hits a button on the table. The door
opens and a SOLDIER appears.

HARKEN
Let's have two M.P.s up here to escort Sergeant
Reynolds to the brig.

MAL
Lock me up. I'll thank you for it. But me and my
crew're gonna be the only ones on this ship that's
safe you don't move to act.

HARKEN
And let's not put him in with his compatriots. In fact, let's see to it they're all separated.

Off Mal's frustration...

INT. SERENITY - FOREDECK HALL

A HATCH OPENS and SIMON, still in his spacesuit, climbs down a ladder. He rips off his helmet as River descends down the ladder. He helps her off with her helmet.

RIVER
Let's go again.

SIMON
Later. Maybe. Captain said once the coast was clear we should lay low in the shuttle.

RIVER
(sensing something)
He's coming back.

SIMON
Yes. Yes, of course he is. They all are. Captain Reynolds is used to these sorts of situations. We just have to be patient. Come on.

They move off. Simon never saw the BLOODY FOOTPRINT nearby. They're not alone.

INT. ALLIANCE CRUISER - INTERROGATION ROOM

The interrogation is over. Harken is off to the side with an M.P. Two more M.P.s are pulling Mal out of his chair, cuffing his hands behind his back.

HARKEN
Your ship and its contents will be auctioned. The proceeds of the sale will be applied to the cost of your defense.

The Ensign now enters, looking a little pale. He moves close to Harken, whispers his report. Harken reacts. We can guess what's being reported to Harken. So can Mal.

HARKEN (cont'd)
(re: Mal)
Get him out of here.
(to Ensign)
Go to full lock down. I want guards on the nursery —

As Mal's hustled toward the door:

MAL
It won't matter. You won't find him.

Harken meets Mal's gaze, a little lost.

MAL (cont'd)
But I know where he'll go.

CUT TO:

INT. SERENITY - PASSAGEWAYS - CONTINUOUS

Simon tries to steer River into the dining

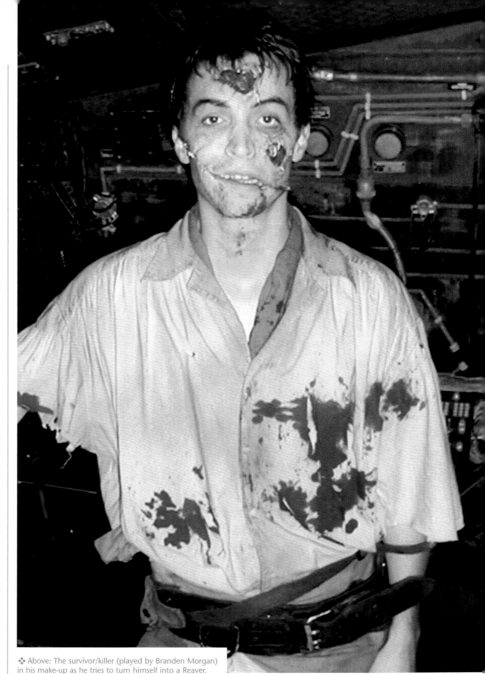
❖ Above: The survivor/killer (played by Branden Morgan) in his make-up as he tries to turn himself into a Reaver.

room/kitchen area. She whimpers. Will go no further.

SIMON
River. It's okay. They've gone. Come on.

But she won't.

SIMON (cont'd)
We don't know how long it's going to be. Once we're settled, I don't think we should move around much. I'll just grab some some food and...

He tries to disengage from her, she's holding him back. He lists away, toward the dining room... CAMERA PULLS back...

...past scattered KITCHEN CUTLERY...

...finally REVEALING the FIGURE just two feet from the oblivious Simon who's trying to back yet closer, as...

INT. ALLIANCE SHIP - AIRLOCK/DOOR TO SERENITY

A DEAD GUARD marks the way of the killer. Mal is there with Harken and armed M.P.s.

HARKEN
Why would he come back here?

MAL
Looking for familiar ground. He's on the hunt.

HARKEN
All right.

Harken nods to his men. They ready themselves to enter. Before they can:

HARKEN (cont'd)
(to an M.P.)
Get him to the brig.

MAL
You should let me go with you.

HARKEN
Out of the question.

MAL
How many more men you feel like losing today, Commander? Nobody knows Serenity like I do. I can help you.

Harken considers that for a beat, then —

HARKEN
We'll let him go first.

MAL
(oh, good)
Great.

Harken is getting set again, Mal makes him pause with:

MAL (cont'd)
Uh — ?

Mal indicates his hands still cuffed behind his back. Harken takes the key from one of his men, undoes the cuffs himself — but just as quick pulls Mal's hands around front, recuffs him with his hands now in front of him.

MAL (cont'd)
Thanks. Now I'll really have the advantage.

HARKEN
(to his men)
Open it.

As his men move to do that —

INT. SERENITY - PASSAGEWAYS - CONTINUOUS

SIMON AND RIVER

She tries to hold him back as he backs close to the unseen (to him) Killer. He absently reaches behind himself, sets his helmet on the dining room table, as —

Simon stops suddenly at the SOUND of the AIRLOCK OPENING in the distance.

SIMON
Someone's coming...

The Killer also hears the approach of footsteps... feints out of frame...

INT. SERENITY - CARGO BAY - CONTINUOUS

Mal leads Harken and his men into the cargo bay.

HARKEN
(hushed)
We'll split up —

MAL
Best if we stick together. Unless you're in the mood to get picked off.

Harken considers, nods. Sighs. Fine.

HARKEN
(to his men)
Keene, Escobar, you two stay here. Watch the door. Don't need this thing back on my ship.

Harken indicates for Mal to lead on. He does.

INT. SERENITY - OUTSIDE INFIRMARY

MOVING WITH MAL

Schmuck bait as he leads the team past the wrecked infirmary. Through the common area, coming up to the steep stairs which lead to the upper levels.

INT. SERENITY - ENGINE ROOM

Mal leads Harken and his men through the engine room, down into the dining area. Mal notes a spacesuit helmet sitting on the table. Knows what that means. He steels himself. Mushes on.

Mal sees the spilled cutlery. He and Harken share a look. They continue on...

Mal steps up into the foredeck hall. Tries not to react as he comes nearly face-to-face with —

SIMON AND RIVER

pressed tight up against a wall just around the corner, hidden by the lip of the passageway.

Harken's right on Mal's ass now, a step down in the dining room. Mal turns to him as —

THE KILLER

leaps from out of frame, attacking one of the men just behind Harken. Harken turns. THE KILLER slashes Harken's man. There is blood, splashing across Harken's surprised face.

Harken fumbles for his gun, the Killer knocks it away, lunges at Harken, as —

Mal leaps at the guy's back, brings his cuffed hands over his head and around his throat —

HARKEN'S POV

Of the HIDEOUS MUTILATED FACE, flesh peeled back, mouth pinned into a grimace by bits of metal. It SNARLS and SNAPS at Harken, trying to get at him. Right the fuck up in his face. Being held at bay only by Mal's strength. It is terrifying. Mal pulls hard. There is a crack.

Mal lets the body drop at their feet.

ANGLE: THE SURVIVOR

Mal uses the tip of his boot to turn the dead man's head slightly... Mutilated flesh. The skin of his mouth remains pulled back and pinned into that hideous grimace. Scarcely human.

MAL AND HARKEN

as they share a look. Harken's face sullied with blood. A baptism of sorts. There are no words. Off this —

EXT. SPACE

Serenity detaches from the Alliance Cruiser, floats down.

INT. SERENITY - BRIDGE

Mal, Wash, Zoe and Jayne. They watch as the big ship gets smaller.

JAYNE
You save his gorram life. And he still takes the cargo. <Hwoon dahn.> [Jerk.]

MAL
Had to. Couldn't let us profit.

Mal doesn't stick around. He turns for the door.

MAL (cont'd)
Wouldn't be civilized.

Through the cockpit window, WE SEE the Alliance Ship send out what look like torpedoes. They connect with the spinning derelict, sending a series of SOUNDLESS EXPLOSIONS through its hull. As the derelict caves in on itself, glows to embers...

BLACK OUT.

END OF SHOW

"HAVE YOU EVER BEEN WITH A WARRIOR WOMAN?"

Zoe's Pistol & Vest

❖ Above: Profile views of Zoe's 'Mare's Leg' pistol.

Zoe's pistol is a fine example of a 'Mare's Leg'; a cut down Winchester rifle. Mike Gibbons, *Firefly*'s armorer, explains its origins: "The Mare's Leg pistols were originally made for a show called *The Adventures of Brisco County Jr.* I had them here in the shop, they saw them, liked them and used them in *Firefly*. The 'Zoe pistol' was inspired by Josh Randall's Mare's Leg in 1958's *Wanted, Dead or Alive*, a TV spin-off from *Trackdown*. Bounty hunter Josh Randall was played by Steve McQueen. He had this pistol which was cut down from a Winchester. The base gun for Zoe's pistol is a 44-40 caliber Rossi 92, a Winchester copy, which was cut down in the shop to remove the stock

and some of the barrel length. We copied pictures of the Josh Randall prop — except that one was, I believe, a Winchester model 73. I did them on a 92 because they work better, they're shorter and lighter. They're more modern, have a shorter action and tend to be more reliable. Besides, at the time, there wasn't a ton of 73s lying around. *Firefly* had a small budget so we provided a lot of stuff for the show right off the shop wall."

Gina Torres would carry a rubber stunt pistol in the holster whenever the Hero (closeup) weapon wasn't required. The rubber guns weigh very little, but the Mare's Leg Hero pistol weighs in at 1.91 kg (4.21 lbs) unloaded.

As on Josh Randall's, the pistol's cocking lever is extended into a loop shape, but not for use as a hand-guard as might be expected. Armorer Mike Gibbons explains, "The loop is so you can 'swing' the gun to reload it. Swinging is the dangerous practice of cycling the gun's action by slinging the entire weapon in an arc around your firing hand. You see John Wayne do it in *True Grit*. It's a great way to shoot yourself or end up with the front sight embedded in your forehead!"

Costume designer Shawna Trpcic designed Zoe's trademark vest, which was made in collaboration with leather artist Jonathan A. Logan. The design evokes the Old West with its natural look and utilitarian economy. The rows of side-buckles were an inspiration of Shawna's.

Logan recalls, "That was a nice piece of work. We had the pleasure of actually fitting the garment to Gina Torres in the studio. We kind of made a vest which molded itself to her body. I have a lot of mock-up garments in fabrics, rather than the final leather material. So, when you have a concept like the vest, we try on a bunch of different bodies, then take whatever is the best for the purpose and apply that shape."

ZOE'S HOLSTER

The holster Zoe wears was also inspired by Josh Randall's. It's a slab of leather with a padded steel spring-clip at the barrel end and a bracket at the top upon which the pistol hangs by its saddle-ring. There's a leg strap, and a leather thong is used to keep the pistol snugly in its clip at the barrel end.

❖ Far left: Zoe's vest.

❖ Left: Zoe's full pistol and holster rig. The rubber stunt pistol is also pictured.

SHINDIG

Written by Jane Espenson
Directed by Vern Gillum

 **JANE ESPENSON**

The idea of Mal having an adventure in Inara's world was one of several ideas that were already underway when I was brought into the process. Mal and Inara's attraction was one of the building blocks of the series. So all the romantic stuff was in place from the beginning of discussions about the story. But I had the immeasurable fun of finding the words. Unspoken attraction is a delight to put into dialogue because it's so unspoken. You get to dance with the words.

I know I came up with the title on my own. I loved the new-Old Western dialect and the chance to dust off an old word like 'shindig' again. Like the Badger-Jayne-Mal scene had a couple of interesting things going on. One of them was Adam Baldwin, as Jayne, constantly filling his cup with sugar. The other was a discussion about how to pronounce 'palaver'. It was another old word I dusted off. You've got to be careful with those old ones sometimes, because no one knows them anymore, except to read them.

I loved inventing sci-fi touches. This episode contains two of my favorites: the floating chandelier and the futuristic hotel key. I wrote the floating chandelier with very little thought. I imagined we'd see it briefly in one shot and then refer to it off-screen for the rest of the scene. But it turned into a major deal. The entire ballroom scene is filled with moving shimmering reflected light that is supposedly coming from the floating chandelier.

The hotel key I had imagined as a small metal knob with a shaft that became the doorknob when it was inserted into the right door-hole. The clever people in charge of such things found the coolest low-tech way of doing this. When Inara screws the knob into the door, the whole back half of the bulb lights up, because it's a light bulb — painted silver in front. Coolest thing ever! I also got to invent the poker descendant, tall card, in this episode.

Once the basic beats of the story were in place, there weren't a lot of adjustments made to them. One thing that I remember is that the first act break changed at least once. The problem was in deciding what exactly Inara was going to see and react to. Kaylee? Mal? Which one should enter first? Should Mal approach Inara in the moment? What we ended up with worked really well.

There is one other small rearrangement that happened after the shooting was done, in the editing process. The scene in which Mal comes to the engine room and tells Kaylee he's got a job for her is now used to break up two chunks of the party. In the shooting draft that scene falls before any of the party material. It's a great change. And the scene in which River is suddenly coherent and speaks to Badger in his own accent came from Joss knowing that Summer could do really good accents. He suggested we use this. I love doing stuff like that, building off the actors — the way they look or move, or stuff they can do.

The Wash-Zoe relationship was my favorite thing on *Firefly* and I was sad that they only had that one scene [the bed scene] alone together. I came up with the joke about Jayne taking over and the idea of Wash jokingly composing poetry for the funeral. Now, given the events of *Serenity*, it just all seems so sad and poignant and foreshadowy. In my version, I didn't have Wash actually quote any of the poem. But Joss liked the idea and he added the line that now ends the scene.

The episode turned out really well, and is one of the very few episodes in my entire career in which I was on the set for almost every take of every scene. I'm terribly proud of it.

TEASER

INT. POOL HALL - NIGHT (NIGHT 1)

It's dark, smoky. Four tables are in play. There are about fifteen people in here, mostly men. A BARTENDER serves beer in heavy wooden bowls. Small tables line the edges of the room.

MAL and JAYNE play two other men, WRIGHT and HOLDER. INARA, in a beautiful outfit, watches and holds a small glass of pink liqueur. She is the only color, only elegance.

WRIGHT is lining up a shot and talking at the same time. His cue has a ring of light right before the tip.

WRIGHT
Didn't hardly have to convert the ship, even.
(re: shot)
Six in the corner. Stronger locks, thicker doors, keep everybody where they're s'posed to be. Don't even need more rations.

As he sights along his cue, all the balls on the table flicker, disappearing for a moment, then reappearing. A general DISGUSTED GROAN comes from every player in the room.

WRIGHT (cont'd)
<Way!> [Hey!]

He looks toward the Bartender, as do other patrons. The Bartender points, bored, to a crude sign: "MANAGEMENT NOT RESPONSIBLE FOR BALL FAILURE" (It also says it in Chinese.)

Wright attempts his shot. Doesn't sink the ball.

WRIGHT (cont'd)
Flicker threw me off.

Mal's turn. He walks around, examines the table.

JAYNE
(to Wright)
You made money?

WRIGHT
Hand over fist, my friend. Border planets need labor. Terraforming crews got a prodigious death rate.

MAL
Side pocket.

Mal makes his shot, lines up another.

MAL (cont'd)
Labor. You mean slaves.

WRIGHT
They wasn't volunteers, for damn sure.

MAL
That why you didn't hafta lay in more rations?

WRIGHT
I didn't hear no complaints.

Wright and Holder laugh.

JAYNE
How much money? Lots?

Mal misses a shot and steps back by Inara. She's brushing cigarette ashes off a chair, making a place to sit.

MAL
There's a chance you may wanna head back to the ship.

INARA
Oh, I'm all right. This is entertaining, actually.

MAL
(amused, disbelieving)
Yeah? What's entertaining?

INARA
I like watching the game. As with other situations, the key seems to be giving Jayne a heavy stick and standing back.

ANGLE ON: Jayne, sinking one of the few remaining balls.

Mal smiles at Inara, but:

MAL
Still think you might oughtta clear out 'fore too much longer. Seems there's a thief about.

INARA
A thief?

Mal leans in close, slips Inara a handful of paper money.

MAL
He took this right off 'em. They earned that with the sweat of their slave-tradin' brows.

INARA
Mal!

MAL
Terrible shame. 'Course, they won't notice it til they go to pay for their next drink—

WRIGHT (O.S.)
<Way!> [Hey!]

MAL
(to Inara)
Good drinker, that one.

Wright's hand falls heavily on Mal's shoulder. Mal spins and LANDS A MIGHTY PUNCH.

Behind them, Holder jumps to help Wright. Jayne TACKLES HIM.

Inara jumps back against a wall, as Wright KICKS MAL'S LEGS from under him. Mal falls.

Holder is up again, swinging a pool cue at Jayne.

Mal, on the floor, grabs the base of a small table and rams it UP at Wright. Wright flies back.

It's a melee. Other patrons jump to join.

Inara jumps when a GLASS SHATTERS near her head. She heads toward the door, fast. She passes the Bartender as she goes.

INARA
(dryly)
Lovely place. I'll tell my friends.

END OF TEASER

ACT ONE

EXT. SERENITY/PERSEPHONE - EFFECT

Descending out of orbit over Persephone.

INT. SERENITY - BRIDGE - DAY (DAY 2)/ EFFECT

WASH pilots Serenity closer to the surface. ZOE stands behind his chair, hand on Wash's shoulder, looking out.

As they approach, Persephone comes between them and this system's sun; the planet's shadow moves over their faces. Zoe bends down close to Wash, a couple enjoying a sunset.

WASH
It seem to you we cleared outta Santo in a hurry?

ZOE
Seems to me we do that a lot. Heard tell though, we're gonna stay a while on Persephone, upwards of a week maybe.

Wash whistles through his teeth.

WASH
Shiny.

ZOE
Yeah? Thought you'd get land-crazy, that long in port.

WASH
Prob'ly. But I been sane a long while now, and change is good.

Mal joins them. Looks out past them at the planet.

MAL
Well, ain't that a joyful sight.

WASH
Gotta love a sunset.

ZOE
Startin' to get familiar, too. Like a second home.

MAL
(firmly)
Persephone is not home. Too many people we need to avoid. Resupply, look for work, move along. We sniff the air, we don't kiss the dirt.

JOSS WHEDON

Ultimately, it's time for a little romantic comedy with Mal and Inara and to see a little bit of her world, and Mal being the fish-out-of-water guy, because that's never not fun. And also, to have Kaylee have a dress, because not since I wanted Willow to have an Eskimo suit [on *Buffy*] have I been so excited about somebody's outfit.

ZOE
Wasn't planning on the dirt-kissing, sir.

WASH
I wouldn't stand for it anyways, Captain. Jealous man like me.
(re: piloting)
Closin' in.

ZOE
Planet's coming up a might fast.

WASH
Just means I'm going down too quick. Likely crash and kill us all.

As Mal exits:

MAL
That happens, let me know.

INT. INARA'S SHUTTLE - DAY

Inara sits facing a Cortex screen that hangs on the wall like a mirror. There is local data across the top of the screen: "Persephone", the local time (ten a.m.), ship's status (docked). The main part of the screen is labeled "Responses". The screen features twelve small pictures — ten men, two women. Text under each picture gives a name. Inara touches three pictures and they disappear.

Inara looks at the ones that remain. She touches one of the pictures and it expands to fill the screen. It's a taped request from a pale YOUNG HOPEFUL (man).

YOUNG HOPEFUL
(on tape, nervous)
I understand your time on our planet is limited. And if you've selected my proposal to hear, then the honor that you do me flatters my...
(searches for words)
My honor... and I hope—

Inara taps the screen. The field of nine photos is back. Before she can select another, a CHIME sounds and the screen fills with the live (not recorded) image of ATHERTON WING.

Atherton is handsome, thirties, with just enough charm to offset his aura of entitlement. Inara smiles at the sight of him.

ATHERTON
(over the link)
Now there's the smile made of sunlight.

INARA
Atherton! How wonderful to see you.

ATHERTON
Did you get my message? I was extra appealing.

INARA
Yesterday. I listened to yours first. What a flattering invitation. I had no idea I was arriving in time for the Social Event of the Season.

ATHERTON
We only have four or five of those a year, you know. So you'll accompany me, I ask, heart in my

throat? There is a certain offer I'm still waiting to hear about.

SFX: KNOCK AT THE DOOR

INARA
Yes, I imagine there is. I'm delighted to say I'll be there. Now, I'm sorry, Atherton, I have to run.

ATHERTON
I understand, I'll see you soon,
<bao bay.> [sweetheart.]

She severs the connection. His image freezes on the screen.

INARA
Come in.

Mal enters. Inara sets the screen on a table.

INARA (cont'd)
Good afternoon, Captain.

MAL
Morning. We're downing, and in case Wash don't kill us all, local time's gonna be in the a.m., ten or so.

INARA
(why are you really here?)
Yes, I saw that.

Mal gestures toward the screen, trying to seem casual.

MAL
Making plans?

Inara tenses. He doesn't wait for an answer from her. He looks closely at the screen.

MAL (cont'd)
"Atherton Wing". He's a regular, ain't he?

Inara blanks the screen.

INARA
I've seen him before.

MAL
Well, I never did. Not what I pictured. Young. Must be rich too, to afford your rates.

INARA
I suppose. He has engaged me for several days.

MAL
Days. The boy must have stamina.

INARA
He does.

Mal tries not to look stung.

MAL
Well... fine. Is he lettin' you out at all?

INARA
Actually, we're attending a ball tomorrow night.

MAL
Tell me, all the men there have to pay for their dates, or just the young rich ones with stamina?

INARA
Most of the women there will not be Companions, if that's what you're asking. Perhaps the other men couldn't attract one.

MAL
Huh. Sounds like the finest party I can imagine getting paid to go to.

INARA
I don't suppose you'd find it up to the standards of your outings. More conversation and somewhat less petty theft and getting hit with pool cues.

Inara moves to the door, a clear invitation to leave.

INARA (cont'd)
I understand, if you need to go prepare for that "it's ten in the morning" issue.

MAL
Yeah. Better do that. Cuz I think this is more of an evening look.

He exits.

EXT. STREET - DAY (DAY 2)

Outside a line of shops on Persephone. KAYLEE, Zoe, Jayne, Wash and Mal are carrying some supplies back to the Mule.

The women and Wash walk ahead, then Jayne, then Mal. Mal carries a heavy burlap sack.

They pass a high-class dress shop. There are three live MODELS behind the window, walking and posing, showing off their gowns. Kaylee stops short, and Zoe almost runs into her.

KAYLEE
Ooh. Look at the pretties.

Zoe looks, and Wash joins her.

WASH
What am I looking at? The girls or the clothes?

Jayne stops short:

JAYNE
(immediately)
There's girls?

ZOE
(answering Wash, overlapping)
The clothes, please.

Jayne looks too. Mal is forced to stop, wait.

KAYLEE
(pointing)
Say. Look at the fluffy one.

ZOE
Too much foofaraw. If I'm gonna wear a dress, I want something with slink.

WASH
(quickly)
You want a slinky dress? I can buy you a slinky dress. Captain, can I have money for a slinky dress?

JAYNE
I'll chip in.

ZOE
(casually, to Jayne)
I can hurt you.

KAYLEE
Only place I ever seen something so nice is some of the things Inara has.

MAL
We'd best be movin'—

ZOE
Guess she needs all that stuff, life she leads.

KAYLEE
Well, sure. And sometimes the customers buy her things. She knows some real rich men—

MAL
Come on. T'ain't feathers I'm toting here, you know.

KAYLEE
I like the ruffles. Inara gets to wear whatever she—

MAL
What would you do in that rig? Flounce around

the engine room? Be like a sheep walkin' on its hind legs.

Jayne snorts a laugh at that. Kaylee's face shows she's hurt. Zoe shoots Mal a hard look. She takes Mal's burden effortlessly. She, Kaylee and Wash head o.s. toward the Mule.

ZOE
(coldly)
See you on the ship, Captain.

Mal instantly regrets what he said.

MAL
<Tee wuh duh pee-goo.> [Kick me in the bottom.]

JAYNE
Is she mad or something?

There's a series of meaningful CLICKS behind him.

Mal and Jayne turn to find themselves facing BADGER, a cockney criminal, a slice of local color with a fine hat.

Three of his LADS are with him, covering Jayne — the clicks were the cocking of their guns.

Mal nods politely, as if this is a normal way to run into an old acquaintance.

MAL
Badger.

BADGER
Captain Reynolds. Heard you was in town. Thought we might have a bit of a sit-down.

MAL
I'd prefer a bit of a "piss off".

BADGER
I'm very sorry. Did I give you the impression I was asking?

INT. BADGER'S LAIR - DAY

Badger, Mal and Jayne sit uncomfortably around a cable-spool table. Badger pours some English tea. Jayne eats from a plate of cucumber sandwiches.

MAL
Seems to me, last time there was a chance for a little palaver, we were all manner of unwelcome...

JAYNE
(re: tea)
That's not bad.

BADGER
(to Jayne, confidentially)
There's a trick to it. Wood alcohol.

Mal continues as if he hadn't been interrupted.

MAL
Now, we're favored guests, treated to the finest in beverages that make you blind. So what is it you need?

Jayne pours himself more tea, reaching across Mal.

JAYNE
'Scuse me.

BADGER
There's this local, name of Warrick Harrow. He's got some property he wants to sell off-planet, to fetch a higher price.

MAL
But the local powers won't let him sell off-world.

BADGER
It's a conundrum. What my man Harrow needs hisself, is a smuggler. 'M willing to cut you in on it.

MAL
Why me? You've got access to ships. You could do it yourself.

BADGER
(reluctant)
He won't deal with me direct. Taken an irrational dislike.

JAYNE
(mouth full)
What happened? He see your face?

BADGER
(ignoring Jayne)
He's a quality gent. Nose in the air like he never <wun gwo pee> [smelled a fart]. Don't find me respectable. You, I figure, you got a chance.

MAL
You backed out of a deal, last time. Left us hanging.

JAYNE
Hurt our feelings.

MAL
You recall why that took place?

BADGER
I had a problem with your attitude, is why. Felt you was, what's the word?

JAYNE
Pretentious?

Mal shoots Jayne a look.

BADGER
Exactly. You think you're better'n other people.

MAL
Just the ones I'm better than.
(then)
Now, I thinkin' that very quality is the one you're placing value on today.

BADGER
I place value on the fact that the stick up your <pee-goo> [bottom] is 'bout as large as the one Harrow's got.

Jayne barks a laugh at that. Mal shoots him

another look.

MAL
How would you even set up a meet, man won't deal with you?

BADGER
I know a place he'll be. Safe place, using some new-tech gun scans. High class, too. They wouldn't let me in there, but you might slip by. 'Course you couldn't buy an invite with a diamond size of a testicle. But I got my hands on a couple.

Mal raises his eyebrows for a pregnant beat.

BADGER (cont'd)
(clarifying)
..of invites. You want the meeting or not?

Mal considers.

BADGER (cont'd)
You want to do business in Persephone, you do it through me. But if you're so well off you don't need it...

INT. SERENITY - ENGINE ROOM - DAY (DAY 2)

Kaylee is working on the engine. Mal enters.

MAL
Kaylee.

She avoids his eyes, busies herself with her work. No answer.

MAL (cont'd)
Kaylee.

KAYLEE
I'm not speaking to you, Captain.

MAL
Got no need to speak... C'mon...

He turns to go, matching her coldness.

MAL (cont'd)
Got a job for you.

INT. PARTY - FOYER - NIGHT (NIGHT 2)

Atherton Wing ushers Inara into the richly decorated foyer of a large public building. They are dressy and elegant.

MARK A. SHEPPARD

London-born Mark A. Sheppard was a successful rock band drummer before he was cast in the docudrama *In the Name of the Father*. Since then, he's worked a lot, but says, "The fondest experience I have had is with *Firefly*. It was a lovely set full of people who actually cared about what they were doing, which is also rare. It's not rare that people care about what they're doing — it's rare that *everybody* cares about what they're doing."

Sheppard loved Badger's costume. "Shawna Trpcic gave me a flamingo pin, which was a great idea with the suit. No socks, an undershirt, a tie but no collar. Everything was slightly broken. We talked about 'very fine hats'. The Western bowler was the coolest-looking hat I'd ever seen. Everything had a reason. They explained to me that Badger having fresh fruit meant he had some power and influence; he also wasn't that interested in opulence, he was interested in enjoying the fruits of his labors."

Adam Baldwin, who had worked with Sheppard before on the films *Lover's Knot* and *Farewell, My Love*, broke the news to Sheppard that Joss Whedon had originally written the role of Badger for himself. "We got through [Badger's scene in 'Serenity'] and Joss said, 'I've got something to tell you,' and I said, 'Yeah, I know!'"

Part of the fun of playing Badger for Sheppard was leading Badger's gang. "The group of extras were extraordinary. I thought the nicest thing that Joss did was, when we went to do 'Shindig', I said, 'Please, get me the same guys.' They went out of their way to get the same guys. There was a wonderful guy, he looks like my accountant — he's sitting with the old adding machine, he's the first guy to draw down. I don't have a gang of big, tough guys — I've got a gang of interesting-looking human beings."

More was shot of the Badger/Mal/Jayne scene than we see in the episode. "Adam and I both have a tape from the editors of the whole scene with all of the pieces that we had put in," Sheppard explains. "Adam's eating my cucumber sandwiches, which is hysterical. It's a big deal to Badger and he's showing off what he has, and there's Jayne, stuffing his face with sandwiches, taking my wood alcohol tea and putting as much sugar into it as he possibly can. We went through the entire case of brown sugar cubes doing takes. They brought us real tea and real sandwiches, so Adam ate basically for about three hours and drank sugary tea. Jayne is staring Badger down, but as he's reaching for more food. It's one of my favorite scenes."

Sheppard helped Summer Glau with her English accent for their scene together. "She and I went to a café, we sat with a tape recorder and just worked on the accent. She said, 'Well, how would you say it?' I said it a few times and she was very self-deprecating, but she got what she needed to learn, she arrived on the set, boom. She won a round of applause after her first take, quite rightly so. She is so open when she does what she does; she's absolutely fearless."

Sheppard recalls his first scene on the Serenity interior. "That moment was about, wow, Badger gets that, Badger doesn't have this [a ship]. Badger thinks he owns it, because for some reason, he likes to think he can control Mal to a point — financially, certainly. I think Badger just wants to be liked — that's his fatal flaw — and I don't know that Malcolm Reynolds likes him that much," Sheppard laughs.

If *Firefly* is ever resurrected, Sheppard says, "It would be wonderful — I'd jump in a minute."

ATHERTON
After you...

The ballroom is beyond, through an ornate arch — there is no visible machinery associated with the arch. Two couples are in front of them, waiting to go through. A DECORATED OFFICIAL stands to the side of the arch.

ANGLE ON THE ARCHWAY

One couple passes through. A PORTER, his back visible through the arch, can be heard, slightly muffled, as he announces them to the room beyond.

PORTER
William and Lady Cortland.

The next couple, equally elegant, heads for the arch. The woman steps through, but the WELL-DRESSED MAN is held in place by something unseen.

A PLEASANT CHIME SOUNDS.

The Well-Dressed Man is not harmed, not struggling, but he can't move forward. He steps back, smiles at the Official. He removes a small pistol from a suit jacket pocket, hands it to the Official. He passes through the arch to join his date.

PORTER (cont'd)
Colonel Cyrus Momsen and escort.

Atherton and Inara step through.

INT. PARTY - BALLROOM - CONTINUOUS

Atherton and Inara enter.

PORTER
Atherton Wing and Inara Serra.

We see the room now, filled with elegant party-goers, circulating waiters, live musicians, a buffet table...

Fresh food means money, so many of the decorations feature huge bowls of fruit. There is also a hovering chandelier.

Atherton and Inara move into the room. Inara waves at someone, exchanges air kisses with another woman.

INARA
Roberta, it's been too long.

She greets an elderly man sitting in a chair:

INARA (cont'd)
<Lao pung yo, nee can chi lai hun yo jing shen.> [You're looking wonderful, old friend.]

They move on. Atherton talks softly into her ear.

ATHERTON
Half the men in this room wish you were on their arm tonight.

INARA
Only half? I must be losing my undefinable allure.

ATHERTON
Not that undefinable. All of them wish you were in their bed.

Inara finds that in bad taste. She looks away, changes the topic.

INARA
I'm looking for the boy with the shimmerwine.

ATHERTON
Oh, she blushes.
(considering)
Not many in your line of work do that. You, you are a singular woman and I find,
(stammering, sincere)

I find I admire you more and more.

Inara stops and looks at him, touched.

ATHERTON (cont'd)
I'm trying to give you something, you know. A life. If you want it.

INARA
Atherton...

ATHERTON
You can live here, on Persephone. As my personal Companion.

INARA
You are a generous man.

ATHERTON
That's not a "yes".

INARA
(after a beat)
It's not a "no" either.

Inara greets another acquaintance.

INARA (cont'd)
(to a woman)
You look gorgeous, dear.

Atherton spots a glass of champagne — a waiter is passing with a tray. Atherton lifts the glass and offers it to Inara in one smooth move. She smiles, delighted.

ATHERTON
You belong here, Inara, not on that flying piece of <gos se> [crap]. You see that, don't you?

INARA
Atherton, language.

ATHERTON
What, "piece of <gos se> [crap]"? But it is a piece of <gos se> [crap].

PORTER (O.S.)
Miss Kaywinnit Lee Frye and escort.

Inara turns her head sharply and a little rudely away from Atherton, startled into looking at the door.

INARA
Kaylee?

ON KAYLEE

She enters, eyes wide, soaking it all in. She wears the ruffled dress from the window and looks beautiful. She carries a glittery evening bag. She's Cinderella at the ball.

Mal steps forward to join her. He is in his Sunday best, something dark and Rhett Butler-y, maybe a cut-away coat.

ACROSS THE ROOM

Inara stares, locking in on Mal.

INARA
Oh <gos se>[crap].

END OF ACT ONE

ACT TWO

INT. PARTY FOYER - CONTINUING

Mal and Kaylee make their way into the party. Her eyes are bright and wide as she takes it all in at once. Mal is trying to look cool and cosmopolitan, but is actually almost as impressed as Kaylee. He tugs at his suit.

MAL
Does this seem kind of... tight?

KAYLEE
Shows off your backside. Didja see the chandelier?

M U S I C

Composer Greg Edmonson: "We used classical music for the ballroom stuff — Beethoven, Haydn. For filming they bought a performance, probably by a European orchestra, and then used the playback on set. Otherwise, they would have had nothing to dance to. Right about the time I got hired, they were already substantially into filming. They said, 'Here's the playback that we used. If you want to write something and replace this, feel free.' The problem was, number one, there was no time, and number two, I didn't have a symphony orchestra to do it with. So I said, 'I will find the scores to this music and go in and add instrumentation, so that it doesn't just sound like something you could just go into a Tower Classical store and pick up today.' I overlaid ethnic instruments, I would double a flute line with a shakuhachi or something, so that it sounded like classical music, except with a little bit of an ethnic twist. A shakuhachi is like a Japanese flute, but it's not polished like an orchestral flute, it's more of an organic, rough-sounding instrument."

It's hovering!

Mal looks up at the chandelier.

MAL
What's the point of that, I wonder?

KAYLEE
Ooh, pineapples.

Mal is still eyeing the chandelier.

MAL
I mean, I get how they did it. I just ain't seeing the why.

KAYLEE
These girls have the most beautiful dresses. And so do I, how 'bout that!

MAL
Well, careful with it. We cheated Badger outta good money to buy that frippery. You're s'posed to make me look respectable.

KAYLEE
Yes sir, Captain Tightpants.

Mal starts looking around, seeking someone out.

MAL
I'm looking for our guy, Harrow.

KAYLEE
And Inara. We should look for her, right? Just to halloo at her.

MAL
(too casual)
If we see her. Think she's wearing gold.

Kaylee is distracted by a passing group of attractive young men in fancy clothes.

KAYLEE
(to Mal, too loudly)
Say, lookit the boys!

Nearby party-goers glance over. Mal winces. Kaylee doesn't notice.

KAYLEE (cont'd)
Some of them's pretty as the Doctor.

She stares, struck speechless, as a waiter passes, carrying a huge BOWL OF ENORMOUS STRAWBERRIES to the buffet table.

MAL
Help me find our man. S'posed to be older, kinda stocky, wearing a red sash crossways.

Kaylee never takes her eyes off the strawberries.

KAYLEE
Why's he doing that?

MAL
Maybe he won the Miss Persephone pageant. Help me look.

KAYLEE
That him?

Mal looks where she's pointing, at the buffet table.

MAL
That's the buffet table.

KAYLEE
How can we be sure? You know, unless we question it?

MAL
Fine. Don't make yourself sick.

Kaylee flashes him a big smile.

KAYLEE
<Sheh-sheh> [Thank you], Cap'n!

And she's off to the buffet. Mal heads off on his own.

INT. SERENITY COMMON AREA/KITCHEN - NIGHT

SIMON, BOOK and Jayne play Chore Poker (it's actually a variant of poker which we'll call tall card). It's played with small metal playing cards. And instead of chips, they're playing for pieces of

METAL CARDS

Prop master Randy Eriksen: "The metal cards were great. I found them down in Chinatown and they were bright, shiny gold things. I ended up spray-painting them black and steel-wooling it off, to age them. The sound guy hated them since they were metal and clanked a lot. Anything that looks that good has got to be bad for sound."

paper. Each man has a collection of paper pieces in front of him — Simon has the least and Book the most. Simon starts to deal.

SIMON
Ante up, gentlemen.
(antes piece of paper)
Dishes.

BOOK
(anteing)
Dishes. Could do with less of them.

JAYNE
(anteing)
Garbage.

Simon completes the deal, five cards to each. The three men study their cards.

Simon lays A SINGLE ROUND CARD FACE-UP on the table.

SIMON
(re: round card)
Tall card... plum. Plums are tall.

BOOK
I'll take two.

SIMON
(giving cards)
Two. No tall card claim.

JAYNE
(re: his hand)
Speakin' of garbage.
(then)
Gimme three.

SIMON
(giving cards)
Three. And...
(taking the round card)
Dealer forced to claim the tall. I'd've cleared flower-side wasn't for this.

BOOK
What do you s'pose the Captain and Kaylee are doing now?
(betting)
Septic vac.

JAYNE
Eatin' steaks off plates made a' solid money, like as anything. I fold.

SIMON
Me too. Tall card's 'round my neck like a weight.

KAYLEE

"Yes sir, Captain Tightpants."

Embarking on an interview about her portrayal of Kaylee, Jewel Staite laughs. "I guess I've established that *Firefly* was the love of my life. I tend to gush like crazy, but it's totally genuine. I don't think anything will ever compare."

Staite began her screen acting career aged nine in the telefilm *Posing* and has since been a series regular on *Higher Ground* and *Da Vinci's Inquest* — she was also tapped for a recurring role on *Wonderfalls* by Tim Minear when *Firefly* ended.

"Initially, I was sent a very brief synopsis of the show and a very brief synopsis of the character," Staite recalls of her introduction to *Firefly* and Kaylee. She videotaped an audition in Vancouver, where she lives, then was asked to meet Joss Whedon in LA. After this she was offered the role, which meant relocating. "It all happened very fast. I had just gotten engaged and my fiancé, who's now my husband, decided to come with me. We just packed up all our things and left and that was that. And it was great. I love LA."

When she was first cast, Staite says she didn't know what the sets for the spaceship, Serenity, would be like. "I didn't know how much was going to be CGI and I didn't know how many soundstages we had access to or anything like that, so when I showed up and saw that each level of the ship was actually one long piece of set, it blew my mind. It was awesome."

As for Kaylee's look, "I remember when we had the hair and makeup test near the beginning and the character read as a bit of a tomboy. She loves boys and she loves dressing up — though she doesn't often get a chance to. I really saw her as this feminine person who loved love and was such a romantic — and she flirts with everybody shamelessly. I really wanted her to have that femininity in her, so I made sure that the hair was a little bit glamorous and she had a little bit of lip gloss — as much as Joss would allow. I really wanted her to be kind of cute and girly, and I really liked that Shawna [Trpcic] was really into that and got a bunch

of flowered shirts and cute, frilly kinds of stuff."

Just how flirty is Kaylee? "Very flirty," Staite laughs. "I think that's how Kaylee gets what she wants — whether she knows it or not, she's a huge flirt. She flirts with everybody on the whole ship. And I think that's part of her charm, whether she's aware of that or not."

One arguable exception is found in Kaylee's relationship with Jayne. "But at the same time, she's soft with Jayne," Staite points out. "I've always said that Kaylee is the one character that everybody trusts on that ship, and I think even Jayne trusts her, and he cares about her. It's obvious when she gets shot in the pilot episode and he's watching her in the infirmary that he really does care about her and really does like her. I think she and Jayne are kind of like brother and sister. I love that they have these scenes where they're just talking about everything that's going on around them and venting at each other. I think Kaylee's loyalty lies with the Captain, and since the Captain's not too hot on Jayne, she's not as nice to him as she could be, but I think she really does care about him."

The relationship between mechanic Kaylee and her beloved ship is key to *Firefly*. "I think Kaylee has always viewed Serenity as the tenth crewmember," Staite says. "It's very dear to her, it's her home, it's probably the only steady home she's ever really had, and I think she's just so proud of it. Right from the very beginning, Joss said that he wanted Kaylee's affection for the ship to be really obvious, so there was a lot of patting of the walls and admiration for the engine. She's just so amazed by how it all works and the fact that she gets to work on it."

As for Kaylee's self-imposed role as peacemaker, Staite says, "I've always thought that the reason why Kaylee steps in and defends people is that she wants everybody to get along. I think one of her biggest goals on that ship is to have everybody finally get along and nobody hate each other; she's always so upset and wringing her hands and doesn't know what to do when people are fighting. She doesn't want any negativity on that boat. She's kind of the only one who really gets the point that all they really have is each other, so it's important to her that everybody gets along." ◐

JAYNE
Take it, Shepherd.

BOOK
Thank you, gents. That's a nice pile of things I don't have to do.

The CAMERA FINDS RIVER, sitting in the kitchen, next to a box of supplies. She takes the label off a can of peaches.

RIVER
There it is, there it is. It's always there if you look for it. Everybody sees and nobody sees it...

BACK AT THE GAME:

Jayne shuffles.

SIMON
The party is probably a buffet. And there'll be dancing. And beautiful women. Dozens of them.

JAYNE
And you can dance with any of 'em?

SIMON
Well, there are social conventions, ways of asking, ways of declining...

BOOK
It sounds very complicated. I'll never understand why it's considered a sacrifice to live a simple life.

JAYNE
Yeah. I wouldn't trade this for nothing, playing cards for a night off from septic vac duty.

IN THE KITCHEN

River has three cans unlabeled, and she's crushing a box of crackers. It has a visible, not emphasized, "Blue Sun" on it. She gets more violent and loud as she continues.

RIVER
These are the ones that take you! Little ones in the corner that you almost don't see. But they're the ones that reach in and do it. They're the ones with teeth and you have to smash them!

AT THE GAME

River's ranting is audible now. Simon drops his cards and goes to her. Book follows.

SIMON
River?

BOOK
Is she hurt?

JAYNE
Better see to her.
(called after)
Bad habit for a fugitive. She's gonna do that in public some day, get herself hauled off.

Jayne moves a few exemptions from Book's pile to his own.

IN THE KITCHEN

Simon has an arm around River, calming her down. Book looks at the supplies. River rants the whole time.

SIMON
(as River rants)
River, it's me. Calm down.

BOOK
(as River rants)
She didn't harm much.
(re: cans)
We'll have a few mystery meals.

SIMON
(as River rants)
River, it's okay. It's okay.

RIVER
A million things, and the little ends of the roots go everywhere and when you brush your teeth or all the little blue things are there but no one says it because, because sometimes they're afraid. And then they come...

She winds down, stops talking. Book and Simon relax.

JAYNE
So, we gonna play cards, or we gonna screw around?

INT. ZOE AND WASH'S QUARTERS - SAME TIME

Wash and Zoe in a post-coital tangle, limbs and sheets, exhausted and happy.

ZOE
Thought you wanted to spend time off-ship this visit.

WASH
Seems like out there it's all fancy parties. I like our party better. The dress code's easier and I know all the steps.

Zoe's eyes are closing.

ZOE
I'd say you do, at that.

WASH
Don't fall asleep now. Sleepiness is weakness of character, ask anyone.

Zoe starts to laugh, her eyes still closed.

ZOE
It is not!

WASH
You're acting Captain. You know what happens, you fall asleep?

ZOE
Jayne slits my throat and takes over?

WASH
That's right!

ZOE
And we can't stop it?

WASH
I wash my hands of it. Hopeless case. I'll read a nice poem at the funeral. Something with imagery.

ZOE
You could lock the door. Keep the power-hungry maniac at bay.

WASH
Don't know. I'm starting to like this poetry thing. "Here lies my beloved Zoe, my autumn flower, somewhat less attractive now that she's all corpse-ified and gross..."

Zoe hits him with a pillow.

INT. PARTY

Back at the party, Kaylee approaches an attractive BOY (early twenties) who is watching the dancers.

KAYLEE
(re: dancers)
Aren't they something? Like butterflies or little pieces of wrapping paper, blowing around...

The boy turns toward her and bows politely and moves away. But there's too much going on for Kaylee to be disappointed.

She joins a group of four GIRLS her age and younger, standing and gossiping. She waits until

JEWEL STAITE

On the hoopskirt: "It wasn't so bad getting in and out of it. It was just sitting in it — I couldn't sit in a normal chair, so I had to sit on an apple box and I couldn't support my back. Every time I had to go to the bathroom, somebody had to come and take my hoop off in front of the whole crew. They had to hike up my skirt and untie the thing and it was sort of embarrassing, but I got over it pretty fast. At one point, I kind of peed on my dress. I totally didn't mean to. But the hoopskirt was so huge and the stall was so small... For the rest of the episode, I had to go around knowing there was pee on the hem of my dress. I just learned to stop drinking so much water and not pee as much!"

---

a group-laugh subsides.

KAYLEE (cont'd)
Hello!

One of the girls, BANNING, seems to be the queen bee. She looks at Kaylee in surprise.

BANNING
I don't... have we been introduced?

Kaylee grabs Banning's hand, shakes it with enthusiasm.

KAYLEE
I'm Kaylee.

BANNING
Banning. And this is Destra, Cabott, and Zelle.

KAYLEE
Don't you love this party? Everything's so fancy and there's some kind of hot cheese over there.

CABOTT
It's not as good as last year.

KAYLEE
Really? What'd they have last year?

CABOTT
Standards.

Destra and Zelle giggle, but Banning looks sympathetic.

BANNING
You're not from Persephone, are you?

KAYLEE
I'm from Serenity. Neat little Firefly class. I keep the engines. She's a sweet runner.

BANNING
Uh-huh. Who made your dress, Kaylee?

KAYLEE
Oh, do you like it? When I saw the ruffles, I just couldn't — <Shuh muh?> [What?]

BANNING
You ought to see to your girl.

KAYLEE
<Shuh muh?> [What?]

BANNING
(confidential)

Your girl. She's not very good. She made you a dress looks like you bought it in a store.

The other girls giggle again, but Banning plays it off with a straight face.

KAYLEE
Oh. I... I didn't know...

BANNING
I'm only trying to help. No one wants you to look foolish...

A nearby guest, MURPHY, a kind-looking man in his fifties, interrupts.

MURPHY
(off-hand, for Kaylee's benefit)
Why Banning Miller, what a vision you are in that fine dress. Must have taken a dozen slaves a dozen days just to get you into that get-up. 'Course your daddy tells me it takes the space of a schoolboy's wink to get you out of it again.

Banning leaves, mortified. Her friends are suppressing giggles.

MURPHY (cont'd)
(to Kaylee)
Forgive my rudeness. I can not abide useless people.

SOME DISTANCE AWAY, MAL

approaches HARROW, who is indeed wearing a red sash. Harrow is upper-crust, an acute observer with a strong code of behavior. He doesn't immediately take to rough-edged Mal.

MAL
Beg pardon, sir. But would you be Mr. Warrick Harrow?

It's a bad start.

HARROW
Sir Warrick Harrow. The sash.

MAL
The sash.

HARROW
It indicates lordhood.

MAL
And it's, it's doing a great job.

Harrow moves a few steps away, dismissing Mal.

Mal has to follow.

MAL (cont'd)
Sir, my name is Malcolm Reynolds. I captain a ship, name of Serenity. I mention this because I have been led to understand you want to move some property off-world...

Mal is distracted as INARA AND ATHERTON DANCE NEARBY. No one makes eye contact, but Mal and Inara are very aware of each other. Harrow observes this.

MAL (cont'd)
...some property off-world, discreetly.

Harrow takes a closer look at Mal. Still not impressed.

HARROW
You're mistaken, sir. I'm an honest man.

MAL
Seems to me, there's nothing dishonest about getting your goods to people what need them.

HARROW
You're concerned about the poor. And yet, for what you're offering, you'd want money, I imagine.

MAL
Well, sir, I think you'll find that working with me is giving to the poor.

HARROW
Whom is it you represent?

MAL
"Represent" isn't exactly —

HARROW
Don't waste my time.

MAL
Fellow called Badger.

HARROW
I know him. And I think he's a psychotic lowlife.

MAL
And I think calling him that is an offense to the psychotic lowlife community. But the deal is solid.

Mal is startled by a touch on his arm. He turns, surprised to see Atherton there. Inara, unsmiling, is at his elbow.

ATHERTON
Sorry to interrupt.
(a greeting)
Sir Harrow. I know you from the club, I believe.

Harrow nods, coolly.

INARA
(resigned)
Captain, this is Atherton Wing. Atherton, Captain Mal Reynolds.

Atherton and Mal shake hands, sizing each other up.

MAL
Pleased to meet'cha. Inara, I didn't realize you were going to this party.

INARA
(icy)
It's the only party.

MAL
And I can see why. How 'bout that floating chandelier?

Atherton circles Inara's arm with his hand... a gesture that is both affectionate and possessive.

ATHERTON
How do you come to be here, Captain?

MAL
Oh I love a party. I was just telling that to my friend here.

ATHERTON
(to Harrow)
I didn't know you were acquainted.

HARROW
It is beginning to seem unavoidable.

Mal watches as Atherton's fingers shift on Inara's arm. We can see the white circle the pressure of his fingers has left. Mal sees that, makes a decision.

MAL
Ath. Can I call you Ath? Inara has spoken of you to me. She made a point of your generosity. Given that, I'm sure you won't kick if I ask Inara the favor of a dance.

Atherton hesitates, can't find a way out.

ATHERTON
Of course.

INARA
In this company, Captain, I believe you are the

Atherton and Harrow end up standing side by side watching as Mal leads an angry Inara onto the dance floor.

HARROW
(to Atherton)
You're a brave man.

ATHERTON
(clipped)
I know what's mine.

Harrow scowls, disliking Atherton.

MAL AND INARA

On the dance floor.

INARA
Why are you here?

The music begins for their dance — it's a courtly and complicated dance, rather Regency England in style. Mal watches the other couples. It's easy at first, lots of walking around each other.

MAL
Business, same's you. I was talking to a contact about a smuggling job, and you came over to *me*.

INARA
You were staring at me.

MAL
I saw you, is all. You stand out.

The dance takes them apart for a few beats, bowing and curtsying to other couples.

Mal starts to make his curtsy mistake as in The Train Job, but he corrects it. They come back together and now dance palm-to-palm.

INARA
one who stands out.

MAL
Maybe I just like watching a professional at work, then. Is this the hardest part, would you say, or does that come later?

INARA
You have no call to try to make me ashamed of my job. What I do is legal, and how is that *smuggling* coming?

MAL
My work's illegal, but it's honest.

INARA
What?!

MAL
While this... the *lie* of it... that man parading you on his arm as if he actually won you, as if he loves you, and everyone going along with it. How can that not bother you?

INARA
"Going along with it"?

MAL
He treats you like an ornament. Other men look at you and discuss if you're worth the cost. The women talk behind their fans, picturing you with their husbands. And to your face, they're sweet as pie.

INARA
That's not true.

MAL
Well, I guess you'd know. It's not my world.

INARA
These people like me, and I like them. I like Atherton too, by the way.

MAL
Well, sure, what's not to like? I'm liable to sleep with him myself.

INARA
And he likes *me*, whether you see it or not.

MAL
(dismissive)
Of course.

INARA
He's made me an offer.

Mal didn't expect that.

INARA (cont'd)
You may think he doesn't honor me. But he wants me to live here. I would be his personal Companion.

MAL
<Wah!> [Wow!] That's as romantic as a marriage proposal. No wait, it's not.

INARA
It would be a good life, Mal. I could belong here. Call me pretentious, but there is some

appeal in that.

Mal reacts to the word "pretentious", startled by it. Beat.

MAL
I... You're right. I got no call to stop you.

Inara accepts that for the concession it is. Then:

INARA
I see Kaylee is here.

MAL
Girl was crying Cinderella tears. Shoulda seen her, when I said she could have that layer cake she's wearin'.

Inara relaxes a little.

INARA
I think she looks adorable.

MAL
Well, yeah, but I never said it.

KAYLEE

She's now surrounded by a group of gentlemen farmers, Murphy and his friends. Many of them are older, some young.

She's enjoying chocolate mints, talking with her mouth full. The men are laughing. The dialogue overlaps as they debate:

KAYLEE
I'm not saying the eighty-oh-four's hard to repair, it just ain't worth it.

OLDER FARMER
It's a fine machine, keep it tuned—

KAYLEE
<Tsai boo shr.> [No way.] The extenders ain't braced.

MURPHY
(re: older farmer)
We've been tellin' him buy an eighty-ten for years!

KAYLEE
(overlapping Murphy)
Those 'tenders snap off, it don't matter how good the engine's cyclin'.

YOUNGER FARMER
(jumping in quick)
Miss Kaylee, I wonder if I could request the honor of—

He's shouted down by the other men:

FARMERS
Dance later!/She's talking./Let her talk.

KAYLEE
(to Murphy)
By the way, the eighty-ten's the same machine. They changed the plating, hoped no one'd notice!

If you knew these machines, oh, you'd find this hilarious. The men laugh, urging her on.

MAL AND INARA

The dance gets more complicated now, some tricky footwork. Inara and all the other dancers do it easily. Mal stumbles. He catches himself with hands around Inara's waist. As the music ends, he straightens himself out, grins at her.

MAL
Possible you were right before. This ain't my kind of a party.

Inara can't help herself and she smiles. Atherton is suddenly there. He's seen enough. He takes her back roughly, hauling her by the arm.

MAL (cont'd)
Watch yourself there. No need for any hands-on.

Guests, including Harrow, look at the public display.

ATHERTON
Excuse me. She's not here with you, Captain. She's mine.

MAL
Yours? She don't belong to nobody.

ATHERTON
Money changed hands. Makes her mine tonight. And no matter how you dress her up, she's still—

Without warning, Mal hauls off and PUNCHES ATHERTON, lays him right down on the floor. Mal smiles and looks to Inara.

MAL
Turns out this is my kind of a party!

Harrow looks impressed, watching everything.

INARA
Oh, Mal...

MAL
What? Man was out of line —

ATHERTON
(as he rises)
I accept!

MAL
That's great. What?

GENTLEMAN
There has been a challenge!

Atherton is on his feet.

ATHERTON
I hope you're prepared, Captain.

MAL
You all talkin' 'bout a *fight*? Well, fine, let's get out of here!

INARA
It's not a fist fight, Mal.

GENTLEMAN
The duel will be met tomorrow morning, at Cadrie Pond.

MAL
Why wait? Where's that guard? He collected a whole mess a' pistols—

GENTLEMAN
If you require it, any gentleman here can give you use of a sword.

MAL
Use of a... s'what?

END OF ACT TWO

ACT THREE

INT. PARTY - CONTINUING

People are where we left them. Mal looks confused. Harrow, Inara and the ballroom full of people look on.

MAL
I laid the fellow out. Seems to me the transaction is complete. Also satisfying.

GENTLEMAN
Everyone, enjoy the party, please! There's no further action here.

The crowd disperses, including Atherton, who

moves away with an evil look at Mal. Kaylee separates herself from the crowd, moving in close to Mal.

KAYLEE
(to Mal)
What's going on?

MAL
Not rightly sure.
(to Harrow)
What's going on?

HARROW
Well, first off, you'll be put up in lodgings for the night, so you don't disappear. I wouldn't blame you, incidentally. Wing may be a spoiled dandy, but he's an expert swordsman. He's killed a dozen men with a longblade and you're the only one gave him a reason.

MAL
This is a joke.

INARA
And he'll need a second.

MAL
What's that?

HARROW
I'll take on the job.

INARA
He fights if you refuse—

ATHERTON (O.S.)
Inara!

ANGLE ON ATHERTON: Waiting impatiently. She hesitates.

ATHERTON
Come with me, please.

MAL
(to Harrow)
You takin' this on, being my second. Does this mean we're in business?

Harrow chuckles.

HARROW
It means you're in mortal danger. But you mussed up Atherton's face and that has endeared me to you somewhat. You might even give him a fight before he guts you.

ATHERTON
Inara!

Inara tears herself away, eyes still on Mal. Finally she turns, goes to Atherton. Mal watches her go.

KAYLEE
(apologetically helpful)
Up til the punching, it was a real nice party.

INT. SERENITY - CARGO BAY - NIGHT

Jayne is in the cargo bay, working out with those hanging rungs under the catwalk. His shotgun leans against a wall nearby.

He's interrupted by a loud metallic BANGING.

Jayne crosses and opens the door (not the ramp, the door into the airlock), revealing Badger, holding a wrench. He's been banging on the door with it.

BADGER
(off-hand)
Your Captain's gone and got hisself in trouble.

TIME CUT TO:

INT. SERENITY - CARGO BAY - NIGHT

Badger stands near the infirmary end of the cargo bay. The assembled crew, Zoe, Wash, Jayne, Simon, Book, are gathered around, back to the closed ramp. (River isn't there.)

BOOK
A duel?

WASH
With swords?

SIMON
The Captain's a good fighter. He must know how to handle a sword.

Simon and Book look to Zoe hopefully.

ZOE
I think he knows which end to hold.

SIMON
All right. So now we just need to figure how to get him out of there.

BOOK
We have until the morning, correct?
(to Badger)
Do you know what lodging he's in?

BADGER
Oh, this is embarrassing. Some of you seem to be misapprehending my purpose in being here.

Zoe stands. It's suddenly clear that now, this is her ship.

ZOE
You're here to make sure we don't do what these men are keen on doing.

BADGER
Penny for the smart lady. Persephone's my home. I gotta do business with the people here. I don't want it known I brought someone in caused this kinda ruckus. We'll just settle in here til this blows over one way or t'other—

Jayne is suddenly there, at Badger's back, shotgun raised. Jayne points the gun at Badger's head.

ZOE
(calm)
Jayne. I wouldn't.

BADGER'S COSTUME

Costume designer Shawna Trpcic notes, "Originally, Badger was supposed to be played by Joss. So we designed it for Joss." However, Mark A. Sheppard wound up playing the role. "Mark was incredibly perfect for the role and fit Joss's clothes like they were made for him, so we just altered a little bit here and there. I love pink and when I bought my house, somebody put two sculpted pink flamingos out front as a welcome, and I adopted them as my mascots. I put my little pink flamingos touch on Badger for his second visit in 'Shindig', but the bowler hat, all that was from Joss. How he tied his cravat and those special touches — that was Mark. We had the cravat, we had the scarf, we had everything, but he added his own little style to it."

For sharp-eyed viewers, do Trpcic's flamingos turn up elsewhere in *Firefly*? "No. I was going to do a Jayne t-shirt with a pink flamingo on it as a print, but we got shut down."

JAYNE
Why not?

Zoe looks toward the doorway. Jayne follows the look...

ANGLE ON THE DOORWAY: FOUR OF BADGER'S LADS: all of them with guns. One of them has a scared Kaylee by the arm.

KAYLEE
(small)
Hi.

Jayne sags.

INT. LODGING - HALL AND ROOM - NIGHT

Inara slips quietly down a hallway, like a modern hotel hall, only with Chinese numbers on the doors. And, oddly, round SHALLOW HOLES INSTEAD OF DOORKNOBS (the holes don't go all the way through the doors). She stops at a closed door.

Now we get to see how a hotel key works. She is holding a small metal sphere with a small protruding round shaft. The sphere is about two thirds the size of a regular doorknob. She holds it near the hole in the door and magnets pull it in. THE SHAFT FITS INTO THE HOLE ON THE DOOR AND, THUS, THE SPHERE BECOMES A DOOR-KNOB! The mechanism hums and A SMALL LIGHT COMES ON. She turns it, unlocking and opening the door.

She enters quietly and we see the room, again, not too different from a modern hotel room. A sword lies on the bed.

Mal, suit coat off, shirt sleeves rolled up, stands, back to her, brandishing a second sword with ridiculous flourishes.

Inara makes a noise and Mal JUMPS. He spins to see her. His sword swings, hits the wall and the tip embeds in the plaster. The sword hangs there.

MAL
What are you doing here?

He tugs at the embedded sword, trying not to be obvious.

INARA
Atherton's a heavy sleeper, night before a big day. He's got the killing you in the morning, then a haircut later.

MAL
It's such a comfort having friends visit at a time like this.

Mal tugs the sword free. Inara looks around the room.

INARA
I knew the accommodations would be nice. Atherton doesn't skimp.

MAL
Don't s'pose I like being kept by him s'much as others do. How come you're still attached to him?

INARA
Because it's my decision. Not yours.

MAL
Thought he made it pretty clear he's got no regard for you.

INARA
You did manage to push him into saying something, yes. Made a nice justification for the punch.

MAL
He insulted you. I hit him. Seemed like the thing to do. Why'd this get so complicated?

INARA
Well, it's about to get simpler. There's a back door. I have the desk clerk on alert. He'll let us out.

MAL
I'm not gonna run off.

Inara looks at him, surprised.

MAL (cont'd)
No matter what you've got into your head, I didn't do this to prove some kinda point to you. I actually thought I was defending your honor. And I never back down from a fight.

INARA
Yes you do! You do all the time!

MAL
Yeah, okay. But I'm not backing down from this one.

INARA
He's an expert swordsman, Mal. You had trouble with that wall. How will your death help my "honor"?

MAL
But see, I'm looking to have it be his death. 'S why I need lessons.

Mal picks the other sword off the bed and throws it to her. She catches it expertly.

MAL (cont'd)
Figure you'd know how. Educated lady like you.

INT. SERENITY - CARGO BAY

It's still a hostage situation here in the cargo bay.

Wash has his head down, trying to sleep. Book reads his bible and prays silently.

Badger leans against the wall, eating an apple.

Jayne, Simon and Zoe talk quietly, pretending to play cards. Kaylee is bending over to talk to them.

KAYLEE
...but he said not to do anything. He'll join us after he wins the duel.

JAYNE
And what if he don't win?

ZOE
It doesn't hurt to have a contingency plan, Kaylee.

Kaylee moves away, unconvinced.

SIMON
I'm thinking, since we're unarmed, we should take them by surprise all at once.

ZOE
Not necessarily. We could lure one or two of 'em away, say, to the infirmary, take 'em out, be on Badger 'fore he knows what happened.

ANGLE ON THE DOORWAY FROM THE INFIRM-ARY: River appears. She looks blank and aimless. No one sees her, and the discussion continues.

JAYNE
Only if his attention's elsewhere. We need a diversion. I say Zoe gets nekkid.

Wash, without raising his head:

WASH
Nope.

JAYNE
I could get nekkid.

SIMON/ZOE/WASH
No!

Book looks up and sees River. He winces, but keeps his reaction small. He gets up casually and makes his way over to Simon. Book puts a hand on Simon's back.

SIMON
What?

BOOK
(whispers)
Don't look now. In the doorway.

ANGLE ON: River. She's stepped over the threshold now...

Simon tenses, starts to stand up.

SIMON
I'll get her out 'fore he spots her.

Simon heads toward River. Badger doesn't look up. Simon is at her, hand on her arm...

ANGLE ON: RIVER AND SIMON

SIMON (cont'd)
(whispers)
River. You can't be here...

RIVER
(whispers)
There's things in the air in there. Tiny things.

SIMON
Come on...

SUMMER GLAU

One moment that really stands out for me is my scene with Badger in 'Shindig'. I love Mark Sheppard so much and he coached me through that scene. He took time out, on his own time, in a little café in Studio City, to coach me on my accent.

Simon tries to lead her back inside, but she pulls back, smiling a little, thinking it's a game.

RIVER
Pull, pull...

SIMON
River! Please!

BADGER (O.S.)
Who's this then?

Simon turns to see Badger, standing close. River avoids Badger's gaze, turning toward Simon for protection.

BADGER
Look at me. What's your story, luv?

River looks around, unfocused.

SIMON
She's just a passenger.

BADGER
(to Simon)
Yeah? Why ain't she talking? She got a secret?

SIMON
No, I'm sure not—

RIVER
(in Badger's accent)
Sure, I got a secret. More'n one.

River raises her head, looks Badger in the eye. She's completely sane, unafraid, and she sounds like she's from his home town. She's also kinda pissed.

RIVER (cont'd)
Don't seem likely I'd tell 'em to you, do it? Anyone off Dyton Colony knows better'n to talk to strangers.

She picks something off Badger's lapel, looks at it, wipes it back onto him.

RIVER
You're talking loud enough for the both of us, though, ain't you? I've known a dozen like you. Skipped off home early, minor graft jobs here and there. Spent some time in the lock-down, I warrant, but less than you claim. Now you're what, petty thief with delusions of standing? Sad little king of a sad little hill.

After a beat...

BADGER
Nice to see someone from the old homestead.

RIVER
Not really.

(to Simon)
Call me f'anyone interesting shows up.

BADGER
(to Simon)
I like her.

ANGLE ON: JAYNE and ZOE.

JAYNE
That there? 'Xactly the kind of diversion we coulda used.

INT. MAL'S LODGING - PRE-DAWN

The furniture has been pushed to the walls. In the center of the cleared room, Inara and Mal face off, holding swords.

INARA
Attack.

He attacks, swinging the sword. She slips out of the way.

INARA (cont'd)
How did I avoid that?

MAL
By being fast like a freak.

INARA
No. Because you always attack the same way, swinging from the shoulder like you're chopping wood. You have to thrust with the point sometimes, or swing from the elbow.

MAL
Swinging from the shoulder feels stronger.

She touches his arm, adjusting his swing, controlling it. It's an intimate touch.

INARA
It's also slower, Mal. You don't need strength as much as speed. We're fragile creatures. It takes less than a pound of pressure to cut skin.

MAL
You *know* that? They teach you that at the whore academy?

Inara backs away, breaking the contact.

INARA
You have a strange sense of nobility, Captain. You'll lay a man out for implying I'm a whore, but you keep calling me one to my face.

MAL
I might not show respect to your job, but he didn't respect you. That's the difference. Inara, he doesn't even *see* you.

INARA
Well, I'm sure death will settle the issue to everyone's satisfaction.

MAL
This <yu bun duh> [stupid] duel is the result of rules of your society, not mine.

She's angry now, waving her sword as she gestures.

INARA
Mal, you *always* break the rules. It doesn't matter which "society" you're in! You don't get along with ordinary criminals either! That's why you're constantly in trouble!

Mal backs away from her sword.

MAL
And you think following rules will buy you a nice life, even if the rules make you a slave.

Inara, turns away, frustrated almost to tears.

Then, Mal, avoiding her eye:

MAL (cont'd)
Don't take his offer.

Inara turns and stares at him.

INARA
What?

MAL
Don't do it. Because, in the case it comes up, that means he's the fella killed me. And I don't like fellas that killed me. Not in general.

He starts practicing again, unable to look at her.

MAL (cont'd)
I said before I had no call to stop you. And that's true. But, anyways... don't.

INARA
I need to get back. He'll be up early.

And she exits, leaving him alone. He swings the sword.

MAL
Right. He's got that big day.

EXT. PERSEPHONE - MORNING (DAY 3)

A grassy pond at dawn would be lovely. Eight spectators, all men, cluster around the duelling area. Among them are a couple of Badger's lads. The crowd shifts and CHATTERS with anticipation.

Mal and Harrow stand, heads together, to one side. Harrow is smiling, Mal looks intense, adjusting and readjusting his grip on his sword. He's still wearing his dressy suit.

Atherton and his Second, another young dandy, are at the other side, talking and laughing easily. Inara stands near them, but her eyes are on Mal.

He meets her look, holds it.

The gentleman who first announced the challenge steps to the center. He raises his hands, commanding attention. Gradually the crowd quiets. He clears his throat.

GENTLEMAN
Ladies and gentlemen, the field of combat is a somber place. A man will here today lay down his life. Let the duel begin.

The last sentence is given no special emphasis, and there is no sound from the crowd. Mal doesn't even realize the fight has begun until the gentleman blends back into the crowd and Atherton steps out, smiling and handling his sword casually.

Mal steps forward, uncertain.

HARROW has moved over by Inara. They exchange a grim look.

MAL AND ATHERTON

face off. Atherton attacks first, an easy swing that Mal parries.

Mal hits back, thrusting with the point of the sword. Atherton barely gets out of the way in time, in fact, his vest is nicked.

MAL
Best be careful, Ath. I hear these things are sharp.

HARROW AND INARA

HARROW
He thinks he's doing well, doesn't he?

INARA
He's being toyed with.

BACK TO THE FIGHT

Mal ducks to avoid a blow.

Atherton brings up his blade to deflect a blow. CLANG.

While Mal hesitates, Atherton tosses his blade in the air and catches it with the other hand, showing off.

Mal gets nicked on the arm.

Atherton parries a blow away with such force it throws Mal off-balance.

Atherton steps back, and PUTS HIS SWORD BEHIND HIS BACK.

HARROW
What's he doing?

INARA
(gritted teeth)
Don't fall for that.

Mal lunges. Atherton steps to the side, the lunge goes past him. Atherton strikes, as he had

planned, attacking sideways with the sword from behind his back, stabbing Mal in the side.

Inara looks stricken.

HARROW
Well, this isn't going to take long, is it?

On Mal, looking down, shocked, at his wound.

END OF ACT THREE

ACT FOUR

EXT. PERSEPHONE - CONTINUING

The crowd is more active now, sensing the end is near.

Mal fights one-handed, his left hand staunching his wound. He's definitely losing now.

Atherton thrusts with the sword. Mal stumbles back clumsily.

Mal lunges. Atherton steps back. Mal lunges again. Atherton steps back again, laughing.

Atherton swings, cutting Mal's defensive arm.

HARROW
(to Inara)
We're coming up on the end, miss. You might not want to watch.

Mal thrusts. He sword CLASHES AGAINST Atherton's sword. MAL'S SWORD BREAKS. And the momentum carries Mal to one knee. Atherton's sword points at his chest.

INARA
Atherton! Wait!

Atherton hesitates, he may be about to get what he wants...

INARA (cont'd)
I'll stay here! Exclusive to you! Just let him live.

ON MAL, still down, as he registers what Inara's doing.

Mal lunges to his feet, catching Atherton under the chin with the hilt and throwing him back, face cut.

Atherton is regrouping, ready to move in for the kill again. He brings his sword arm back...

But Mal KICKS HIS BROKEN SWORD POINT OFF THE GROUND and up into his hand. He THROWS the broken sword point at Atherton like a dart!

Atherton takes the sword point in the shoulder. It sticks there, and Atherton, furious, reaches to pull it out.

Mal raises the hilt, still around his right hand, and brings it down like a gun butt, over Atherton's head. Atherton sprawls on the ground.

GENTLEMAN
He's down!

Mal scoops up Atherton's dropped sword off the ground and holds it, point at Atherton's heart. He freezes there.

HARROW
You have to finish it, lad. For a man to lie beaten and yet breathing, it makes him a coward.

INARA
It's a humiliation.

Mal pulls the sword back a little.

MAL
Sure. It would be humiliating, having to lie there while the better man refuses to spill your blood. Mercy is the mark of a great man.

Very quickly, offhandedly, Mal STABS Atherton!

MAL (cont'd)
Guess I'm just a good man.

He STABS him again!

MAL (cont'd)
Well, I'm all right.

Mal grins and tosses the sword aside. Inara goes to him.

Atherton gets up slowly. The crowd draws back, whispering behind their hands.

ATHERTON
Inara! Come here!

She ignores him.

ATHERTON (cont'd)
Inara!

Harrow puts a hand on Atherton's arm.

HARROW
You've lost her, lad. Be gracious.

Atherton shakes off Harrow's hand and staggers to Inara.

ATHERTON
You set this up, whore. After I bought and paid for you. I should have uglied you up so no one else'd want you.

MAL
(to Inara)
See how I'm not punching him? I think I've grown.

ATHERTON
(to Inara)
Get ready to starve. I'll see to it you never work again.

INARA
Actually, that's not how it works. You see, you've earned yourself a black mark in the client registry. No Companion is going to contract with you ever again.

HARROW
You'll have to rely on your winning personality to get women. God help you.

Inara and Mal start to walk away. Harrow joins them.

HARROW (cont'd)
You didn't have to wound that man.

MAL
I know, that was just funny.

HARROW
You willing to fight that hard to protect my property, I'll have it in your hold before midnight.

Mal nods. The deal is struck. Mal and Inara walk away, Mal a little unsteady.

MAL
(through pain)
Mighty fine shindig.

INT. SERENITY - CARGO BAY - DAY

Morning. Badger stands with his lads. Simon talks quietly to Book. Jayne pours coffee for Kaylee and Wash and Zoe.

JAYNE
(softly to Zoe)
Doc is filling the Shepherd in on the plan. We're ready to move on your signal. Doc's the diversion—

MAL (O.S.)
Did you ever see such a lazy crew?

CAMERA FINDS Mal and Inara in the doorway. Inara is helping hold him up, and he's still got a hand over his wound.

KAYLEE
Captain!

Kaylee runs to him. The others follow.

SIMON
You're hurt.

Badger approaches Mal.

BADGER
You get us a deal?

ZOE
(to Badger)
Back off, he's injured.

MAL
I got a deal. Now get off my ship.

Badger's heard all he needs to. He's a happy man.

BADGER
Ta very much for a lovely night then.

Badger exits. Inara and Simon guide Mal into a chair. The others gather around. Quickly:

BOOK
Are you badly hurt?

JAYNE
We was just about to spring into action, Captain. A complicated escape and rescue op.

WASH
I was gonna watch. It was very exciting.

EXT. SERENITY - IN FLIGHT - EFFECT

Serenity against a star field.

INT. SERENITY - DAY (DAY 4)

In the engine room, a grease-smudged Kaylee finishes installing a replacement engine part.

Humming, she wipes her hands on a rag and heads out...

Down the hall...

Down the ladder into her quarters...

She crosses to her Cortex screen. Kaylee's Cortex has no casing. The circuitry is exposed so she can tinker with it.

Kaylee hits some keys. Nothing happens. She frowns, presses a chip more firmly into place in the machine's guts.

TINNY DANCE MUSIC plays, like the kind at the party. This is what she's been humming.

PULL BACK FROM THE CORTEX

to find Kaylee, sitting on the bed, eating some of the CHOCOLATE MINTS from the party.

Pull further back to see she is looking at her party dress, which hangs from an exposed pipe.

INT. SERENITY - CARGO BAY - DAY (DAY 4)

Mal and Inara sit on the catwalk/balcony over the bay. Mal's midsection is bandaged. Inara wears another elegant kimono-type robe.

A bottle of wine sits between them and they drink from battered metal cups.

Inara sips her wine, makes a little face.

INARA
Thank you for the wine. It's very... fresh.

MAL
To Kaylee and her inter-engine fermentation system.

He raises his cup to toast, winces from the wound.

INARA
Are you in pain?

MAL
Absolutely. I got stabbed, you know. Right here.

INARA
I saw.

MAL
Don't care much for fancy parties. Too rough.

INARA
It wasn't entirely a disaster.

MAL
I got stabbed. Right here.

INARA
You also lined up exciting new crime.

MAL
It is good to have cargo. Makes us a target for every other scavenger out there, a' course, but sometimes that's fun too.

INARA
(beat, then)
I am grateful, you know, for the ill-conceived and high-handed attempt to defend my honor although I didn't want you to.

MAL
Gracious as that is, as I look back, I probably shoulda stayed outta your world.

INARA
My world. If it is that. I wasn't going to stay, you know.

MAL
Yeah? Why's that?

A little disingenuous:

INARA
Oh, someone needs to keep Kaylee out of trouble. And all of my things are here... Besides, why would I want to leave Serenity?

We ARM BACK to REVEAL

the cargo bay is full of mooing milling CATTLE.

MAL
Can't think of a reason.

BLACKOUT.

END OF SHOW

SAFE

Written by Drew Z. Greenberg
Directed by Michael Grossman

JOSS WHEDON

The idea was one that spoke to me and to [episode writer] Drew Greenberg very strongly, why was Simon so attached to his sister? So to show a world where he had the most genial and delightful father, and now he's stuck with this irascible, untrustworthy bastard [Mal]; and then, over the course of a series of flashbacks, to have him realize, as he has sort of always known, that his father is genial because everything is going his way. When the chips are down, he's nobody, and Simon has always been the only person there to look after his sister. However loving his parents may have seemed, he knew that, scratch the surface, and they'd scream and run away. And here he's confronted with a guy who is just everything he thinks is wrong about a person, who comes back for him when the chips are down because he's on his crew. To me, that's a *real* parent, and that is an extremely beautiful thing to get to, and I think it's very real. Having the 'she's a witch' thing was something we had planned to explore, because River had this power and she was a little strange and with the psychic, but we did want to show how backwoodsian people could become when they were left to their own devices. But the most important thing about 'Safe' was that relationship. I will say, by the way, that that is a show that, again... this is why I love my crew and my actors and that whole experience so much. We needed to do a lot of reshooting on a lot of stuff and we came in short [the episode was not long enough for its running time] and I was worried that we weren't going to get a sense of them being off the ship and what that meant, so I literally said, 'Lock the show [do a final edit], give me thirty seconds here and twenty seconds there and I'm going to write two scenes.' And they were the scene of Jayne going through Simon's stuff and the scene of Jayne welcoming Simon back on board. And they're two of the best scenes we ever did on the show [laughs] — we literally had already locked the show, so Adam had fifteen props to pick up and a thirty-second monologue that he had to do to the second, with that precision, and be hilarious and true to character, and the precision with which he did both those little scenes was phenomenal. When you feel something like that, to be able to drop that in moments before it went to air — that's really fun.

TEASER

CLOSE ON:

Rich expensive BRANDY as it pours into a rich expensive snifter. Pull back to see:

INT. TAM ESTATE - DAY

The room, tasteful, lit by candlelight, feels warm. SIMON holds the snifter. He swirls the brandy around a bit to warm it, inhales the aroma, looks up and smiles.

SIMON
This is a joke, right?

We see Simon's father, GABRIEL, fifty, refined, used to having control, standing in front of him. At the moment, he seems warm and jovial.

GABRIEL
Yes. That's exactly right. Because brandy is funny.

SIMON
It's just, this is... this smells like New Canaan brandy.

Gabriel pours brandy for himself and for Simon's mother, REGAN, late forties, elegant.

SIMON (cont'd)
Aged New Canaan brandy. How much did you pay for this? I thought business was slow.

GABRIEL
Pierre owed me a favor. Seeing how it's a special occasion.

SIMON
Is it?

Simon tries to read his father's grin. Then:

REGAN
For god's sake, Gabriel. Just tell him.

Gabriel chuckles.

GABRIEL
Fine, spoil my fun.
(to Simon)
I had a talk today with Jerome Stuart. Seems he's about to take over as Head of Surgery at AMI. Said when you're done with your internship, there'll be an attending position waiting for you.

This is a huge moment for Simon. He's thrilled.

REGAN
(smiling)
Congratulations, son.

Simon stares into his glass, embarrassed.

SIMON
It's not a big deal.

GABRIEL
Oh. Well, all right then.

Playing along, Gabriel reaches for Simon's glass. Simon pulls it away, grinning.

SIMON
Okay, okay. It's an enormous deal. AMI, that's, I can really do good work there —

GABRIEL
Good work, good pay. There'll be an announcement at the term-end ceremony.

REGAN
We're so proud, sweetheart.

SIMON
Is River coming back?

Gabriel and Regan stare at Simon.

SIMON (cont'd)
For the ceremony. Did she say she'd be able to get away?

REGAN
We didn't...
(brightly)
We'll write to her immediately, tell her all about it.

GABRIEL
I doubt she'll come. You saw the schedule at that school of hers. I took one look at it, had one of those school dreams. You know, "I didn't study"...

Gabriel chuckles to himself.

SIMON
I just... I haven't heard from her in a while. I thought she'd come home sometimes, or at least send a wave, but there's only been the occasional letter, and half the time she doesn't sound like herself.

REGAN
She's changing. Finally starting to fit in. You should be happy for her.

Simon forces a smile.

SIMON
Of course.

GABRIEL
Your position will still be there for her to admire when she gets home, *Doctor* Tam. Come on... let's have a toast. I've been working on this all day.

The three of them rise and lift their glasses...

GABRIEL (cont'd)
May your future always be as bright as it is this very moment —

The three glasses meet... CLINK.

CUT TO:

EXT. JIANGYIN/CARGO BAY - DAY

Squish. Simon has stepped in cow poop on the ship's ramp. Future not lookin' so bright right this second.

SIMON
<Niou fun.> [Cow poop.]

JAYNE passes him, amused.

JAYNE
'Bout time you broke in them pretty shoes.

Jayne takes us further, showing us that the crew is off-loading the cows (from ep 3) into an open prairie at the edge of the woods. We're on Jiangyin, a planet heavy on the nature — woods and scrubby grazing ground.

Simon continues down the ramp, moving around cows, trying to keep out of the way of all the activity:

MAL leads a cow as Jayne SMACKS another steer on its rump, urging it to move.

JAYNE (cont'd)
Ha! Git along!

MAL
They walk just fine if you lead 'em.

JAYNE
I like smackin' 'em.

Simon looks down to see WASH AND ZOE, at the base of the ramp, where they are sending the cows off to the side, where BOOK directs them into a makeshift pen.

BOOK
Hope this corral's strong enough to hold them.

SIMON'S COSTUMES

Costume designer Shawna Trpcic: "Simon was the dandy, if you will. His was a classic look. Certain things in men's fashion throughout thousands of years haven't changed, so his classic lines were just to show his schooling, that he wasn't sloppy, that he was neat, and that even if he became more casual, his sweaters fit well and his pants fit well and it just happens to be a very Banana Republic look," she laughs. "We toughened him up as he became more and more part of the group with the big nubby sweaters. We really wanted to separate him from the others, who are very earth-toned and very down to earth. They had cotton and he was always very put-together with wools and the stiffer fabrics and the more expensive satins and silks. At first, Joss wanted him to have a vest on, so we used Asian fabrics and Asian buttons to reflect the Asian influence, but his character went through a transformation as the show went on, especially as he started the relationship with Kaylee. We got him to be more romantic and softer, but still staying in those color tones."

"Shepherd" is a purely figurative title, you know.

ZOE
Next time we smuggle stock, let's make it something smaller.

WASH
Yeah, we need to start dealing in those black-market beagles.

ANGLE ON: Simon again. He's made his way off to one side. He scrapes at his shoe with a stick. Mal approaches him.

MAL
What're you doing out here, Doc? Besides the scraping.

SIMON
I thought perhaps I could help. With the cows.

MAL
I'll let you know, any of 'em start complaining of palpitations. Til then, not much call for a doctor.

SIMON
(off Book)
But there is call for a preacher?

MAL
I was surprised myself, but turns out he's converted five of 'em. Not easy, neither. Seems they got this natural inclination toward Hinduism.

SIMON
Captain, my sister and I have been on your ship for more than two months. You've stopped collecting fare from us... no one's required my services in some time... I'm starting to feel a little —

MAL
Useless?

SIMON
Restless.

MAL
Ah.

SIMON
Is that your feeling? That I'm useless?

MAL
Well, Doc, useful man don't have to ask to be put to use. Usually just finds himself something to do.

SIMON
Sorry if my criminal instincts aren't as sharp as the rest of your crew.

EXT. TREETOPS - MOMENTS LATER

We move off them to find a man, STARK, staring from cover not far away. He scurries away to two other men.

STARK
Got a good look. They waitin' fer a payment. Somethin' there worth takin', too.

He turns to look back...

STARK (cont'd)
They got precious cargo.

On Stark's crafty look, we —

BLACK OUT.

END OF TEASER

ACT ONE

EXT. JIANGYIN/CORRAL - DAY

CLOSE ON RIVER and a cow. She's looking into one of its eyes and murmuring:

RIVER
Little soul big world. Eat and sleep and eat...

Jayne appears, bringing another cow, sees her communing with the bovine. She's reaching back toward the animals.

RIVER (cont'd)
Many souls. Very straight, very simple...

JAYNE
(calling, re: River)
Captain! This one's in the way!

Mal appears. On his approach, trying to get to her:

MAL
Cattle on the ship three weeks, she don't go near 'em. Suddenly, we're on Jiangyin and she's got a driving need to commune with the beasts?

River looks at Mal very seriously.

RIVER
They weren't cows inside. They were waiting to be, but they forgot. Now they see sky and they remember what they are.

MAL
Is it bad that what she just said makes perfect sense to me?
(reaching for her)
Come on, now. Let's move you clear of the work.

River recoils from him. He's not Simon. Now Simon appears, approaching. Sees River backing away from Mal. Some cows might get agitated by this.

SIMON
What's going on?
(off Mal)
What are you doing?

MAL
I was fixin' to do some business. Buyers'll be along soon. I can't be herding these steers and your sister, too.

SIMON
I'll keep her out of the way. But you don't need to say things like that in front of her.

MAL
Yes, I've clearly upset her.

River is looking at the ends of her hair now, completely tranquil. Jayne, still nearby, snorts. Simon bristles.

SIMON
She understands more than you think. Anyway — she didn't mean any harm.

RIVER'S COSTUMES

Costume designer Shawna Trpcic: "The first thought was, when she came on to the ship, that [once dressed] she would be wearing Kaylee's clothes. We got hippie-looking clothes, but in jewel-colored tones and in grays and blues, to make them kind of colder, to show that she was from a different world than the Serenity crew, and then we started to find her own look. In 'Safe', I lightened her up with pinks, but still staying with the garnet sweater, still staying with the jewel-like tones. We made the majority of the stuff, except for the classic hippie dress, and used boots to differentiate River from the softness of a normal girl in those kinds of soft fabrics. I like to contrast the really soft and flowing fabrics with the hardcore boots, because that's who she is — she's this soft, beautiful, sensitive girl, but with this hardcore inner character."

MAL
Never figured she did. But when a man's engaging in clandestine dealings, he has this preference for things being smooth. She makes things not be smooth.

SIMON
Right. I'm very sorry if she tipped off anyone about your cunningly concealed herd of cows.

MAL
You know, I'm starting to remember you asking if there wasn't something you could "do". Think now I got a notion regarding that. How about you take your sister for a little walk?

Simon looks startled, worried.

SIMON
A walk?

MAL
Yeah. Someplace... away.

SIMON
Probably best if we stay close. The Alliance has us marked as fugitives—

MAL
Closest Alliance is the Cruiser Magellan, hours out from here. And I promise you, they ain't coming to a backwater like Jiangyin.

SIMON
Still... I'm not sure it's such a wise suggestion.

MAL
Might not wanna mistake it for a "suggestion".
(off Simon's look)
Don't worry. We won't take off without you.

Mal continues with his back to Simon. Off Simon —

INT. "GENERAL SUPPLY" - DAY - LATER

A dusty local store. Mostly ranching supplies: feed and branding irons and horseshoes. Along one wall there are some local crafts. A bored-looking proprietor reads a Chinese-language newspaper at the counter.

KAYLEE and INARA browse among the crudely made items.

KAYLEE
Everything's dusty.

INARA
Does it seem every supply store on every border planet has the same five rag dolls and the same wood carvings of...
(looking at one)
What is this? A duck?

KAYLEE
That's a swan. And I like it.

INARA
You do?

KAYLEE
It looks like it was made with, you know... longing. Made by a person really longed to see a swan.

INARA
Perhaps because they'd only heard of them by rough description.

Kaylee holds up a little painted souvenir dish with painted Chinese characters on it.

KAYLEE
You think this'd make a nice gift?

INARA
A gift? For whom?

Kaylee just studies the dish.

KAYLEE
I just think it's nice. Kinda rich, you know.

INARA
Oh. For Simon.

KAYLEE
I didn't say that.

INARA
Well, you don't do a very good job of hiding your interest.

KAYLEE
He's just so <swai> [cute]. You wanna take a bite out of him all over, you know?

Just then, Simon and River enter. Simon is nervous about being out and visible, a little frazzled at having to watch River constantly.

INARA
(to Kaylee)
Careful.

KAYLEE
Did he hear? I don't think he heard.
(louder, maybe too loud)
Mornin', you two!

Kaylee's over-bright greeting just makes Simon more jumpy. He forces a smile, nods.

INARA
We don't usually see you two out and about planetside.

SIMON
(tense)
We're trying something different today.

River immediately goes to the farming equipment, starts touching things.

SIMON (cont'd)
River, careful with that, that's...
(helplessly to Kaylee)
What is that?

KAYLEE
That's a post holer. You dig holes. For posts.

SIMON
(to River)
It's dirty and sharp. Come over here.

He steers her over to the crafts section with the women. He picks up the little dish Kaylee was admiring.

SIMON (cont'd)
(reads the Chinese)
"Jiangyin, Prairie Paradise."
(then)
Good god. They ask money for this <go se> [crap]?

Kaylee flinches, but recovers.

KAYLEE
Hard to believe, ain't it?
(then)
I'm glad you're out.

He smiles absently, politely. His focus on River.

KAYLEE (cont'd)
Give you a chance to loosen up a bit.

Tiny delayed reaction to Kaylee's perfectly innocent comment.

SIMON
What's that supposed to mean? Loosen up?

KAYLEE
Nothing... I just... Well. You never seem to have any fun, is all.

His attention's split. He moves to take something breakable out of River's hand.

SIMON
Fun. Right. I consider this "fun". It's "fun" being forced to the ass-end of the galaxy, get to live on a piece of <luh-suh> [garbage] wreck and eat molded protein while playing nursemaid to my <boo-tai jung-tzahng-duh> [not entirely sane] sister. "Fun."

Simon may not have noticed how that all stung. Kaylee just stares at him. He glances at her. Sees her looking at him. A beat.

KAYLEE
<Luh-suh?> [Garbage?]

SIMON
Sorry?

KAYLEE
Serenity ain't <luh-suh> [garbage].

SIMON
I didn't mean...

KAYLEE
You did. You meant everything you just said.

SIMON
(trying to lighten things)
Well, no... actually I was being ironic. So in the strictest sense, I didn't really —

KAYLEE
You were being mean, is what. And if that's what you think of this life, then you can't think much of them that choose it, can you?

He's got nothing to say. She turns and heads for the exit. Inara falls in with her, walk out side by side. As they go:

INARA
(softly, to Kaylee)
You're getting better at hiding it.

Simon, already regretting the altercation, takes a beat, sighs a "god am I an asshole today" sigh. Then he turns to collect River.

SIMON
River?

But River is gone.

EXT. JIANGYIN/CORRAL - DAY

The ship's ramp is empty of cows now. But littered with that which cows leave behind. Mal stands at the base of the ramp, surveying the damage.

MAL
This is the last time. Last time with cows.

Zoe approaches Mal.

MAL (cont'd)
I heard there was some idea regarding beagles. They got smallish droppings?

ZOE
I believe so, sir. Also, the disreputable men are here.

THE OUTER PLANETS

Carey Meyer says that the production design for the outer planets "was based a lot on what we were able to find as a location to shoot. Obviously, once you start driving outside of Los Angeles, you end up with a real dirty dust-bowl feel and that's where a lot of the Western frontier town concepts started to play into it. There was a lot of discussion about, 'Do we really go with just a Western feel or do we try to recreate this concept in every episode or should we come up with a fully-realized design for each planet?' Our budget meant we had to go with a lot of existing locations. I think in the end the feel was that we wound up using a lot of places or exteriors that just felt too Western and we didn't necessarily want to go that way; but at some point, it just became the lesser of two evils — what could we actually create in three days?"

Mal turns to see the GRANGE BROTHERS standing near the makeshift corral, looking at the animals. Jayne stands nearby. Book is not far off, seeing to the fencing.

MAL
(to Zoe)
I better go take their money.

Mal heads toward the brothers. Zoe turns and heads into the ship.

ANGLE ON: THE GRANGE BROTHERS

There are two of them, shabby low-life types. They're looking over the cows critically now,

examining their hooves, eyes, teeth. Mal approaches.

MAL
Good morning, gents. You must be the Grange brothers. Hope you're hungry for beefsteak.

They say nothing. Continue to examine the cattle.

JAYNE
Attractive animals, ain't they?

OLDER GRANGE
They ain't well fed. Scrawny.

MAL
<Fei hua.> [Nonsense.] Hay and milk three times a day. Fed to 'em by beautiful women.

JAYNE
It was something to see.

YOUNGER GRANGE
They ain't branded.

MAL
You boys're hitting all the selling points. Unregistered. Claim 'em as your own.

The Granges continue to look sour.

OLDER GRANGE
Twenty a head.

MAL
That's an amusing figure in the light of you already agreed on thirty with Badger.

OLDER GRANGE
That's afore we seen 'em. They're atrophied, standin' 'round on a ship for near a month.

MAL
My comprehension is, less muscle, more tender the meat. Thirty.

The Grange boys step back to talk — they look nervous, casting looks toward Mal and Jayne, toward the surrounding woods...

Mal and Jayne eyeball them. A RUSTLING in the trees. Seems it could be the wind. Before Mal can take much note, Book approaches.

BOOK
(off the brothers)
Problem?

MAL
Nope. Minute from now we'll agree on twenty-five.

A NOISE. The Granges spin, hands go near their guns (they don't draw). WASH is on the loading ramp, dumping a bucket of water. The Granges relax. Wash re-enters the ship.

BOOK
They seem a mite jumpy to you?

Off Mal, watching the men, considering that...

EXT. "GENERAL SUPPLY" JIANGYIN - DAY

Simon, more than jumpy, standing in front of the store, just catches a glimpse of River's dress as she disappears around a corner. He dashes after her. He rounds the corner to see...

LOCAL COPS, a group of five, heading toward him with some purpose. He freezes.

But River is there, a block ahead of him. He bravely heads toward her. As he passes the cops:

SIMON
(comes out way too loud)
MORNING, OFFICERS.

The cops pass him harmlessly. We stay with him as he winces.

He continues on, spots River going around a corner. Follows.

EXT. JIANGYIN/CARGO BAY - DAY

Mal and Jayne are talking with the Grange brothers again. Book is visible in the b.g., tending to the corral fencing.

MAL
See, the problem we got with twenty-three is that it ain't thirty.

YOUNGER GRANGE
These cows ain't as young as you said.

JAYNE
They're babies. Half of 'em born on the trip.

OLDER GRANGE
I'm thinking maybe we walk away entirely.

MAL
I'm thinking you do that and we got ourselves trouble — morning, ladies...

Kaylee and Inara, returning to the ship, walk right past the group. The Granges' eyes follow the women. This isn't lost on Mal who steps into their purview with:

MAL (cont'd)
(without a break)
...serious trouble. Of the you-owe-us variety.

OLDER GRANGE
We can go to twenty-five.

Mal and Jayne exchange a look. The transaction is coming to a close.

MAL
Well, we'd be takin' a loss, but you seem like clean and virtuous boys... done.

The Elder Grange takes out a little cloth bag, starts counting money into Mal's palm. But freezes when he hears:

HEAD COP (O.S.)
Marcus and Nathaniel Grange!

CHINESE COINS

Prop master Randy Eriksen: "I got the Chinese coins for 'Safe' in Chinatown. There are a lot of Asian characters on the graphics, the money and the ships. Joss came up with the Sino-American Alliance, which was basically East meets West, and made the show quite visually interesting."

BANKNOTES

Prop master Randy Eriksen: "The number forty-seven appears on the banknotes because forty-seven is the most commonly occurring random number. It's been my lucky number since before high school. I was number forty-seven in the football team. It's kind of nonsensical but we try to work it in to most things. If you look at the notes in the canvas moneybag from 'Safe', it's on the money. You could probably go back to *Buffy* and find a bunch of forty-sevens. There's a whole forty-seven society on the Internet. It's funny, if you're looking for something, you find it. When you have a big hammer, pretty much everything starts looking like a nail."

SIMON

"How do I know you won't kill me in my sleep?"

Family. It's what truly drives the stories of *Firefly* and connects the disparate crew of Serenity. While Captain Mal and his crew may not be blood, they have evolved into their own kind of kin that squabbles, loves and protects just like any other. Yet, in the pilot of *Firefly*, a true brother and sister invade Serenity and their love and protection of one another ends up mirroring the relationships of those on the ship that takes them in. Dr. Simon Tam, a young man of privilege who risks his life and career to rescue his sister, River, from the Alliance, is a man with a lot to learn from the Serenity crew. Initially contemptuous of Mal and his people, Simon comes to learn that the eclectic personalities on board all have something to offer him and his wounded sister. It's certainly not the kind of sci-fi role an actor would expect to be offered and Sean Maher said during the press launch for *Firefly's* cinematic reincarnation that that is what made him open to auditioning. He remembers getting the script from his agent and being told, "'Here's this Joss Whedon new sci-fi thing.' I was like, 'Hmm, sci-fi. I don't really know much about that.'"

Maher ended up reading for the part and while Simon Tam was interesting enough on his own, it was Whedon that sealed the deal for the actor. "Sitting down with him — he was just so intriguing. He's such a wonderful man and I'd just like to say it was love at first sight with him. When I met him, I wanted to do anything that he was part of."

Luckily, the entire cast felt the same way as Maher, and the legendary rapport among the cast and crew made for a chemistry and magic that the actor still marvels at. "Joss always says that in casting *Firefly*, he really looked for the person before the acting ability or the actor. Not that we're all not great actors, but that he just made sure that he connected with the person, and it was somebody that he really got a good vibe from — somebody with great energy. So then he just sort of put us all together,

and I think it was very quick, like right out of the gate, we all instantly bonded."

In describing the show from his perspective, Maher says, "The words 'science fiction' come to mind, but it's not actually science fiction. It feels more like a Western, like a post-apocalyptic Western. It's obviously set after there is no more Earth. Humans have colonized other planets. So it's a glimpse into the future. There's a huge Asian influence, more specifically a Chinese [influence]. Even on the set, little keyboards have American italics and also Chinese, so everyone is bilingual because of the meshing of the two cultures.

"Simon is picked up on Persephone," he continues. "He's looking for transport, so he picks Serenity because it looks disreputable and he tries to fly anonymously. The crew has stuff that they're hiding and they don't want the passengers to know about, because they are running goods illegally." It ends up being a match made in space as the denizens of Serenity all hold their own secrets as tragic and dangerous as the Tam's.

Yet despite that connection, Simon has a hard time conforming to Malcolm Reynolds' ship and his crew. "Simon has a huge contrast with the rest of the crew because he's definitely from a more privileged background," Maher says. "It's an entirely different level, an entirely different class of people. He's very well off. Simon is a very gifted doctor. He was a surgeon in the trauma centre on Osiris." It's through his profession that Tam finds a place amongst the Serenity crew and proves his worth to everyone, including himself. "When stuff goes down he turns out to be invaluable to the survival of a few people."

While Simon and Summer's path may have been hellish on *Firefly*, the actor says the experience of working on the series was incredible. As Maher told *TV Guide*, "Honestly, wherever Joss goes, I follow. And the cast, I would do anything with this group of people, whether it's television or film... even if we take a circus act on the road. I feel blessed to have been a part of this. The more and more it continues, it's overwhelming. We had this little show that could, you know?"

They all turn to look — A COP, one of the ones Simon saw in town, stands nearby, gun drawn.

HEAD COP
You are both wanted in connection to the illegal killing of Rance Durban. You are bound by law to stand down!

The other four cops emerge variously about the scene. As Mal puts his hands in evidence, surrounded:

MAL
You know, I'm startin' to find this whole planet very uninviting.

Off that —

INT. CORRIDOR/INT. TENT - DAY

Simon enters a low ceilinged, long corridor/hallway. He catches a glimpse of River up ahead, she disappears around a bend in the corridor.

WITH SIMON

moving down the dark, scary corridor. Moving... River is nowhere to be seen, but Simon speaks to her anyway...

SIMON
River. Please...

He turns a dark corner which opens into —

TENT

An open, beautiful airy space. A decorated tent.

Music plays.

Local women fill the floor, dancing an intricate folk dance.

River stands on the edge of this, not seeing Simon. Never taking her eyes off the dancers.

EXT. JIANGYIN/CARGO BAY - DAY

The cops, guns drawn, are moving in on the scene. They disarm the Granges and also Mal and Jayne. Firearms are dropped into a neat pile on the dirt.

Another cop is rousting Book nearby. No gun.

MAL
Appears we have ourselves a situation...

HEAD COP
Who are you?

MAL
Just a bystander.

HEAD COP
This your beef?

MAL
No, sir.
(re: the Granges)
You're looking at the proper owners right there.

HEAD COP
Like to see some paper on that cattle.

The Younger Grange suddenly lunges at the cop who is frisking him. Wrestles the cop's gun away from him, turns to kill, but suddenly BANG!, the gun is shot out of his hand by —

ZOE

who is on the ramp at the ship, never far from her Captain's back.

And now all hell breaks loose. The Elder Grange pulls a concealed gun that the cops hadn't yet got to. More gunfire.

Mal and Jayne drop to the ground, reach for their guns from the pile...

JAYNE
Here we go.

MAL
It never goes smooth. How come it never goes smooth?

Now Mal notices — THE CLOTH MONEYBAG in the dust. Just a little more than arm's length away. Mal reaches for it, fingertips brushing the edge of it. Reaching... reaching... MAL grabs it —

— just as a BULLET kicks up dust. Mal rolls clear, but has the cash as

fire fight!

INT. TENT - DAY

River watches from the sidelines. She watches intently, studying. Simon tries to make his way to her. But she DARTS INTO THE DANCE.

SIMON
River!

She works her way into the pattern, mimicking the others' steps perfectly. She dances.

EXT. JIANGYIN/CORRAL - DAY

The fire fight continues. Mal and Jayne are on the ground between the other parties. The Grange boys fire at the five cops.

The cops return fire.

Mal and Jayne keep low, bullets sailing over them.

MAL
I hate it when this happens.

The Granges make a break for it, disappear into the corral. Still firing —

Mal looks back to Zoe on the ramp, she indicates where the Granges have gone.

Mal nods back. Mal and Jayne use the cows for cover as they do a mini-pincher move around the Grange boys —

INT. TENT - DAY

River continues to dance. As Simon watches, she throws back her head. We see what Simon sees: she wears a huge grin.

Simon notices, a look of amazement, wonder, on his face. He is in awe of her. Even Simon's starting to smile now, loosening up. The music continues, and so does...

EXT. JIANGYIN/CORRAL/INT. TENT - INTERCUT

The gun battle.

We're INTERCUTTING now. Between River as her dance gets more and more frenzied and...

...the gun fight. Chaos and confusion. The cops firing into the herd. The Granges firing back. And Mal and Jayne closing in on the Granges.

MUSIC

Composer Greg Edmonson says he was not responsible for the timing of the gunshots being percussively interspersed with River dancing with the villagers. "We used a traditional piece — 'The Sailor's Wife', I believe it's called — that I arranged for River's dance. The gunshots just happened — it's just the way they cut it together."

❖ Right: The hood that is pulled over Simon's head by the kidnappers.

IN THE TENT. River dances...

AT THE CORRAL. The Younger Grange is hit! He goes down, but he's only wounded. He reaches for his gun.

The Elder Grange comes to his aid, firing back at the cops. But suddenly —

— Mal appears, sailing at him, taking him down. The cops swarm in. None of them hit.

Mal sighs as the cops take the Granges into custody. He looks around. Reacts to something, as...

IN THE TENT. River stops dancing suddenly. Reacting to something as well. Sensing something terrible, as...

AT THE CORRAL. Mal and Jayne rush to find...

BOOK

on the ground. Hit. Blood blooms on his shirt. His eyes roll up. He blinks at Mal, confused. It's bad.

INT. TENT - CONTINUED

Simon grows concerned, seeing River through the undulating crowd. Sees she is caught up in one of her premonitions.

Simon strains to see her...

She is covered by the crowd, then revealed again, getting a bit jostled. Simon starts to move toward her when —

A HOOD is pulled down sharply over Simon's head. We reveal STARK and his two MEN — They spirit Simon off. Silent and fast. Off River, alone among the dancers —

BLACK OUT.

END OF ACT ONE

ACT TWO

EXT. JIANGYIN/CARGO BAY - DAY

Book lies in the dust of the corral, staring up at the milling cows. And also Mal, who is perched over him, trying to stem the blood flow. Jayne is there, too. Looking at something off screen.

MAL
Stay with me, Shepherd.

Book tries to focus, bleary-eyed. He looks down his body, tries to take it in...

BOOK
That's... that's quite a lot of blood, isn't it?

MAL
Just means you ain't dead.

BOOK
'Fraid I might be needin' a preacher.

MAL
That's good. You just lie there and be ironical.
(to Jayne)
Stretcher.

But Jayne's looking off toward —

— the COPS taking away what they came here for: the Grange brothers in rough custody.

MAL (cont'd)
Jayne.

JAYNE
They're goin'.

MAL
'Course. Got what they came here for.

JAYNE
(after a beat)
You get the cash?

Mal flashes him a look.

CUT TO:

INT. CARGO BAY - DAY

Mal and Jayne, along with Zoe carry Book onto the ship. Kaylee appears as they move through, toward the infirmary.

KAYLEE
What's going on — ?

She stops asking, sees it.

KAYLEE (cont'd)
Oh god, Shepherd! Shepherd can you hear me?

They carry the stretcher across the cargo bay toward the infirmary.

INT. SERENITY/INFIRMARY - DAY

They move Book from the stretcher onto the operating table. Zoe rips open Book's shirt, revealing the wound — gunshot high in the chest.

JAYNE
Don't look good.

Mal shoots him a look that says both "duh" and "shut the fuck up". Mal hits an intercom:

MAL
Wash! Get down to the infirmary! <Ma-Shong!> [Now!]

Mal moves with a purpose.

MAL (cont'd)
(to Zoe)
We gotta try and stop this bleeding.

Mal moves for the cabinet. As he does he tosses the cloth moneybag onto the infirmary counter — it leaves a bloody smear. He grabs more blood rags and bandages, like that.

Kaylee has drifted closer and closer to Book, tearing up.

KAYLEE
You don't worry now, Shepherd Book. Cap 'n Zoe got lots of experience with this kinda thing. Seen lots worse in the war.
(beat)
Shepherd? Shepherd Book?
(then, closer)
He ain't breathin'!

Book starts to CONVULSE VIOLENTLY.

ON KAYLEE, tears brimming as she backs away from the horror. Zoe rips open the package of a disposable stylette and hands it to Mal, who plunges it into Book's arm.

Finally the convulsions subside. Mal turns away

from the scene. Looks to Kaylee.

MAL
(calm down, be brave, I haven't the time)
He ain't dead. But he is bad off. Now we gotta see what we can do to help him.

Wash appears now. Takes in the sight before him.

WASH
<Lao-tyen, boo.> [Oh, god, no.]

MAL
Wash, I need you to go into town, see if you can find that <jing-tzahng mei yong-duh> [consistently useless] Doctor.

Wash nods, heads off. Mal rejoins Zoe at Book's side. Kaylee stares at her dying friend...

KAYLEE
Hurry...

EXT. WOODS - DAY

Simon is dragged through the woods by Stark and his men. Stark moves ahead, the Shabby Man drags Simon, stumbling, by the arm.

STARK
Faster. Gotta go faster. Wanna get there afore dark.

SIMON
Get where? Where are we going? Are you with the police?

STARK
Shut up.

SIMON
Please. If it's ransom you want, I... I can arrange something.

STARK
No talking.

SIMON
You don't understand. My sister...

Stark turns and shoves him hard and he falls. On impact —

INT. TAM ESTATE - NIGHT

Our second flashback. [Note: this scene takes place several weeks after the previous flashback, so wardrobe should change.] Simon stands facing his mother. It's tense.

REGAN
Your sister is fine, Simon.

SIMON
She's not fine. Didn't you look at the letters? Look at the letters!

Gabriel is at his desk, looking over a sheaf of papers. He stands up, bringing the papers with him.

GABRIEL
They seem perfectly normal to me.

Simon points at the pages frantically, pointing things out:

SIMON
She talks about last summer at the lake.

GABRIEL
So?

SIMON
We weren't at the lake, we were in the mountains.

REGAN
Oh honey, I'm sure there's a lake up there.

SIMON
No. These phrases... they don't sound like her. And look here — some of these words, they're misspelled.
(off parents' blank looks)
She started correcting my spelling when she was three. She's trying to tell us something. I think there's a code.

Regan and Gabriel share a look — that just sounded nuts.

GABRIEL
A code?

SIMON
Yes.

GABRIEL
Simon... have you talked to anyone about this?

SIMON
What? No. What do you mean? I'm talking to you.

GABRIEL
Good. Don't mention this to anyone outside the family.

SIMON
What?

GABRIEL
You don't hear what you sound like, Simon.

SIMON
I don't care —

GABRIEL
You should. Because it sounds insane.
(then)
Look, son, if your sister was in danger, we'd be right beside you. You know that.

SIMON
Then let's go and find out.

GABRIEL
Government schools don't allow visitors.

SIMON
And why do you suppose that is?

GABRIEL
You can't go charging in there ranting about "spelling codes" and nonexistent lakes.

REGAN
It'll hurt your future at the hospital. It'll hurt River in the school.

GABRIEL
(then, not without affection)
I always thought it was River who was lost without her big brother... now I'm starting to wonder if it isn't the other way 'round.

Now Simon's less sure.

GABRIEL (cont'd)
I know you miss her.

SIMON
Yes...

GABRIEL
You want to see her.

He nods. Gabriel puts a paternal hand on his boy's shoulder.

GABRIEL (cont'd)
You will, son. Just be patient.

Simon, his anger dissipated, looks uncertain.

EXT. WOODS - DAY

SUNLIGHT GLARES through the trees. Simon squints against it as he is still being forced along in front of Stark and his men. He's a little dizzy from the earlier fall. He blinks through the glare up ahead... sees...

A FIGURE

Feminine, fragile, a nearly angelic vision up ahead.

SIMON

blinks again. Slows.

Stark gives him a mighty push that sends him stumbling ahead... but he doesn't take much note of the violence, he's still looking toward the figure that stands among the trees, looking at him now.

SIMON
No... Oh, no...

Stark and his men are noticing the figure now, too. It's River. And she's smiling.

SIMON (cont'd)
Oh, god...

The men exchange looks, grow wary —

RIVER
Found you!

SIMON
River! River, no! Run, RUN!

Her smile fades into confusion.

RIVER
Found you?

Simon manages to tear himself away by sheer force of will, the sight of his sister giving him sudden strength. He bolts toward her.

But Stark and his men chase him down. Simon is nearly to her, now. In desperation Simon PUSHES RIVER away roughly.

SIMON
RUN! GO!

River looks at him, tears in her eyes. She doesn't know why he pushed her.

And then one of Stark's men has her by the arms. She's caught too.

STARK
Bring her.

And now they're both being forced forward, Simon utterly defeated now as —

INT. CARGO BAY - DAY

Kaylee paces in the cargo bay. Inara and Jayne are nearby. They both react to the SOUND of the MULE. Kaylee perks up.

KAYLEE
(calling)
They're back! Doctor's back!

Mal appears from the infirmary area as Wash drives up in the Mule. Alone. The others register this. Wash parks the Mule, climbs off.

KAYLEE (cont'd)
Where's the Doctor? Why isn't he with you?

WASH
He wasn't in town. Wasn't anywhere.

KAYLEE
He was in town. We saw him there. Him and River. I can show you —

WASH
Town's not that big, Kaylee. Believe me when I say he wasn't there.

JAYNE
Knew it. Probably saw them cops, turned tail.

MAL
Doctor could be called a lot of things — coward wouldn't be one of 'em, though.

INARA
You don't think they were arrested, do you?

WASH
Worse than that, probably.
(then)
Looks like maybe they got snatched.

INARA
Kidnapped?

WASH
I went by the sheriff's office. Seems if we'd looked at the posted alerts for this rock we mighta known it. Settlers up in the hills take people sometimes. Usually tradesmen and the like.

MAL
And now they got themselves a doctor.
(then)

And we don't.

Mal moves to the controls that work the doors. Kaylee reacts as the ramp starts to rise, closing up.

KAYLEE
What are you doing?! What about Simon and River?

MAL
Forget them. We lost two people today. If I can help it, we won't lose a third.

THUNK! The ramp door closes.

MAL (cont'd)
Wash, get us in the air.

Wash obeys, heads off. Mal moves off, too. We hold on Kaylee, registering what's happening, surprised, devastated —

EXT. WOODS - DAY

As SERENITY RISES UP over some trees in the distance, then takes off heading for space — CAMERA TILTS DOWN TO...

SIMON

pausing in his trek, watching as he and River are left behind. Stark appears.

STARK
You just keep movin'.

And with a helpful shove from Stark, he does. He keeps moving. Moving and looking back for a moment, until the SOUNDS of Serenity hitting atmo and getting fainter cause him to

turn forward, stumbling toward whatever awaits him —

END OF ACT TWO

ACT THREE

EXT. SERENITY - EFFECT

The ship moves through space, fast.

INT. SERENITY - INFIRMARY

Book is laid out on the examining table, apparently unconscious. Zoe stands over him, cleaning the wound. He opens his eyes, watches her for a moment before she's aware he's awake. She looks grim.

BOOK
(re: her expression)
That bad?

She looks at him, a little caught.

ZOE
Battle wounds are nothing new to me, Preacher. Seen men live with a dozen holes in 'em that size.

BOOK
That right?

ZOE
It surely is. Knew a man with a hole clean

through his shoulder once. He used to keep a spare hanky in there.

BOOK
Where's the Doctor? Not back yet?

ZOE
We don't make him hurry for the little stuff. He'll be along.

Book's losing it, starting to drift away again.

BOOK
He could hurry a little...

INT. SERENITY - BRIDGE

Wash is piloting. Mal leans over his shoulder. They're looking at a star chart on a display.

WASH
Well, there's Greenleaf. They'd have med help there.

MAL
Too far, more'n ten hours. Man's worse off'n that.

Inara has just entered, overheard that last line.

INARA
You know where to find what you need.

MAL
Don't recall inviting you onto the bridge.

INARA
You didn't. Mal, you know where you can find a doctor. You know exactly.

MAL
Inara — he was dumb enough to get himself grabbed in broad daylight. Don't have the time to be beatin' the trees lookin' for him now. No assurance we'd find him. Or that he wouldn't need a doctor himself.

A beat as her pain and worry for Simon and River crosses her face, then, pushing on:

INARA
I'm not talking about Simon. I'm talking about medical facilities.

A beat as Mal realizes what she means, even if we don't at the moment. He turns away from her:

MAL
That's not an option. Nor is it a discussion I much want to have at the moment.

INARA
It doesn't matter what you want. He's dying.

He looks at her. Off that eye contact —

INT. SERENITY - INFIRMARY

Kaylee enters the infirmary, joining Zoe, who is watching Book — genuinely unconscious now. Kaylee makes a move to hold his hand.

KAYLEE
(re: holding hand)
Can I?

ZOE
Sure. He's out, though.

KAYLEE
He did this for me once. How's he doing?

ZOE
I cleaned it out, wrapped it up. Best I could do. I don't know.

KAYLEE
But we're headed for help, right?

ZOE
Captain'll come up with a plan.

KAYLEE
That's good, right?

ZOE
Possible you're not recalling some of his previous plans.

After a beat:

KAYLEE
We left 'em back there.

ZOE
Yeah.

KAYLEE
Don't seem right.

CUT TO:

EXT. WOODS/BACKWOODS SETTLEMENT - DAY

They come to a small community. Falling down gray wood shacks. A frontier town that lost the battle with the forest, and was overrun. The general look is Appalachian village.

A few beaten-looking people sit in front of the shacks: thin men cooking on crude clay ovens, grim-faced tattered women tending to dirty children in sack-dresses.

Stark pulls Simon roughly by the arm, out into the center of the cluster.

STARK
Look at what we got! It's a doctor! Got ourselves a doctor!
(proud, relieved)
A doctor. A real doctor.

Simon looks to Stark who suddenly seems less threatening — because he's smiling and not malevolently, but with a kind of relief.

Simon looks back to the village as more and more TOWNSFOLK begin to emerge...

STARK (cont'd)
(nudging him, sotto)
Stand up straight.

Simon does, as many of the townsfolk draw nearer, tentative, curious... some in awe...

INT. BRIDGE

Wash is looking with some awe himself at a thing just outside the cockpit window.

Mal looks less awestruck and more or less just grim.

WASH
You sure this is where you wanna be?

MAL
Oh, I'm fairly certain it ain't.

EXT. SPACE - CONTINUOUS

SERENITY moving (slowly now) through space. CAMERA PANS with Serenity, revealing just what it is she's moving toward...

AN ENORMOUS ALLIANCE CRUISER. A GRAPHIC comes up over this image: Alliance Cruiser, Magellan, Outer Rim.

INT. BACKWOODS SICKHOUSE - DAY

A DOOR is pushed open. Dusty SUNLIGHT pours into this dark place. Simon and Stark are silhouetted against it.

STARK
In here.

He ushers Simon inside.

STARK (cont'd)
Don't figure it's near as fancy as you're used to, but it's what we got.

River enters with them. Simon tries to make his eyes adjust to the dimness. It's dark in here, and there are eight or nine people inside, all ages. There are a few cots around the edges, but mostly people sit on the dirt floor. Everyone is thin, haggard, hopeless. They look at him with dead eyes.

SIMON
What... what is this place? Am I in prison?

INT. BRIDGE - CONTINUOUS

Mal and Wash looking out at the imposing Alliance Cruiser which fills the entire bridge window.

MAL
(to Wash)
Be sure to ask nicely.

Wash nods, he's already got his hand mic poised to speak into:

WASH
Alliance Cruiser Magellan, this is Firefly Transport Serenity, requesting permission for docking...

As Wash says this, Mal moves to exit the bridge, passing...

... Inara who stands there. He doesn't even look at her. Off Inara, and before Wash's request can be answered...

STARK (V.O.)
T'ain't a prison...

INT. BACKWOODS SICKHOUSE - DAY

The sad, dark place.

STARK
...it's the sickhouse.

There is some COUGHING and MOANING. Simon looks to River who gazes with sadness and compassion on those there. Stark calls out to a young woman, DORALEE.

STARK (cont'd)
(to Doralee)
Got yer doctor.

DORALEE
(joining them)
Praise the Lord!

STARK
Doralee here'll show you what's what.

Stark turns and exits. Simon looks around, moves closer to the patients.

DORALEE
What's your name?

RIVER
(appearing)
Simon.

Doralee looks over, sees River.

DORALEE
Well, hello there. Who're you?

SIMON
That's River.

River tries to move toward the sick people. Simon holds her back.

SIMON (cont'd)
River.
(indicates chair)
Just... sit down over there.

She does. Doralee looks to River; Simon looks to the assembled.

SIMON (cont'd)
(to Doralee)
Has there been... is there a sickness here?

DORALEE
Nothing especial. Just, people get sick. Or injured. Mostly people heal on their own, but sometimes...

SIMON
Sometimes you need a doctor.
(then)
Bring me light and any supplies you have.

As Simon rolls up his sleeves —

EXT. SERENITY - EFFECT

We dock with the huge ship Magellan.

INT. SERENITY - AIRLOCK

Mal and Jayne carefully lower Book onto a large crate in the cargo bay that's near the sliding airlock doors. Zoe starts rolling back the inner airlock doors.

ZOE
You sanguine about the kinda reception we're apt to receive on an Alliance ship, Captain?

MAL
Absolutely.
(then)
What's sanguine?

ZOE
Hopeful. Plus, item of interest, it also means bloody.

MAL
Well, that pretty much covers the options, don't it?

Mal moves to the smaller inner door on the ramp, hits a button — WHOOSH, it opens, and Mal finds himself facing a PHALANX OF GUNS held on him by Alliance soldiers.

INT. BACKWOODS SICKHOUSE - DAY

Doralee has brought a hurricane lamp and a wicker box presumably with medical supplies. Simon kneels in front of a child with a bandaged arm. He unwraps the bandage. As he examines the child —

SIMON
This all seems pretty minor. There's no epidemic? Nothing more serious? I was brought here just to tend to these people?

DORALEE
They need tendin', don't they? Last year, the place needed builders. Got two men. Five years ago, they decided they needed a teacher.

SIMON
So they... went and took one?

DORALEE
Went and took me.

Simon looks up from his work.

SIMON
You're... are you a prisoner here too?

DORALEE
I just live here now. Teach the children their sums, their bible lessons, how to live the Lord's way. Don't choose to leave.

SIMON
And you think they'd let you?

DORALEE
(shrugs)
Never thought to try. They needed a teacher. That's what I do. Teach.

Off Simon's incredulous reaction we return to...

INT. SERENITY AIRLOCK - CONTINUED

Mal, Zoe and injured Book face an array of guns. There are three soldiers, a COMMANDER in charge, and an ENSIGN.

Mal and Zoe are not wearing weapons and keep their hands in evidence as the Commander and his team moves into the cargo bay area. Regard the injured Book.

MAL
We're requesting aid. No other purpose.

ZOE
We got papers.

She carefully pulls a little folder of papers from her vest, hands 'em over to the Ensign. As he looks at them...

COMMANDER
What's your business?

MAL
We're a supply ship. Freelance. Had an accident this morning. Crewman got injured...

Mal indicates with his head — back toward Book.

ZOE
We need medical help.

Mal's getting twitchy — Book might be dying.

MAL
Fast'd be better'n slow.

The Ensign looks up from the papers. He hands them to the Commander. He looks at them.

COMMANDER
(to the Colonel)
Official seal's out of date, Captain...
(checks paper)
Harbatkin?

Book opens his eyes, looks up at the Commander.

MAL
We ain't been through a checkpoint in a while, sir. You gonna see to my man?

COMMANDER
How did this happen?

ZOE
He was —

MAL
(preemptively)
Bystander in a gun fight. Back on Jiangyin. You can check. Not he nor any of ours were the aggressors.

❖ Below: The ship's papers for Serenity.

❖ Opposite page: Book's ident. Note the issue number: 20 47 20, Randy Eriksen's lucky number makes another appearance!

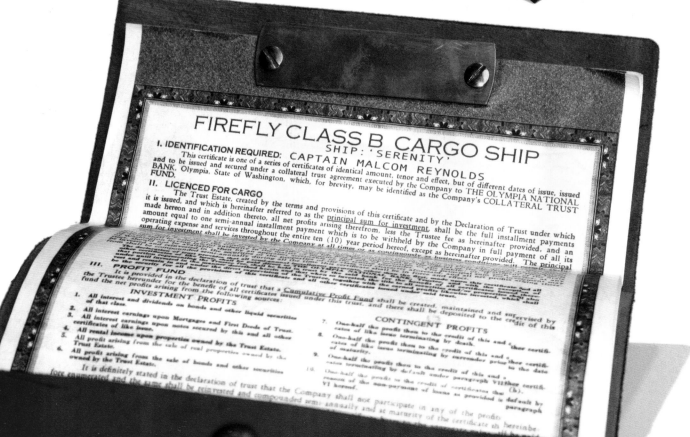

FIREFLY CLASS B CARGO SHIP
SHIP: 'SERENITY'

I. IDENTIFICATION REQUIRED: CAPTAIN MALCOM REYNOLDS
This certificate is one of a series of certificates of identical amount, tenor and effect, but of different dates of issue, issued and to be issued and secured under a collateral trust agreement executed by the Company to THE OLYMPIA NATIONAL BANK, Olympia, State of Washington, which, for brevity, may be identified as the Company's COLLATERAL TRUST FUND.

II. LICENCED FOR CARGO
The Trust Estate, created by the terms and provisions of this certificate and by the Declaration of Trust under which it is issued, and which is hereinafter referred to as the principal sum for investment, shall be the full installment payments made hereon and in addition thereto, all net profits arising therefrom, less the Trustee fee as hereinafter provided, and an amount equal to one semi-annual installment payment which is to be withheld by the Company in full payment of all its operating expense and services throughout the entire ten (10) year period hereof, except as hereinafter provided. The principal sum for investment shall be invested by the Company at all times or as continuously as business conditions will

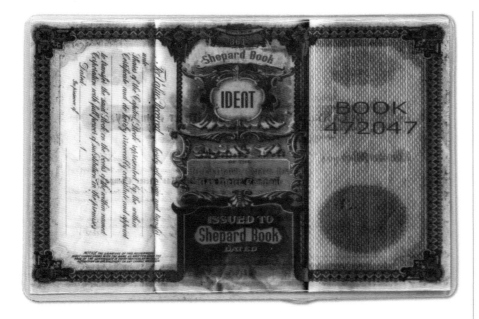

DORALEE
No. She was fine until two years ago when she stopped talking.

ANGLE ON: River and the little girl.

DORALEE (cont'd)
Place like this might be good for your sister. Quiet, safe. Place where folks take care of each other.

SIMON
Yes, it seems like a lovely little community of kidnappers.

COMMANDER
We aren't an emergency facility, Captain. Our services aren't simply available to any—

BOOK
(weakly)
Commander...

The Commander looks at Book, startled.

BOOK (cont'd)
My ident card... pocket...

Book tries to reach into his own pants pocket, winces...

The Commander nods to the Ensign. He helps Book, comes up with an ident card... a square of electronic paper.

Mal and Zoe watch with interest — weren't expecting this and don't quite know what to make of it.

The Ensign takes the card, slides it into a reading device (size of a credit card imprinter) which overrides its privacy code, and takes in secured information on it. He hands it to the Commander. WE CAN SEE information scrolling across the card. The Commander looks at it. Then, to the Ensign:

COMMANDER
(no nonsense)
Get this man to the infirmary at once.

The soldiers carry Book off to the infirmary. Zoe and Mal exchange a look.

INT. BACKWOODS SICKHOUSE - NIGHT

Simon has brought in even more light. Some of the people, having been treated, have left. The few remaining ones seem happier, livelier... Simon is making a difference.

Simon is treating a woman's infected hand when

another woman approaches him. As Simon finishes treating the first woman, Doralee enters and approaches him. She has River with her.

DORALEE
I found her. She wasn't far.

SIMON
Thank you. She's... It's important she stay close.

River wanders to a corner of the room, sits among some small children.

DORALEE
She's not quite right, is she?

Simon finishes what he's doing...

SIMON
(to the patient)
You keep that bandage clean now, you understand?

Simon sits back and looks toward River.

SIMON (cont'd)
(to Doralee)
River's been through some trauma. She's recovering though.

DORALEE
She in a restful situation these days? Getting a chance to get better?

SIMON
Not... well. We're trying. But it's... difficult.

They watch as River looks at a little girl, age around seven, we'll know as RUBY. The little girl looks back at her, apparently unresponsive.

DORALEE
She won't get a good conversation out of Ruby, I can tell you that much. That little girl's mute.

SIMON
Do you know the cause? Was she born deaf?

DORALEE

Costume designer Shawna Trpcic: "We had a lot of research about peasants from all around the world and whenever we went to a poor planet, we would tap into that. Doralee was very reminiscent of the Civil War period, of almost a Mammy, the kind, soft, helpful woman. We even put a little turban on her, which could be Hindu or it could be a classic turban or a scarf. Whenever we went to a planet, we always tried to blend the cultures and blend the influences, because that's the whole idea of pioneering, that you're taking people from all over the world and planting them in one spot together."

RIVER

"Two by Two, hands of blue."

With her luminous eyes, dancer-lithe body and gentle spirit, it's hard to imagine anyone better born to play the character of River Tam than actress Summer Glau. In her first speaking role, Glau brought an amazing depth to her portrayal of the tortured, teenage lab experiment fleeing from the Alliance with her brother, Simon. It's under the protection of Captain Mal Reynolds and his crew that this wounded bird of a girl begins to heal from her traumatic past, and her story truly created the compassionate heart of *Firefly*. For the actress, her association with Joss Whedon and being cast as River signified the start of a new facet of her career, not to mention an amazing period of personal growth and discovery. Glau made her first impression on Whedon when she worked as a ballerina in his *Angel* episode, 'Waiting in the Wings'. When casting for *Firefly* took place soon after, Glau says it was that small role which opened the door for River. "I heard I was suggested as a good fit from that," she says. "Joss had me come in and work with him and the casting director, Amy Britt. He had to get me ready for the test because testing for a series is very intense. I had never done it before, or auditioned for a pilot. So I went in and worked with them and from that audition, I went straight to the test [for the network]. It was one of the most vivid days of my life; I remember everything about it. I remember when I did the read, it was in a very dark room with all these different faces, except that Joss was sitting in the front row and I remember looking at him afterwards and him smiling at me and looking proud, like he was happy with my read. He had called me after my audition, because he knew how nervous I was and how badly I wanted it, and told me that I did well.

"But they didn't want to cast me right away," she continues. "A lot of times they tell you a few days after or

even on the day, but in my case, because I was the youngest person in the cast and it was a smaller role, they wanted to focus more on Inara and Zoe, so I had to wait and wait and wait. Finally, it was Joss that actually called and told me I got the role, which was really special. He called me two weeks after and said, 'You're my girl!' I just cried and cried. I really believe that I got cast as River because I wanted the part more than any other girl."

While River might have been a major trial to decipher or understand for some actresses, Glau says she connected with the character from the start. "A lot of people ask me how I got inspired to play River because she is such a challenging, different person. It's funny, as soon as I read it, I knew exactly how I wanted to do it. I did. It was like we were meant to be together. I went in and I read for Amy and Joss and I was shaking like a leaf, I was so nervous. I always felt whenever I had to show someone a River scene, I had to go out on a limb. It was scary. But Amy looked at Joss when I was done and said, 'That's how you do it.' So it was just a fit, it felt right. I feel like my background and who I was before I was an actress helped me. I was really shy growing up, and dancing was my way of getting people to look at me and showing how I felt. You never talk in ballet and you are always so separated from everyone and there is a safety in that. River was a great transition for me because she was kind of distanced from the rest of the cast. She was in her own world, on her own stage, so I had a special relationship with her that way."

Of her first day Glau remembers, "The very first thing I did was go to the production office for a hair, makeup and costume test. Of course, they didn't have very much to do with River's hair. All we did was make it look dirty," she laughs. "The first person I met though was Jewel. I met her in the production office with Joss and instantly fell in love with her. She is so stylish and fabulous and fun and girlie and lovely and smelled so good. Her shoes were fantastic!

"Then I went down to get my hair done and they described her as the wacky, odd, sort of child of the group so they were trying all kinds of weird things with my hair. Of course, they had my hair stuck in some weird shape and in walks Sean. I was so awestruck and captivated by him," she blushes. "I couldn't even look at him for the first month, I just thought he was so fantastic. He treated me with care from the very beginning, just like Simon." ◐

DORALEE
The Lord says "judge not".

SIMON
They took us off the street.

DORALEE
Life sometimes takes you places you weren't expectin' to go.

SIMON
Life didn't bring us here. Those men did.

DORALEE
You were on a transport ship, right? Takin' a journey? It's the way of life in my findings that journeys end when and where they want to. And that's where you make your home.

SIMON
This isn't our home.

DORALEE
If it isn't here, where is it?

We linger on Simon as he considers that, having honestly no answer.

INT. ALLIANCE CRUISER - INFIRMARY/ VIEWING ROOM

Mal, Zoe and Jayne in an observation room just off the big, hi-tech Alliance Cruiser infirmary. Within we see ALLIANCE DOCTORS working on Book. This has none of that E.R. urgency — it's all very staid and antiseptic.

JAYNE
This place gives me an uncomfortableness.

ZOE
So what do you figure — Shepherd's got some sort of Alliance connection?

MAL
Know what it looks like. Still — it'd surprise me if he did.

JAYNE
See, this is my whole problem with picking up tourists. They're never what they claim to be.

MAL
Does seem like everyone's got a tale to tell...

INT. BACKWOODS SICKHOUSE - NIGHT

Simon pulls a blanket over a patient who is asleep. He stands. Work done for the day. He turns. River is not there. Nor is little Ruby.

SIMON
River? River?

Doralee appears.

DORALEE
What's wrong?

SIMON
River's gone. So's the little girl.

DORALEE
Ruby —
(then, as she goes)
I'll check out back.

Simon nods. Doralee moves off. Simon moves to the entrance. He pulls open the door —

— and there's River. Alone. She's using her dress as a pouch for something.

SIMON
River, don't... what is that?

RIVER
For you.

She reveals a skirt full of BERRIES.

SIMON
Oh.

RIVER
I picked them.

He looks around for a bowl. He finds a wooden water bowl and she pours the berries from her skirt into it.

SIMON
Well, here... you'll stain your dress.

RIVER
You have to eat.

She feeds him one. He smiles. It tastes good.

SIMON
Blackberries. Do you remember when we found those giant blackberry bushes on the Cambersons' Estate... We thought they'd grown wild, but...
(his smile fades)
...long while ago.

He puts the bowl aside. River watches his bitter-sweet reverie.

RIVER
I took you away from there.

SIMON
No, no...

RIVER
I know I did. You don't think I do, but... I get confused. I remember everything, I remember too much and some of it's made up and some of it... can't be quantified, and there's secrets and ...

She's getting upset now, eyes welling up...

SIMON
It's okay...

RIVER
But I understand. you gave up everything you had to find me, and you found me broken and it's hard for you, you gave up everything you had —

SIMON
<Mei mei> [Little sister]... Everything I have is right here.

She feeds him another berry.

RIVER
You have to eat. Keep up your strength and we won't be here long, Daddy will come and take us home and I'll get better. I'll get better.

He clouds over at the reference to home and family, though he tries to hide it. Eats another berry.

SIMON
These are better than the Cambersons' berries.

RIVER
They are. Except they're poison.

He spits it out, horror on his face — and she laughs delightedly... He smiles, busted.

RIVER (cont'd)
He believed her, made a face.

SIMON
(genuinely happy)
You're such a brat.

Doralee appears with Ruby.

DORALEE
(relieved to see River)
You found her.

Ruby moves off to her makeshift bed, one of the many mats.

SIMON
Yes, she... there are berries.

DORALEE
Fruit of the ground. God's reward for a hard day's work.
(to Ruby)
You get to bed, now.

SIMON
(re: he and River)
We should probably think about doing the same. It's been a big day, what with the abduction and all.

DORALEE
Ya'll don't have to sleep here. There's a house set aside for you. We've been looking for a doctor for a good while. So things are ready.

SIMON
Really...

RIVER
(mouth full of berries)
Her sister got killed. Her mother got crazy. Killed the sister. That one lived.

DORALEE
Ruby talked to you, honey?
(to Simon, excited)
It's true what she's saying. Poor woman went out of her mind, tried to kill her two girls. Ruby lived.
(to River)
Sweetheart, you are an angel! No one's been able to get Ruby to speak even a peep! It's a miracle! That's what it is!

RIVER
Ruby doesn't talk. Her voice got scared away. I hear crickets.

DORALEE
I don't understand... if Ruby didn't talk, how do you...?

SIMON
My sister is... She's very good at —
(off Doralee's face)
What's wrong?

DORALEE
(reciting softly)
"And they shall be among the people, and they shall speak truths and whisper secrets... and you will know them by their crafts..."

SIMON
What are you talking about?

Doralee takes a troubled, horrified step backward...

DORALEE
"Thou shall not suffer a witch to live."

She runs into the night. Simon is, understandably, alarmed.

END OF ACT THREE

ACT FOUR

INT. TAM ESTATE - NIGHT

We're in Simon's third and final flashback. [Note: again, this is on a different night, new wardrobe.] We're in the same room. Regan looks out the window, alone. Face etched with worry, drink in hand. It's POURING RAIN outside. She hears the front door open O.S. Simon enters wearing an overcoat, walking briskly, followed by his father.

REGAN
Simon! Thank god! I was so worried.

SIMON
I'm fine.

REGAN
Then what were you doing in a police holding center?

GABRIEL
Your son was caught in a vice unit raid. Downtown, in a red-light tenement bar.
(to Simon)
Never expected I'd be dragged out of the house in the middle of the night for something like this, Simon.

SIMON
Weren't you even listening? I had to go there! It was the only place the man would meet me.

REGAN
Man? What man?

SIMON
Someone with information about the Academy. Someone with the contacts we're going to need. Other children have disappeared into that school, Mother. And the ones who do come out, they're... wrong... aphasic or psychotic...

She just stares. Gabriel looks more annoyed than worried.

GABRIEL
Can you believe this? This is what I've had to listen to for the last two hours.

SIMON
I've been working on her letters. There is a code. She says someone is hurting them.

Gabriel goes to the phone-screen, starts to make a call.

GABRIEL
I'll call Johan. He should be able to scrub this off his record, with a small transfer of funds...

Simon slams the shut-off, stopping the call.

SIMON
Dad! Forget my record! River is in trouble!

REGAN
River isn't here!

Simon looks like he's been slapped across the

---

face. Stunned.

GABRIEL
We are. And we have to be careful how we act. This is a government school, Simon. People in our position... it's important that we show support for this government.

SIMON
You're talking about politics? This is about your daughter!

GABRIEL
This is about our lives.

Simon stares at them both for a beat, taking this in. Simon turns, heads for the door. Gabriel follows —

GABRIEL (cont'd)
Where are you going?

SIMON
To get her out.

GABRIEL
This isn't something you want to do.

SIMON
You're right. This isn't something I want to do. But if I don't, then no one will. So I'll do it. I'll take care of her. Just like I always have.

GABRIEL
That's <tsway-niou> [bullcrap]. We gave both of our children everything they could possibly want.

A beat as Simon stares at his father.

SIMON
(hardens, starts to turn)
Right.

GABRIEL
If you do this thing, they will find you, and they will put you away. And know this: when they do, I will not come for you. If you leave here, if you do this... I will not come for you.

Simon turns and walks away into the night.

EXT. BACKWOODS SETTLEMENT - NIGHT

Simon and River watch as Doralee rings the town bell. It's at the side of the little street, rigged to a pole. She pulls repeatedly at the cord that swings the clapper.

Townspeople, about a dozen, emerge onto the streets. Stark among them. Doralee yells to them as they appear.

DORALEE
Witch! The girl's a witch!

SIMON
This is lunacy. You're supposed to be the teacher here. What exactly is it you teach?!

An older man, an official known as the town PATRON, comes to Doralee, puts a hand on her arm, makes her stop ringing the bell. He's got a long coat over pajamas, an air of authority, and he seems completely rational and comforting.

PATRON
What's going on, woman? Why are you knocking us out of our beds this hour?

DORALEE
That girl, the new Doctor's sister... she read Ruby's mind. Saw things she couldn't —

River is clinging to Simon, confused and scared.

SIMON
River's not a witch. She's just a troubled girl —

The Patron smiles at the brother and sister.

PATRON
I'm sure that's true.
(to River)
You're not a witch, are you, <nyen ching-duh> [young one]? I'm the Patron here — do you know what that means?

RIVER
(to the Patron, pleasantly)
Yes. You're in charge. Ever since the old Patron died.

PATRON
That's right.

RIVER
He was sick and you were alone in the room with him.

The Patron slaps her across the face.

SIMON
No!

Simon makes a rush for him and is restrained.

PATRON
This girl reads minds and spins falsehoods! She has had congress with The Beast!

The Patron motions to two men who step forward, take River.

PATRON (cont'd)
We will purge the devil from her.

She KICKS... struggling to break free. This isn't delicate squirming, but an all-out fight.

She lets out a horrible long SCREAM — as if she's being killed. It's shocking. It doesn't help.

SIMON
No! She didn't mean anything!

PATRON
Bind her. She must be purged. With fire.

INT. SERENITY/INFIRMARY - NIGHT

We're back on Serenity. Book is on the recovery table. Comes around. Sees Mal hovering over him.

BOOK
Well. That's not a face I expect to see in heaven. Guess I survived.
(then)
Thank you, Captain. It was very resourceful of you.

MAL
Had no reason to think it'd work. Just took a chance.

BOOK
Reckon that's how you do lots of things.

MAL
Majority of the time it turns out bad. I may want to rethink my governing principle.

BOOK
Well, it worked out this time.

MAL
Yeah. They let us come and they let us go. What kind of ident card gets us that kind of reception and send off?

BOOK
I'm a shepherd. Folks like a man of God.

MAL
No they don't. Men of God make everyone feel guilty and judged. That's not what I saw. You like to tell me what really happened?

BOOK
I surely would. And maybe someday I will.
(then)
It's good to be home.

INT. SERENITY - INFIRMARY/COMMON AREA - CONTINUOUS

Jayne is seated at at little table, carefully drying money between little towels. He sets the last dried bundle in a tidy stack. Zoe enters from the cargo bay as Mal steps out of the infirmary.

ZOE
Badger just hailed us. Getting impatient for his share. Wants us to drop it to his men on the Kowlan Fed base.

JAYNE
Well, that'll be a hell of a lot easier to do without the "two most wanted" on board.
(excitedly)
Life would look to be simpler all round, us not carrying fugies.

Mal, and Zoe with him, go, neither wanting to say;

ZOE
He's right, you know.

MAL
Yeah. Simpler.

EXT. BACKWOODS SETTLEMENT - NIGHT

The villagers are constructing a witch-burning set-up... vertical pole, kindling... you know how it goes.

Men SCURRY UP TREES, like Stark before. They go into the high branches, drop down dry, dead kindling.

River, being held, is calm again. But Simon is losing it. Stark is there now, too, looking regretful.

SIMON
Don't do this. There has to be another way...

STARK
You asked for time, Doctor. The Patron give you that. But you don't offer him nothin'.

The men holding River spirit her over to the stake. They start to tie her to it. She doesn't struggle. They're piling kindling there. One of the men fires up a small TORCH.

SIMON
(to Patron)
Take me instead! Take my life for hers!

PATRON
The witch must burn. God commands it.

The man with the torch moves to the pile of kindling. Is about to light it.

SIMON
NO!

Simon manages to rip free, rush over, shoves that guy aside.

SIMON (cont'd)
Get away from her!

He gets hit. Hits back. More of the men come at him. He stands between them and River. Sees that he's woefully outnumbered. A few show up with old, rusty rifles pointed at him.

SIMON (cont'd)
She doesn't understand! Can't you see what you're doing? Please...

The mob just stares back, unmoved. Simon sees the odds. Nothing to do now. He turns, climbs up onto the pile of kindling —

STARK
That's not gonna stop us, Doctor.

He doesn't even look back to Stark. Looks at River.

RIVER
Post holer. For digging holes. For posts.

She smiles at him. Doesn't seem frightened. He smiles back, tries not to explode with the emotion. He looks at her bonds, at the mob converging. At the man with the torch. So he just wraps his arms around her. She rests her head on his chest. Then, all defiance, he turns to the mob.

SIMON
Light it.

SUMMER GLAU

In 'Safe', I got to dance. It was a really special episode that I remember very vividly. It's such a powerful image for me, being up on the stake — and it was cold. I remember the wind blew my hair up and it got stuck on the stake. Also the stake wouldn't stay in the ground: it kept tipping over so I would have to jump off of it.

The Patron nods to the man with the torch. He brings it up. Touches it to the pile of kindling. It starts to SMOKE and IGNITE. Simon holds on tight.

RIVER
(clear and still)
Time to go.

Then the wind picks up and it gets darker, as

SERENITY RISES UP

huge and gray. THUNK. The BOMB BAY DOORS open on the belly of Serenity and there's Jayne, hanging out of them, big ass rifle with a flashlight

strapped to it aimed down on those assembled. He could pick off any of them at any time.

THE VILLAGERS back away, stunned.

And into the clearing strides Mal, hero shot, big ass rifle in his hands, Zoe close behind. He speaks up, for everyone's benefit.

MAL
Well, look at this. Appears we got here just in the nick of time. What does that make us?

ZOE
Big damn heroes, sir.

MAL
Ain't we just. Sorry to interrupt, people, but you all got something of ours, and we'll be needing it back.

PATRON
This is a holy cleansing. You cannot think to thwart God's will.

MAL
Do you see the man hanging from the spaceship with the really big gun? Now I'm not saying you weren't easy to find, but it was kinda out of our way and he didn't wanna come in the first place. Man's looking to kill some folk, so it's really his will y'all should worry 'bout thwarting.

He moves past the Patron, addresses Simon.

MAL (cont'd)
Gotta say, Doctor, your talent for alienating folks is near miraculous.

SIMON
Yes, I'm very proud.

Mal turns to the Patron.

MAL
(to Patron)
Cut her down.

PATRON
The girl is a witch!

MAL
Yeah. But she's our witch.
(cocks his gun)
So cut her the hell down.

Off Mal's won't-take-no-for-an-answer look...

INT. SERENITY - INFIRMARY/COMMON AREA

Mal comes into the common area, glances into the infirmary, notes that it's empty. He turns

and there's Simon.

SIMON
I've moved him to his room.

MAL
How's he fairing?

SIMON
He's going to be fine. They took good care of him.

MAL
Good to know.

An awkward beat between them. Then:

SIMON
Finally a decent wound on this ship and I miss out. I'm sorry.

MAL
Well, you were busy trying to get yourself lit on fire. It happens.

Mal starts to go.

SIMON
Captain...
(Mal turns back)
...why did you come back for us?

MAL
You're on my crew.

SIMON
You don't even like me. Why did you come back?

MAL
You're on my crew. Why we still talking about this?
(his back to him, as he goes)
Chow's in ten. No need to dress.

As we hold on Simon:

INT. SERENITY/DINING ROOM - NIGHT

The crew gathered for supper. Everyone's there except for Book. Simon appears, ushers in River. She goes across the table, takes a seat in between Jayne and Wash.

Kaylee appears carrying a bread basket, sets it on the table. She glances at Simon. He smiles at her. She smiles back. He holds a chair for her. She sits.

There's lots of chatting and laughing and arguing.

WE FOLLOW the serving dish as it's passed around. Jayne takes a big hunk of bread, puts it on his plate, passes the dish. He looks back — the bread is gone. River's got it, is eating it.

Simon takes in the communal experience happening around him. And as we pull back on this milieu —

FADE OUT:

END OF SHOW

> Some scenes in this episode changed quite substantially from the shooting script and some extra scenes were added in at the last minute. Here are those scenes as aired.

EXT. LARGE MANSION - NIGHT

Establishing shot. High-tech security fence surrounds the mansion.

INT. LARGE MANSION - NIGHT - CONTINUOUS

We're in a study or living room. Spacious, lushly appointed, a fire crackling in the fireplace.

Chyron reads:

TAM ESTATE, 11 YEARS AGO

Young Simon Tam sits on the couch doing his homework.

Young River Tam is playing behind the couch.

YOUNG RIVER
(peeping up from behind couch) We're in trouble. (beat) We got cut off!

YOUNG SIMON
Cut off from what?

YOUNG RIVER
Our platoon, Simon. We got outflanked by the Independent squad, and we're never gonna make it back to our platoon. (beat) We need to resort to cannibalism.

YOUNG SIMON
That was fast. Don't we have rations or anything?

YOUNG RIVER
They got lost. We're gonna have to eat the men.

YOUNG SIMON
Aren't you supposed to be practicing for your dance recital?

YOUNG RIVER
I learned it all. (re: his homework) That's wrong.

YOUNG SIMON
It's from the book, River.

YOUNG RIVER
No, the book is wrong. This whole conclusion is fallacious.

Simon smiles, puts his homework away. Turns to River.

YOUNG SIMON
So... how'd the Independents cut us off?

YOUNG RIVER
They were using dinosaurs.

YOUNG SIMON
(incredulous) <Jien tah-duh guay!> [Like hell!]

GABRIEL TAM enters the study.

GABRIEL
Language, young man.

YOUNG SIMON
Sorry, Dad. The Independents attacked us with dinosaurs.

YOUNG RIVER
Simon lost his head in the heat of battle.

GABRIEL
(chuckling) <Nah mei guan-shee.> [That has nothing to do with it.] Because there were dinosaurs involved, I think we'll let it slide.

YOUNG SIMON
Did you get my wave?

GABRIEL
I got it. Your text shorted. I got the whole thing during a board meeting. Thank you.

YOUNG SIMON
If I had a dedicated source box, it wouldn't short out. I lost half my essay.

GABRIEL
Yes, and you'd have access to any <tyen-shiao duh> [heaven knows what] that filtered in from the Cortex. I absolutely forbid it!

YOUNG SIMON
(pleading) Dad...

YOUNG RIVER
Dad...

GABRIEL
I will not have it in my house. (beat) But since your mother's already ordered you one, I guess I should give up the fantasy that this is my house!

YOUNG SIMON
Are you kidding?

GABRIEL
You will repay me by becoming a brilliant doctor. That's the deal. Dedicated sourcebox — brilliant doctor.

YOUNG RIVER
When do I...?

GABRIEL
(dismissive) Many years.

YOUNG SIMON
Dad, this is so <da bianhua> [big change]! It's really gonna —

GABRIEL
I know. You think I'd let you work with something second-rate?

YOUNG SIMON
Thank you.

GABRIEL
You're worth it. (beat) Now do you think it's possible for you two geniuses to give your tired old dad a couple minutes' quiet?

INT. SERENITY - COMMON AREA - CONTINUOUS

Back to the present. River is struggling and shouting.

Simon is attempting to calm her.

RIVER
(collapses onto couch) No! No, I don't wanna go back to the...

SIMON
It's okay. It —

RIVER
It's not okay! (beat) You can't just dig into me, shove twenty needles in my eyes and ask me what I see!

SIMON
I... we won't go in. Look. (shuts infirmary doors) No test today.

RIVER
No rutting tests? Stupid son of a bitch, dress me up like a gorramn doll!

SIMON
No tests, no shots... (beat) I'm, uh, I'm just gonna give you a smoother that'll...

River stands, takes Simon's case of medical supplies, and tosses it.

SIMON
River!

Mal is walking down the steps to the infirmary as this happens. None too pleased.

RIVER
(to Mal) You're not him? (beat) <Liou coe shway duh biao-tze huh hoe-tze duh ur-tze.> [Stupid son of a drooling whore and a monkey.]

River wilts and sits back on the couch.

Mal continues down the stairs.

MAL
So, she's added cussing and hurling about of things to her repertoire. She really is a prodigy.

SIMON
It's just a bad day.

MAL
No, a bad day is when someone's yellin' spooks the cattle. Understand? (beat) You ever see cattle stampede when they got no place to run? It's kind of like a... a meat grinder. And it'll lose us half the herd.

SIMON
She hasn't gone anywhere near the cattle.

MAL
No, but in case you hadn't noticed, her voice kinda carries. We're two miles above ground and they can probably hear her down there. Soon as we unload, she can holler until our ears bleed. (to River) Although I would take it as a kindness if she didn't.

RIVER
The human body can be drained of blood in 8.6 seconds given adequate vacuuming systems.

MAL
(to Simon) See, morbid and creepifying, I got no problem with, long as she does it quiet-like.

SIMON
This is paranoid schizophrenia, Captain. Hand-crafted by

government scientists who thought my sister's brain was a rutting playground. I have no idea what'll set her off. If you have some expertise —

MAL
(firmly) I'm not a doctor. And I'm not your gorramn baby-sitter, either. Gag her, if you have to. We got trade to be done.

Mal exits via the stairs. Simon sighs heavily.

EXT. PLANET - DAY

Establishing shot of Serenity landing on the planet's surface.

REVERSE camera to reveal three hill folk sitting in a copse of trees, all men.

One of the men is skinning a rabbit hung from a tree.

STARK
You see that? Fancy vessel such as that don't land here 'less they got something to sell. And if it's something we need...

He RIPS the skin off the rabbit in one move.

STARK (con't)
We take it.

BLACK OUT.

END OF TEASER

INT. TAM ESTATE - FLASHBACK - NIGHT

Forward in time from the last flashback. Simon is an adult now.

REGAN
Your sister is fine, Simon.

SIMON
She's not fine. Didn't you look at the letters? Look at the letters.

GABRIEL
Uh, I'm looking at letters.

SIMON
These phrases — they don't sound anything like her. Some of these words — they're misspelled. (off their looks) She started correcting my spelling when she was three. She's trying to tell us something. I think there's a code.

REGAN
A code?

SIMON
Yes.

GABRIEL
(chuckling) I always thought it was River who was lost without her big brother. Now I'm beginning to wonder if it isn't the other way around.

SIMON
Did you have a good time at the D'arbanville's ball this year?

GABRIEL
What are you...?

SIMON
River thought it was duller than last year. But since we don't know anybody named D'arbanville, I'm having trouble judging. (angrily) Did you even read these?

GABRIEL
Well, of course I did.

REGAN
It's one of her silly games. You two are always playing.

SIMON
She is trying to tell us something that somebody doesn't want her to say.

REGAN
Simon, this is paranoid. It's stress. If they heard you talking like this at the hospital, it could affect your entire future.

SIMON
Who cares about my future?

GABRIEL
You should.

REGAN
You're a surgeon in one of the best hospitals in Capital City. On your way to a major position, possibly even the Medical Elect. You're going to throw all of that away? Everything you've worked for your whole life?

GABRIEL
Being a doctor means more to you than just a position, I know that.

REGAN
A few months time, you'll turn around and there she'll be. Now, nothing is going to keep you two apart for long.

INT. SERENITY - SIMON'S ROOM - CONTINUOUS

Jayne is tossing Simon's room, stealing all the valuables he can find. He comes across a journal of Simon's, opens it up, reads to himself out loud:

JAYNE
(mock reading)
"Dear Diary, Today I was pompous and my sister was crazy."
(flips page)
"Today, we were kidnapped by hill folk never to be seen again. It was the best day ever."

Jayne tosses aside the journal and continues searching Simon's belongings. He finds some money, pockets it.

JAYNE (cont'd)
Now we're talkin'.

Jayne pulls out a fancy maroon shirt and shakes it out, holding it up as if sizing it.

JAYNE (cont'd)
Amazing we kept him this long.

INT. CAPITAL CITY PENITENTIARY - FLASHBACK - DAY

Gabriel Tam is waiting in a lobby. Simon is escorted in by a guard.

GABRIEL
Have you completely lost your mind?

SIMON
Pretty nearly.

GABRIEL
We got the wave at the Friedlich's. I had to leave your mother at the dinner table.

SIMON
(snidely) I'm sorry, Dad. You know I would never have tried to save River's life if I had known there was a dinner party at risk.

GABRIEL
Don't you dare be flippant with me. I just spent two thousand credits to get you out of here, and I had to walk through that door which goes on my permanent profile. (beat) Are you trying to destroy this family?

SIMON
I didn't realize it would be so easy. (beat) Dad, I — I didn't do anything.

GABRIEL
You were in a blackout zone!

SIMON
Talking! To someone who might be able to help River. And I'm going right back there.

GABRIEL
[Whispering in Chinese.] This is a slippery slope, young man. You have no idea how far down you can go, and you're not taking us with you.

SIMON
Meaning what?

GABRIEL
I won't come for you again. You end up here, or get mixed-up in something worse, you're on your own. I will not come for you. (beat) Now, are you coming home?

INT. SERENITY - SIMON'S ROOM

Close shot of Simon's bed. Someone's dumping a bagful of loot onto it. It's Jayne, hastily returning his ill-gotten gains. Jayne darts out of Simon's room into

INT. SERENITY - CORRIDOR - CONTINUOUS

Jayne's beating his retreat when he sees Simon walking past.

JAYNE
(looking guilty) Hey, there, Doctor. Glad you're back now on the ship.

SIMON
Thanks.

Simon keeps walking. Jayne bolts up the stairs.

COSTUME DESIGN

An interview with Shawna Trpcic

The original costume designer on *Firefly* was Jill Ohanneson; however, the vast bulk of the series' apparel was designed by Shawna Trpcic [pronounced "Trip-chick"]. Trpcic, who began her professional career by designing forty episodes of *Power Rangers* and went on to assist Albert Wolsky on the Costume Oscar-nominated *Toys*, had worked as Ohanneson's assistant designer on a show called *The First $20 Million Is Always the Hardest*. The duo got along well, so when Ohanneson got the gig to design the *Firefly* pilot, she invited Trpcic to work with her again; the job called for Trpcic to do the physical sketches of all the designs. "We pretty much designed the pilot together," Trpcic says. "When the series started, they asked her to come back, but she had gotten *Six Feet Under*, so she told them that she would

design the first episode, but that they should hire me to do the rest."

Trpcic worked closely with *Firefly* production designer Carey Meyer. "We had a lot of the same styles. It's funny, because we have a lot of the same comic book collection," Trpcic laughs. "So when we walked in, the tone that we wanted was the same."

Firefly borrows from many different historical eras. Trpcic says especially influential periods for the look were: "World War Two and the Old West, 1876 and the American Civil War, 1861, mixed in with 1861 samurai Japan."

Regarding use of colors, Trpcic says, "If you look at Asian culture, with the red lamps and the colors they use to highlight emotions and feelings, I tried to do that with a brush stroke, with a deep red or a deep orange to constantly bring us back to the heart and the humanity of these people and the reality of their struggle, trying to separate them from the coldness of the Alliance. When we went to the hospital [in 'Ariel'], I wanted everyone to be wearing white and blue, and grey and purple, cold colors. Whereas, when you think of the Old West, you think of golden lights burning and coming home. I wanted people to feel at home with the characters, and to convey that with color."

Collaboration with the hair and makeup departments was also crucial, says Trpcic. "Sometimes I would get the character dressed and think, 'Oh, my gosh, I totally fell short, this isn't what I was trying to convey — what am I going to do?' And then they would go into hair and make-up and then come out, and I'd be like, 'That's what I was trying to do!' The hair and makeup people would complement the costume, or they would come to me with ideas, and then we'd go off of each other. They were an amazing group of incredibly talented men and women and I'm so grateful for them, because they would literally finish the idea I had in my head that I couldn't get out."

Some examples: "With Kaylee's ball gown [in 'Shindig'], I showed them the initial pencil sketch that I had done and they made Kaylee look so soft and so beautiful. And Inara — she would come out of hair and make-up looking drop-dead sexy gorgeous and I'm like, 'Yeah, the dress is doing what it's supposed to do.' Also, on 'Shindig', we dressed something like three hundred extras and I was just assembly-lining them, throwing these things together, trying to think of colors and shapes and

❖ Below: Designs for Mal as a civilian and as a soldier.

❖ Opposite: Costume design for Inara.

❖ Over the page: A selection of Trpcic's designs for Kaylee, Inara, Wash and Jayne, along with Rosie the Riveter (inspiration for Kaylee's look), and costume continuity photos.

We Can D

WAR PRODUCTION CO-ORDINATING COMMITTEE

ylee ideas.

& Paint

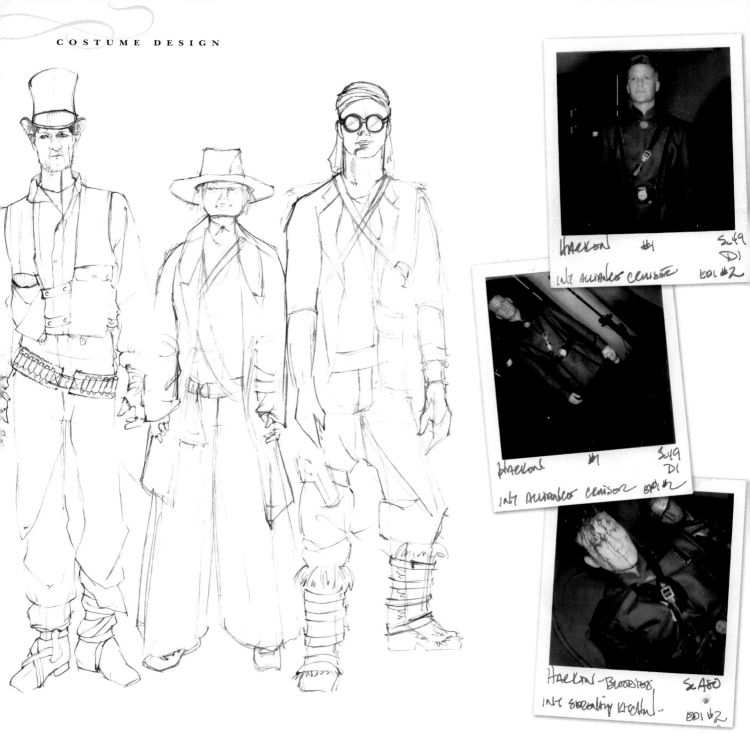

Above left: Design sketches of Patience and her men from 'Serenity'.

Above right: Continuity photos of Commander Harken from 'Bushwhacked'.

Opposite page left: A design for an Alliance soldier.

Opposite page right: A design for Simon.

going, 'Oh, this isn't working,' and then all the extras came out of hair and makeup, and they were beautiful! They looked like we had spent millennia planning this instead of just the few days that we had to do it."

When designing costumes for individual episodes, Trpcic says, "I took my cues off the script and then I would create boards of images. Say, for the mud episode ['Jaynestown'], I went to the library at Fox and talked to [Fox researcher] Brian, and said, 'I need people who farm mud, people who farm oil, people who farm different things from the earth.' And he would give me tons of images and I would put them on a board and send them to Tim or Joss, whoever was supervising that particular episode, and fine-tune the look for that planet. No two planets were ever the same."

The crew of Serenity and their adversaries had a tendency to get shot, which meant that their clothes got bloody. Wardrobe accommodated repeated takes of clothes getting gored by having multiple copies of costumes. "Up to six," Trpcic explains. "Sometimes, even that was not enough and we had to use a bloodied one over again and try to hide the blood or wash it really quick while they shot the last take. Squibs are the little explosions that look like a bullet hole, and sometimes they go off before the camera's rolling and we lose our shirts even before they catch it on camera. Sometimes, when they say there'll just be a small amount of blood, they will push the gage too quickly and there will be tons of blood. Most often, they want us to have a lighter-colored outfit to show the blood. I think with

Mal one time, it was a dark red shirt, so it didn't show a lot, but we just got it really wet so it looked really gooey."

It was also Shawna's job to costume the actors when the characters were supposedly naked. "We talk to them in the morning and say, 'What do you want to wear?' and we get the appropriate little pasties or G-strings or whatever it takes to make them feel comfortable with being in front of the crew."

Of the *Firefly* experience as a whole, Trpcic says, "Working with Joss is the dream job and doing *Firefly* was obviously a design dream job, because we were in a different universe every week. He's an incredibly gracious, humble, talented man who just has a gift for creating these worlds that are really fun to play in."

OUR MRS. REYNOLDS

Written by Joss Whedon
Directed by Vondie Curtis Hall

When I wrote 'Our Mrs. Reynolds', it was Tim who said, 'He's got to be married before the opening credits.' I'm like, 'I just don't think I can do that.' And then of course he was totally right. And then that episode — and I will never say these words again, and believe me, I wish to god I could — wrote itself.

❖ On-set prop master Skip Crank relaxing with the cast, while filming the teaser for 'Our Mrs. Reynolds'.

TEASER

EXT. RIVER IN WOODED GLADE - DAY

[NOTE: If a river is an impossibility, wagon in a glade will suffice. But water makes it cooler.]

A farmer in a broad-brimmed hat (Amish-ish) sits by his bonneted wife on the front of a flat-boat. There's a pole that sticks out to one side harnessed to a team of two horses. The boat is covered with a tarp, almost covered-wagon style.

We see it from a distance, through the trees — and in the foreground, horses snort and paw.

Someone else is watching as well.

A beat, and the riders — four of them — clear the woods and circle the boat (the river being shallow enough to ride in). The men are bandits, the main one (BANDIT 1) facing the cowed couple.

BANDIT 1
Pardon me for intruding, but I believe y'all are carrying something of mine.

The Farmer doesn't lift his head, barely whispers:

FARMER
T'ain't your'n.

BANDIT 1
(pissed)
You talking words to me? You <jung chi duh go-se dway> [steaming crap pile], you gonna mouth off after what you done? Did you think we wouldn't find out you changed your route? You're gonna give us what's due us and every damn thing else on that boat, and I think maybe you're gonna give me a little one-on-one time with the Mrs.

The Farmer lifts his head — it's JAYNE, smiling.

JAYNE
You might wanna reconsider that last part. I married me a powerful ugly creature.

MAL looks up from under his bonnet, shocked.

MAL
How can you say that? How can you shame me in front of new people?

JAYNE
If I could make you prettier, I would.

MAL
You're not the man I met a year ago.

Over this is the extreme confusion of Bandit 1, who finally gets pissed enough to go for his gun —

— and Mal and Jayne, in mid-spat, raise theirs first, targeting 1 and 2.

MAL (cont'd)
Think very hard. You been birddoggin' this township a while now, and they wouldn't mind a corpse of you. Now you could luxuriate in a nice jail cell but if your hand touches metal, I swear by my pretty floral bonnet I will end you.

A beat. The Bandits all look to each other —

Bandit 4 in the back raises his rifle — and a shot from the covered boat knocks him off his horse.

Then everybody's firing, Mal and Jayne dropping 1 and 2 as ZOE dives from the wagon, dropping 3

as she hits the water.

Much falling, much splashing and —

EXT. TOWN - NIGHT

Much celebration, the town gathered around a bonfire dancing, laughing... all the trimmings.

Mal walks through the celebration with INARA, who is dressed down (for her).

MAL
We'll head for Beaumonde in the morning, give you a chance to do some work of your own.

INARA
I appreciate it. This place is lovely, but —

MAL
Not your clientele. I'm wise. You got to play at being a lady.

INARA
Well, yes. So explain to me again why Zoe wasn't in the dress?

MAL
Tactics, woman. I needed her covering the back. Besides, them soft cotton dresses feel kind of nice. There's a whole air flow.

INARA
And you would know that because...

MAL
You can't open the book of my life and jump to the middle. Like woman, I am a mystery.

INARA
(laughing)
Best keep it that way. I withdraw the question.

MAL
Care to dance?

INARA
I've seen you dance.
(off his mock hurt)
Go enjoy yourself. You got hired to be a hero for once. It must be a nice change.

ANGLE ON: JAYNE: he sits by the fire, drunk as a butter-churn, as a townsperson, ELDER GOMMEN, hands him a big wooden stick filled with beads, that sounds like rain when you turn it over.

ELDER GOMMEN
It makes the rain come when you turn it. The rain is scarce, and comes only when needed most. And such it is with men like you.

Jayne's eyes fill with tears.

JAYNE
This is the most... you, friend. You're the guy.

He hugs the Elder hard.

JAYNE (cont'd)
I'll treasure this.

ANGLE ON: BOOK. He stands far off from the noise and light, by a sheet with four pairs of boots sticking out of it, silently reading last rites. Looks over and sees:

ANGLE: BOOK'S POV

Mal sits in a circle, next to Jayne. Book watches as a shyly pretty girl kneels before Mal and places a wreath on his head.

Book goes back to praying.

ANGLE: Mal — as the girl hands him a bowl of wine. Mal drinks and she smiles, moves off into the dance. Others draw Mal and Jayne into the dance as well, Mal finishing his wine sloppily and Jayne not letting go of his rainstick. Mal looks to Zoe, but she is making out with WASH like mad. These are three soused heroes.

Mal and Jayne join in the dance, noise and movement filling the frame, cutting to —

EXT./INT. SERENITY AIRLOCK/CARGO BAY - MORNING

The noise of the whirling engine coming to life — we pan from it to Mal and Elder Gommen on the ramp, as a couple of townsfolk load crates onto the ship.

MAL
Elder Gommen, thank you for your hospitality.

ELDER GOMMEN
We owe you a great debt. I'm sorry we have so little to pay it with. Though I hope our gifts will show our regard.

MAL
I don't think Jayne's ever letting go of that stick.

Zoe runs up to Mal from inside, whispers in his ear:

ZOE
Alliance patrol boat is heading into atmo right now.

Mal smiles at Elder Gommen as Zoe runs back up.

MAL
Well, we gotta fly.

He steers him off as Elder Gommen replies:

ELDER GOMMEN
We will pray for a safe voyage, and hope to lay eyes on you again 'ere too long, my friend.

MAL
Count on it. Bye now.

He runs back up, the ramp closing on the still waving Elder.

EXT. SERENITY

As she takes off and heads up.

INT. CARGO BAY - CONTINUOUS

As Mal is squaring away the goods he comes upon —

❖ Above and below: Before and after the Zoic effects have been added to the cargo bay scene.

MAL
Ahh!

— the girl from last night, huddled shyly in the corner between various boxes. She wears the same potato-sack shift she sported before, and sandals. And an expression of extreme subservient fear. Her name, we will learn, is SAFFRON.

MAL (cont'd)
Who the hell are you?

SAFFRON
What do you mean?

MAL
I think I was pretty clear. What are you doing on my boat?

SAFFRON
But you know! I'm to cleave to you.

MAL
To wabba hoo? You can't be here.

SAFFRON
Did Elder Gommen not tell you...

MAL
Tell me what? Who are you?

SAFFRON
Mr. Reynolds, sir... I am your wife.

We hold on his very stupid expression for a long, long time.

END OF TEASER

ACT ONE

INT. CARGO BAY - CONTINUING

Mal is still looking dumb for a while. Finally:

MAL
Could you repeat that please?

SAFFRON
I am your wife. That was your agreement with Elder Gommen, since he hadn't cash or livestock enough to —

MAL
I'm sorry. Go back to the part where you're my wife.

SAFFRON
(downcast)
I don't please you.

MAL
You can't please me. You've never met me.

Zoe and Jayne enter.

MAL (cont'd)
Zoe, why do I have a wife?

JAYNE
You got a wife?

ZOE
What's she doing here?

JAYNE
All I got was that dumb-ass stick that sounds like it's raining. How come you got a wife?

MAL
I didn't.
(to Saffron)
We're not married.

SAFFRON
I'm sorry if I shame you...

MAL
You don't shame me! Zoe, get Wash down here.

ZOE
(hits com)
This is Zoe. We need all personnel in the cargo bay.

MAL
All — I said Wash!

ZOE
Captain, everyone should have a chance to congratulate you on your day of bliss.

MAL
There's no bliss! I don't know this girl.

JAYNE
Then can I know her?

ZOE
(tough)
Jayne...
(sensitive)
Don't sully this.

MAL
Zoe, you are gonna be cleaning the latrine with your face, you don't cut that out.

Everyone is in now.

BOOK
Who's the new recruit?

ZOE
Everybody, I want you to meet Mrs. Reynolds.

ANGLE ON: INARA

True pain crosses her face.

SAFFRON
Costume designer Shawna Trpcic: "Saffron [Christina Hendricks] was a lot of fun. She had a challenging figure, because usually on TV, actresses are shaped like little boys and she was an incredibly shapely woman, so she was one of my favorites."

KAYLEE
(excited)
You got married?!

SIMON
Well, that's — congratulations...

WASH
We always hoped you two kids would get together. Who is she?

MAL
She's no one!

Saffron starts to cry.

KAYLEE
Captain!

MAL
(at a loss)
Stop that.

SAFFRON
I'm sorry...

WASH
You brute.

Kaylee goes up to Saffron —

KAYLEE
Oh, sweetie, don't feel bad. He makes everybody cry. He's like a monster.

MAL
I'm not a monster! Wash, turn the ship around.

BOOK
(to Simon)
Have you got an encyclopedia?

SIMON
<Dahng ran.> [Of course.]

He goes off. Wash and Mal are still talking throughout:

WASH
Can't.

MAL
That's an order.

WASH
Yeah, but can't.

MAL
What the hell is wrong w—

WASH
Alliance touched down the second we left. And there's already a bulletin on the Cortex as to the murder of a prefect's nephew — that's right, one of our bandits had some family ties. So unless you feel like walking into a gallows, I suggest we continue on to Beaumonde and you enjoy your honeymoon.

MAL
This isn't happening.
(to Saffron)
Will you stop crying?

INARA
Oh, for god's sake, Mal, can you be a human being for thirty seconds?

WASH
Speaking as one married man to another...

MAL
I am not married!
(to Saffron)
I'm sorry. You don't shame me, you have very nice qualities but I didn't ever marry you.

BOOK
(holding encyclopedia)
I believe you did. Last night.

Mal hesitates. As does everyone.

MAL
(to Jayne, quiet)
How drunk was I last night?

JAYNE
I don't know. I passed out.

BOOK
It says here, the woman lays the wreath upon her intended — which I do recall — which represents his sovereignty.

MAL
(to Saffron)
That was you?

BOOK
And he drinks of her wine. This represents his obeisance to the life-giving blood of her — I'll skip this part — and then there's a dance, with a joining of hands.
(closes book)
The marriage ceremony of the Triumph Settlers, been so over eighty years. You, sir, are a newly-wed.

A beat.

MAL
So what does it say in there about divorce?

Saffron runs from the room, to the infirmary.

KAYLEE
<Nee boo go guh, nee hwun chiou.> [You don't deserve her, you fink.]

MAL
<Gwan nee tzi-jee duh shr.> [Mind your own business.]
(starts after her)
Everyone go back to... whatever.

ZOE
Really think you're the one to talk to her, sir?

MAL
Way I see it, me and her got a thing in common. We're the only ones who don't think this is funny.

His words ring true, and he storms out, passing Inara last, who doesn't particularly feel like laughing either.

INT. PASSENGER DORM - CONTINUOUS

Mal enters, finds no one. A quick look —

MAL
Hello? Woman-person?

He starts up the stairs.

INT. ENGINE ROOM - CONTINUOUS

Mal enters, finds Saffron huddled in the corner. She has been crying, but has stopped.

MAL
You all right?

SAFFRON
I thought last night during the ceremony... you were pleased.

MAL
Well, yeah, last night I was. I had some mulled wine, pretty girl gave me a hat made out of a tree, nobody said I was signing up to have and to hold...

SAFFRON
You don't have marriage where you're from?

MAL
Well, sure, we just... we do it different.

Awkward beat.

SAFFRON
Are you going to kill me?

MAL
What? What kind of crappy planet is that? Kill you?

SAFFRON
In the maiden's home, I heard talk of men who weren't pleased with their brides, who...

MAL
Well I ain't them. And don't you ever stand for that sort of thing. Someone tries to kill you, you try to kill 'em right back. Wife or no, you're no one's property to be tossed aside. You got the right same as anyone to live and to try to kill people. I mean, you know. People that are... That's a dumb planet.

SAFFRON
What will you do with me?

MAL
Not rightly sure. We're bound for Beaumonde, it's a decent kind of planet... might be able to set you up with some sorta work...

SAFFRON
I'll not be anyone's doxy.

MAL
I don't mean whoring, there's... factories and the like. Some ranches, if you're more for the outdoors... I don't know — near a week before we get there, we'll figure something.

Small beat.

SAFFRON
I'd be a good wife.

MAL
Well, I'd be a terrible husband. You got five whole days to figure that out.

SAFFRON
Five days, we'll be together?

MAL
We'll be together on the ship, not in any —

She stands, visibly cheered.

SAFFRON
That'll be fine, I'll do for you or not, as you choose.

MAL
Well, shiny. You hungry? Kitchen's just through there.

And she slips by him, excited.

SAFFRON
I'll cook you something!

MAL
No, I meant if you —

SAFFRON
I'm a fine cook, everyone says.

MAL
Yeah, but —
(she's down the hall)
Hold it!

She turns.

MAL (cont'd)
I ain't ever even —

SAFFRON
(smiling)
My name is Saffron.

And she goes. He stands there, bemused. Book appears from the infirmary hall. He has seen that nice moment between the two.

BOOK
Divorce is very rare and requires dispensation from her pastor. I can send him a wave, see what I can do.

MAL
I'd appreciate it. She's a nice girl.

BOOK
Seems very anxious to please you.

MAL
That's their way, I guess.

BOOK
(bright, casual)
I suppose so. If you take sexual advantage of her, you're going to burn in a very special level of hell. A level they reserve for child molesters and people who talk at the theater.

MAL
Wha — I'm not — Preacher, you got a smutty mind.

BOOK
Perhaps I spoke out of turn.

RON GLASS

There was no ad-libbing, but that was okay with me because I prefer not to have that kind of pressure. I like to come in and feel like the writer has written something significant enough and important enough that it needs to be said just as it was written. It worked out very well for me.

MAL
Per maybe haps, I'm thinking.

BOOK
I apologize. I'll make her up a room in the passenger dorm.

MAL
Good.

Book goes back. A beat and his head pops back in:

BOOK
The special hell...

And he's gone again. Mal sighs.

INT. DINING ROOM

Mal sits as Saffron places a plate in front of him, mostly mush (and a few bao), but well presented and aromatic.

MAL
Thank you.

Zoe and Wash enter as he tucks in.

WASH
Something smells good...

ZOE
Having yourself a little supper, Captain?

MAL
Well, Saffron insisted on... I didn't want to make her feel... It's damn tasty.

He can't figure out who to be careful around — so he just starts shoveling it in.

WASH
Any more where that came from?

SAFFRON
(downcast)
I didn't think to make enough for your friends.
(to Zoe)
But I've everything laid out if you'd like to cook for your husband...

Wash looks at Zoe for a microsecond of hope — her eyes narrow — and he laughs overcompensationally.

WASH
Ta-ha-ha— isn't she quaint? I'm just not hungry.

He sits, Zoe sitting as well. Her hilarious mood has abated. Saffron retires to the pantry.

ZOE
So, are you enjoying your own nubile little slave girl?

MAL
(mouth full)
I'm not... nubile...
(swallows)
Look, she wanted to make me dinner. At least she's not crying...

WASH
I might. Did she really make fresh bao?
(off Zoe's glare)
Quaint!

ZOE
Remember that sex we were planning to have ever again?

MAL
Y'all are making a big deal and I would appreciate it if one person on this boat did not assume I was an evil, lecherous hump.

ZOE
Nobody's saying that, sir.

WASH
Yeah, we're mostly just giving each other significant glances and laughing incessantly.
(to Mal)
Is that cider?

MAL
(finishing his)
By the stove.

WASH
(going for Mal's glass)
Yum. I'll give you a refill.
(to Zoe)
Hon?

Saffron is suddenly in frame, grabbing Mal's glass from Wash.

SAFFRON
That's for me to do.

She fills Mal's glass, places it by him. Everyone is quiet and uncomfortable as she stands by Mal, waiting for him to continue eating.

MAL
You know, you weren't lying about your cooking. If I hadn't just eaten...

SAFFRON
You don't want to finish.

MAL
No, I just, I have captain-y stuff I have to do, but truthfully, that's a fine meal. Thank you.

He rises.

SAFFRON
Do you need anything else?

MAL
(rising)
No, no. You just, you eat something yourself, I'm gonna go... captain.

SAFFRON
If you're done with supper, would you like me to wash your feet?

There is a pause. Mal exits.

Saffron goes back into the kitchen. A moment and Wash grabs Mal's plate, digging in. Zoe goes for it as well, elbowing in with a fork.

EXT. SHIP - LATER

Through space she floaty.

INT. INARA'S SHUTTLE - LATER

Inara is working her screen, talking to it as the graphics change accordingly.

INARA
Beaumonde, City of New Dunsmuir. Arrival, October 24, Departure...

Mal comes to the door.

MAL
Can I come in?

INARA
(touches screen to deactivate voice command)
No.

He does anyway.

MAL
See, that's why I usually don't ask.

INARA
What do you want?

MAL
I just needed to, um... hide.

INARA
So I take it the honeymoon is over?

MAL
She's a fine girl, don't misread — hell of a cook, too.

INARA
(pointedly)
I'm sure she has many exciting talents.

MAL
Do you ever, um, wash your client's feet?

INARA
(no)
It's my specialty. We'll be on Beaumonde at least two weeks, right?

MAL
Can't be exactly sure, but —

INARA
Well, I need you to be exactly sure, Mal. I can't make commitments and then not keep them. That's your specialty.

MAL
I'm sorry. Are you tetchy 'cause I got myself a bride or 'cause I don't plan to keep her?

INARA
I find the whole thing degrading.

MAL
That's just what Saffron said about your line of work.

INARA
Maybe you should think twice about letting go of "Saffron". You two sound like quite a match.

MAL
Maybe you're right. Maybe we're soulmates.

INARA
Yes. Great. I wish you hundreds of fat children.

MAL
(laughing fondly)
Can you imagine that? Me with a passel of critters underfoot? Ten years time, I could teach 'em to —

INARA
(standing)
Can you leave me alone for five minutes please?

Mal is surprised by the force of her outburst. He exits.

INT. CARGO BAY - CONTINUOUS

He calls back as he goes:

MAL
I wasn't looking for a fight...

Turns and sees Jayne standing with meanest looking future shotgun imaginable. He cocks it, stone-faced.

MAL (cont'd)
I always do seem to find one, though...

END OF ACT ONE

ACT TWO

INT. CARGO BAY - CONTINUOUS

JAYNE
Do I have your attention?

MAL
We're kind of going to extremes here, ain't we?

JAYNE
There's times I think you don't take me seriously. And I think that oughta change.

MAL
Do you think it's likely to?

JAYNE
You got something you don't deserve.

MAL
And it's brought me a galaxy a' fun, I'm here to tell you.

JAYNE
Six men came to kill me one time, and the best of them carried this. It's a Callahan fullbore autolock, customized trigger and double cartridge thorough-gage.

He holds it out to Mal.

JAYNE (cont'd)
It's my very favorite gun.

MAL
<Da-shiang bao-tza shr duh lah doo-tze> [The explosive diarrhea of an elephant], are you offering me a trade?

JAYNE
A trade? Hell, it's theft! This is the best gun made by man, and it's got extreme sentimental value! It's miles more worthy 'n what you got.

MAL
"What I got" — she has a name.

JAYNE
So does this! I call it Vera.

MAL
Well, my days of not taking you seriously are

certainly coming to a middle.

JAYNE
Dammit, Mal, I'd treat her okay...

MAL
She's not to be bought. Nor bartered, nor borrowed or lent. She's a human woman, doesn't know a damn thing about the world and needs our protection.

JAYNE
I'll protect her!

MAL
Jayne! Go play with your rainstick.

Mal heads downstairs. Jayne clearly not letting it go, but heading back up to his quarters.

Mal comes to ground level and runs into Saffron — he jumps a bit.

MAL (cont'd)
Gah! You do sneak about, don't you.

SAFFRON
You're a good man.

MAL
You clearly haven't been talking to anyone else on this boat...

SAFFRON
I don't wish to be wed to the large one. I'd rather... if I'm not to be yours, I'd rather have that work you spoke of. I could be useful on a ranch.

MAL
That's good work. My momma had a ranch, back on Shadow where I'm from. Ran cattle, mostly — wasn't nobody ran 'em harder or smarter. Used to tell me, don't brand the cattle, brand the buyer — he's the one likely to stray.

SAFFRON
She raised you herself?

MAL
Well, her and about forty hands. I had more family for a kid who —

He stops, looking at her.

MAL (cont'd)
Well, that is odd.

SAFFRON
What?

MAL
I just don't — I'm not one talks about his past. And here you got me...

SAFFRON
Does your crew never show interest in your life?

MAL
No, they're, they're... They just know me well enough to... What about you? What's your history?

SAFFRON
Not much to say. Life like yours, I fear you'd find mine terrible dull.

MAL
Oh, I long for a little dullness. Truth to say, this whole trip is getting to be just a little too interesting.

EXT. SPACE

Serenity passes a small (tiny) cracked moon. Zoom in to see a device webbed about the surface of the moon, with a dozen tiny camera faces all firing flashes one after another.

ANGLE: A COMPUTER

As a 3D image forms (fed by the camera's info) of Serenity. Pull back to:

INT. CHOP SHOP OFFICE

as two men, CORBIN and BREED, look at the screen. They are clearly disreputable, their outfits as hodge-podge and junky as the room they're in. Corbin is tough, strong, in charge. Breed is seedier, but also not to be underestimated. Bad guys.

BREED
It's a wreck.

CORBIN
No, no. This is good.

BREED
It's parts. A lot of cheap parts we'll never unload.

CORBIN
This is why you'll never be in charge, Breed. You don't see the whole. The parts are crap —

BREED
I said exactly that —

CORBIN
— but you put 'em together, you got a Firefly. Thing will run forever, they got a mechanic even half awake.

BREED
It's got no flash...

CORBIN
Some people ain't looking for flash. She's a good catch. She comes our way, you prep the nets.

BREED
Lotta effort we're going through here... hoped we'd hit a t-bird, at least.

CORBIN
Just keep complaining. The sound is soothing.

He's on his way out.

BREED
Kill the crew?

CORBIN
Save me the pretty ones. You know the drill.

IF POSSIBLE — This entire talk has been one slow pull-out from the screen, and now pull-out further, through the window, to see:

EXT. SPACE - FLOATING CHOP SHOP - CONT.

Which is basically a giant floating ring — the office sits on top like a giant crab, the rest of the ring made up of connecting tunnels and chambers, and mostly by ships and parts of ships. Some gleam enticingly, some are cannibalized. Electricity crackles silently along the rim, fired up at six key points (this, we will see, forms the net). Ten Serenities could pass through the ring at once.

A flash of electricity flares us out to:

INT. ROOM/PASSENGER DORM - LATER

Book is making up a room for Saffron, making the bed. He finishes smoothing it out, admires his work. We hold a still, wide frame as River enters and pulls the bed apart quickly and calmly and exits again, taking the pillow. Book sighs, starts out after River.

Simon is coming the other way, interrupts River. She takes him by the hand, turns back to Book.

SIMON
<Tzuh muh luh?> [What's going on?]

BOOK
Seems River doesn't want me making up a bed for our young guest. Or she's starting a pillow collection, I'm still collating data.

SIMON
I'm sorry. I'll take care of the room —

RIVER
It's not important!
(to Simon)
Tell him.

SIMON
Tell him what?

RIVER
(to Book)
We want you to marry us.

SIMON
What? We — no! What?

RIVER
Two by two. Everyone a mate, a match, a dopple. I love you.

SIMON
No, River, mei-mei, of course I love you too, but we can't be married.
(to Book, mortified)
She's... really crazy.

River kicks him in the shin.

SIMON (cont'd)
OW! I don't mean crazy — that's just not something brothers and sisters do. I mean on some planets, but only pretty bad ones.

RIVER
The Captain took a wife...

BOOK
Well, that's also complicated.

SIMON
I don't know where this is coming from...

RIVER
We'll take care of each other. I'll knit. You don't love me.

Mal enters with Saffron.

MAL
What's going on?

SIMON
I really couldn't say.

MAL
I was gonna show Saffron her quarters, did they get squared away?

BOOK
Once upon a time...

SAFFRON
I don't need anything, I'm really just fine —

RIVER
(turning)
You're a thief.

Slight beat as Saffron recoils from River's accusation. Book notices that she shrinks a bit toward Mal, who puts a protective hand to her back.

MAL
Well, ho, let's play nice here.
(to Simon)
Your sister's got some funny notions.

SIMON
That's not untrue.

SAFFRON
I'm sorry...

They all turn to her, surprised, as she pulls a packet of food from her dress pocket. River responds by stuffing her pillow under her shirt.

SAFFRON (cont'd)
(handing the packet to Mal)
I didn't know when I was to be fed, and I was afraid...

MAL
You made that fine meal, didn't eat nothing yourself?

SAFFRON
That was for you. Weren't but pot lickings left, so I took this for later, I didn't know she saw me.

RIVER
(to herself)
Didn't see you...

BOOK
Well, there's certainly no harm done...

MAL
(forcefully)
And I'd say there is. Good deal a' harm, and it's starting to tick me off.

Saffron is frightened, and Mal turns her to him.

MAL (cont'd)
Now, I got no use for people sneak around taking what ain't theirs.

BOOK
(wryly)
Yes, we frown on that here.

MAL
But what I got even less use for is a woman won't stand up for herself. Five days hence we're puttin' you in the world, and you won't last a day by bowing and sniffing for handouts. You want something, you take it, or ask for it. You don't wait to be told when to breathe, you don't take orders from anyone. Except me — and

that's just 'cause I'm the Captain, and people take orders from captains even in the world. But for the rest, damnit, be like a woman is. Not no petrified child. There's more'n seventy little earths spinning about the galaxy, and the meek have inherited not a one. Do you understand what I'm saying to you?

SAFFRON
(with quiet strength)
I do.

He tosses the food back to her. Looks to Book.

MAL
Shepherd, would you show Saffron her room please?

Mal exits, Book leading Saffron the other way. Simon is left with pillow-belly River.

RIVER
Now we have to be married.
(hands on belly)
I'm in the family way.

Simon cannot think of a response.

ZOE (V.O.)
She's clearly out of her mind.

INT. BRIDGE - LATER

Zoe and Wash in mid-conversation.

WASH
Well, she's led a sheltered life.

ZOE
Did you see the way she grabbed that glass from you?

WASH
Every planet's got its own weird customs. 'Bout a year before we met, I spent six weeks on a moon where the principal form of recreation was juggling geese. My hand to god. Baby geese. Goslings. They were juggled.

ZOE
Of course the man rushes in to defend her...

WASH
(huh?)
I'm talking about geese.

ZOE
Captain shouldn't be baby-sitting a damn groupie. And he knows it.

WASH
Okay, when did this become not funny?

ZOE
When you didn't turn around and put her ass back down on Triumph where it belongs.

WASH
Oh, hey, now it's even my fault! Is there anything else on your mind I should know about? There's all sorts of twists and cul-de-sacs, it's wild.

ZOE
She's trouble.

WASH
I'm getting that.

ZOE
I'm going to bed.

She exits.

WASH
I'm gonna stay here, where it's safe and quiet, and I'm gonna play with some of these dials and stuff.

He's watching her go, confused and unhappy.

WASH (cont'd)
I might, you know, steer.

She's long gone. He spins back around.

INT. JAYNE'S ROOM - LATER

Jayne sits on his bed, unhappily turning his rain-stick over and listening to it.

INT. FOREDECK HALL - NIGHTPHASE

It's empty as Mal starts down his ladder, we follow him into:

INT. MAL'S ROOM - CONTINUOUS

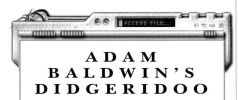

ADAM BALDWIN'S DIDGERIDOO

Prop master Randy Eriksen: "Adam Baldwin had a didgeridoo he brought down to the set that he wanted to use in the show, but Joss didn't like it. He was always playing it like 'Mmmoooo'. It was very cool."

CHRISTINA HENDRICKS

Christina Hendricks's upbringing likely helped her generally as an actress and more specifically as the nothing-if-not-multifaceted Saffron. "I was born in Tennessee," the actress says, "but I grew up all over — in Georgia, Oregon, Idaho, Virginia, New York — moving from city to city, very different kinds of places and things, seeing different kinds of people and how people deal with things in their own way."

How did Hendricks view Saffron? "I decided that Saffron is so good at what she does, and she does it so often, that she has to almost convince herself. So I never tried to play the secret — I just tried to play what was happening at that moment, because I think *she* believes it and she was so convincing. I tried to just be honest about each one of those people that she was, each time. I loved all parts of her. I like the little moments where she may do an eye-roll or a smirk behind someone's back, and they don't know it's happening."

Favorite scenes? "Well, clearly the seduction scene was fun," Hendricks laughs. "What a beautifully written scene — and I loved the reveal at the end of that, when Mal passes out. Running with Alan up on deck and then going into action mode was really fun, trying to seduce him and then knocking him out."

There's usually a difference between coming onto a series as a first-time guest actor and coming back but, Hendricks says, "less so on *Firefly* than on any other show. I mean, the cast on *Firefly* were so warm and just giving and immediately made me feel comfortable; whereas other casts — including the show that I'm on this week! — don't even speak to you. *Firefly* made me feel *so* comfortable. They showed respect for me as an actress immediately, so that was really, really nice."

Mal enters, pulls off his shirt. Tosses it in the corner, turning to see:

ANGLE: IN THE BED is Saffron. She is quiet, a bit apprehensive and more than a bit naked.

MAL
(jumps)
Wah! Yo— hey. You're, um... well, there you are.

SAFFRON
I've made the bed warm for you.

MAL
It, uh, looks warm.

SAFFRON
And I've... made myself ready for you.

MAL
Let's ride right past the part where you explain exactly what that means. Didn't you see you got a

room of your own?

SAFFRON
And... I'm to sleep there?

MAL
That's the notion. Assuming you're, yeah, sleepy...

SAFFRON
But we've been wed. Aren't we to become one flesh?

She is soo insouciently sexy. Mal looks up where his shipmates would be, resolve wavering...

MAL
Well, no, I think we're still two fleshes here. And that your flesh oughta sleep somewhere else.

SAFFRON
I'm sorry. When we talked, I'd hoped... but I don't please you.

BOOK

"Wasn't born a Shepherd, Mal."

A respected, veteran actor with thirty years in the business appearing in such classic television series as *Barney Miller*, *All in the Family* and *Friends*, there were nevertheless a couple of genres Ron Glass hadn't explored in his career — until he was approached to play Shepherd Derrial Book. Called by his agent to take a look at the new series by Joss Whedon, Glass says he had his reserv-ations about taking a role in a space Western. "Before *Firefly*, I had always stayed away from science fiction and for that matter, Westerns too. I never made a point of seeking that kind of material once I got past ten years old," he laughs. "I had never seen much of Joss's work prior to that time. Of course, I read the pilot script... and fell in love with it. I loved all the characters, the story and the world and I especially loved the Book character. The thing that was galvanizing for me was the characters, so the environment was secondary. I was happy to see how Book would unfold in that kind of environment and it worked really, really well."

With his priest's collar and meager belongings, Book's physical presence was a strong reflection of the character right from the pilot. "Joss and the costumer had a pretty clear idea of how they wanted him to look," Glass says. "I concurred because it was really simple, but very definitive at a moment's glance. The only thing I had some curiosity about was whether that collar would be the only thing that he'd ever be seen in. As it worked out, there were some variations that I wore. For example, when I was working out and lifting weights and another time when we were playing Calvinball. I loved that huge coat that Book wore in the pilot episode.

"I used to tease Morena a lot because she has such a wide variety of costume changes. One time, there were bunches of people 'oohing and ahhing' over some new wardrobe Inara had and just to tease her, I walked around the corner and stepped back and said, 'Oh my gosh! What is this? A carnival act?' Everyone thought it was hysterical," he chuckles.

A devout Buddhist in real life, Glass says tackling Book's faith was intriguing from the start. "I did have some in-depth conversations with Joss in terms of suggesting that Book have more of a Buddhist persuasion in his Christianity. Joss explained to me that he really wanted Inara to be the Buddhist in the group and Book to be more of a fundamentalist Christian guy. The wonderful thing was the commonality in terms of the two philosophies. What I was able to bring to the Christian part of it was the humanism and the humanistic point of view. It was the hook in terms of being able to make that adjustment. I wasn't born Buddhist, so I do have some other traditions to pull from too.

"One of the things I was most delighted about as far as Book's character was concerned was that he was not a saint and he had not always been a preacher. Though rather mysterious, it was absolutely clear that he had had a very full life before he went off to the monastery and took on that responsibility. I loved the fact that he could save your soul but he could also kick your ass. That's a really great combination to play."

Remembering his first day on set, Glass says, "There was some commonality of the newness of the project for me as well as the newness of Book's experience, in terms of joining the crew of this ship that he also did not know. He was learning and unfolding in the script at the same time as I was learning and unfolding on the set. It was a happy circumstance that I was able to use real life experience to come to express what was happening on the page as well. On the first day I'm always a little tentative because you need to start picking up what the ground rules are, in terms of how the director is, if the director is going to be flexible or how much input you are going to have. It's part of the excitement and the learning process. I think the very first script and on one of the early days, I got to knock somebody out and at the same time have this wonderful, gentle experience with Kaylee, presenting her with the strawberry. In the same script, I also had this wonderful shared experience with Inara, explaining how conflicted I felt. It was a really full, dimensional exploration and really contributed to the feeling of great expectations." 🟢

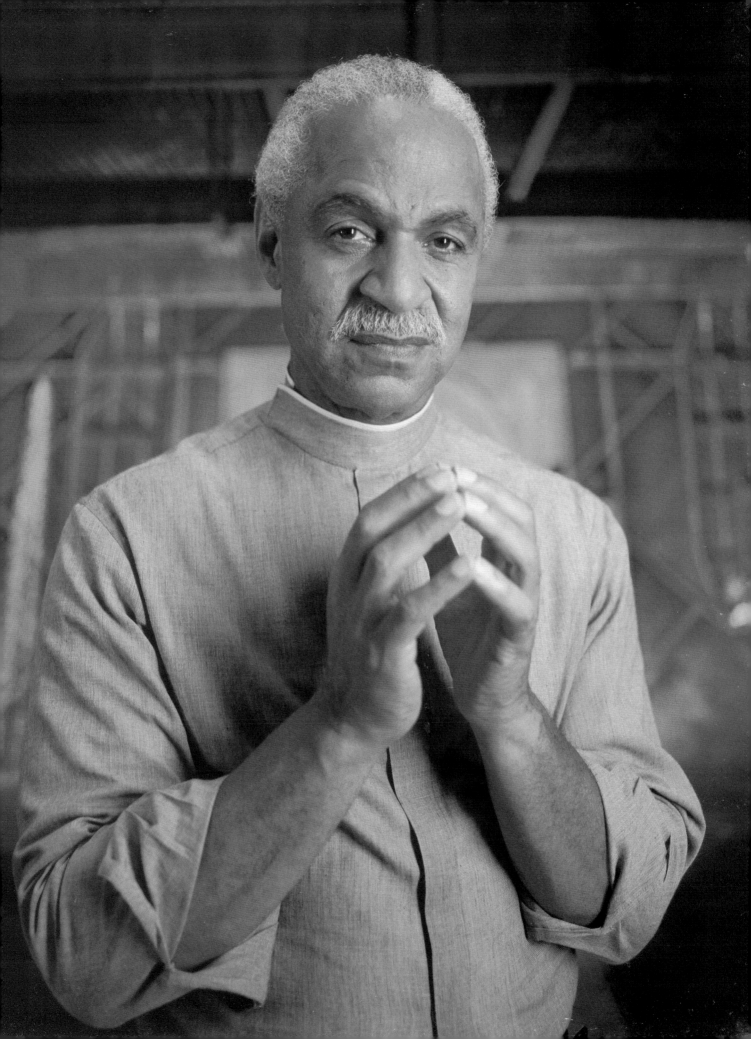

She says it shamefacedly, the covers slipping down as she sits naked before him.

MAL
Hey flesh! Look, Saffron, it ain't a question of pleasing me. It's a question of what's... uh... morally right.

SAFFRON
I do know my bible, sir. "On the night of their betrothal, the wife shall open to the man, as the furrow to the plough, and he shall work in her, in and again, 'til she bring him to his fall, and rest him then upon the sweat of her breast."

Beat.

MAL
Whoah. Good bible.

SAFFRON
I'm not skilled, sir, nor a pleasure to look upon, but —

MAL
Saffron. You're pleasing. You're... hell, you're all kinds of pleasing and it's been a while... a long damn while since anybody but me took a hold a' my plough so don't think for a second that I ain't interested. But you and me, we ain't married. Just 'cause you got handed to me by some <hwun dan> [bastard] couldn't pay his debts, don't make you beholden to me. I keep trying to explain —

SAFFRON
Let me explain.
(he waits, surprised at the grown up tone)
I lived my life in the maiden house, waiting to be married off for trade. I seen my sistren paired off with ugly men, vicious or blubberous, men with appetites too unseemly to speak on. And I've cried for those girls, but not half so hard as I cried the night they gave me to you.

MAL
(suddenly insecure)
Well, what — you — is there blubber?

SAFFRON
I cried for I'd not dreamed to have a man so sweet, so kind and beautiful. Had I the dare to choose, I'd choose you from all the men on all the planets the night sky could show me.

She stands, getting close to him.

SAFFRON (cont'd)
If I'm wed, I'm a woman and I'll take your leave to be bold. I want this. I swell to think of you in me, and I see you do too.

Mal looks down, embarrassed.

MAL
Well, that's just...

SAFFRON
Leave me at the nearest port, never look on me again, I'll make my way with the strength you've taught me... only let me have my wedding night.

They're inches apart. He's dying.

MAL
(looking up at the door)
I'm gonna go to the special hell...

She kisses him, slowly and sweetly. He pulls away, his face still close to hers, sad resolve in his eyes.

MAL (cont'd)
I really wish it was that simple, girl. But I just —

She kisses him again, and he gives massively in, putting his arms around her, their tongues intermingling...

He takes a step back, confusion on his face. Puts a hand to his lips.

MAL (cont'd)
Son of a —

He is already stumbling as he goes for his gun — it drops to the ground with the same lifeless thud as he does.

She looks at him a moment as he snores. The expression on her face, one we've not seen before, is sly triumph.

SAFFRON
Night, sweetie.

END OF ACT TWO

ACT THREE

INT. BRIDGE - NIGHT

Wash pilots alone. Saffron enters, tentatively — all shy girl (and dressed) again. Wash hears, turns —

WASH
Well, if it isn't the master chef. Not sleepy?

SAFFRON
Am I let to be up here?

WASH
Well, sure, why not. Not like anyone else is taking up space.

She enters, eyes on the window.

SAFFRON
I've never been off world before.

WASH
Beautiful, isn't it? Endless. You stare at it long enough, as long as I have, it becomes almost... preternaturally boring.

SAFFRON
(brow furrowed)
I don't think you're serious.

WASH
(smiling)
'Bout half. You stop seein' 'em after a spell, but they are your very first charts. Time and again, you look up from your screens and remember that.

SAFFRON
It's like a dream.

WASH
Planet I'm from, you couldn't see a one, pollution's so thick. Sometimes I think I entered flight school just so I could see what the hell everyone was talking about.

She smiles at him, her warmth enfolding his sweet reminiscence. A beat, and she moves to the door, quietly shuts it.

WASH (cont'd)
What are you doing?

She moves to the middle of the room, stands there, almost trance-like.

SAFFRON
Now we're alone. Us and the stars. No ship, no bellowing engines or crew to bicker at each other... look. Come look...

He's hesitant, but comes to stand next to her. They stare out at the brilliant black.

SAFFRON (cont'd)
Do you know the myth about Earth-that-was?

He can feel her closeness, her excitement — tries to be cool amidst the hard-on.

WASH
Not so much.

SAFFRON
That when she was born, she had no sky, and she was open, inviting and the stars would rush into her, through the skin of her, making the oceans boil with sensation, and when she could endure no more ecstasy, she puffed up her cheeks and blew out the sky, to womb her and keep them at bay, 'til she had rest some, and that we had to leave 'cause she was strong enough to suck them in once more.

Beat.

WASH
Whoah. Good myth.

She turns to him, eyes nearly moist with pleading.

SAFFRON
My whole life, I saw nothing but roofs and steeples and the cellar door. Few days I'll be back to that life and gone from yours. Make this night what it should be. Please...

Her face is inches from his.

SAFFRON (cont'd)
Show me the stars.

They're practically touching and she moves to kiss him, but he pulls away at the last minute.

WASH
<Wuh duh ma huh tah duh fong kwong duh wai shung> [Holy mother of god and all her wacky nephews] do I wish I was somebody else right

now. Somebody not married, not madly in love with a beautiful woman who can kill me with her pinky.

SAFFRON
I've been too forward.

WASH
No. Well, yes. But I actually like that in a woman. That's part of why Zoe and I are, as previously mentioned, married.

SAFFRON
I thought... she didn't seem to respect you.

WASH
Not everybody gets me and Zoe at first glance. Did it get very hot in here? I need airflow.

He moves to the door. She stops him with...

SAFFRON
You love her very much.

WASH
Yeah.

He turns to open the door. Saffron rolls her eyes with bored exasperation as he continues heading for the door —

WASH (cont'd)
I never did meet a woman quite like her. The first time we —

And Saffron sidekicks him in the back of the head, slamming his face into the door. He slides down, unconscious.

She pulls the door open, drags the body into the space before the stairs, hidden off to the side from view. Shuts the door again, locking it.

She moves to the console, hits the screens, working the nav like an expert. We see the course setting come up on the screen, see her change the coordinates and lock them in. Hits another screen and opens a channel to signal the new destination of arrival.

Just as swiftly and expressionlessly, she slides under the console, chooses a few wires and rips them out, sparks flying. Crosses a couple others (we see the nav screens wink out) and she's up, back at the door, opens it, looking to see she's alone.

She reaches under her dress and pulls a strip of tape from the hem, sticks it on the interior lock of the door and pulls off a layer, which causes a bubbling not unlike the burning glue of the pilot. As the lock begins to melt and fuse she slams the door shut, locking herself out of the bridge.

INT. CARGO BAY - MOMENTS LATER

She comes down the stairs, gets her bearings for a sec, then heads to the second shuttle. Opens the door and runs smack into:

INARA.

SAFFRON
Oh!

INARA
Are you lost?

Instantly she's subservient Saffron again, looking down. She backs up as Inara comes down a few stairs.

SAFFRON
I'm sorry. I thought the other shuttle was yours.

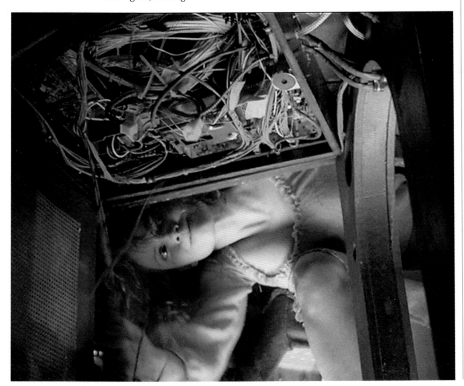

INARA
It is. I was on the Cortex and my screen shorted. This one's out too.

SAFFRON
Looking for customers?

INARA
What were you looking for?

SAFFRON
I don't mean to be rude... A Companion's life is so glamorous and strange... I wish I had the skill for such a trade...

By god, she's moving from subservient to seductive...

INARA
You'd like to please your new husband.

SAFFRON
Oh, he'll have none of me... For true I'm somewhat relieved... if I'm to learn of love, I'd want it to be at the hands of someone gentle... someone who could... feel... what I feel...

Their faces are close. Inara is as intimate in tone as Saffron:

INARA
But Mal said... you don't approve of my work...

SAFFRON
Sure and he said that to keep you from me... I was too curious about you, ever since I saw you...

They are face to face.

INARA
Come to my shuttle.

SAFFRON
You would... you would lie with me?

The alarm goes off, red lights spinning — Saffron looks around in innocent alarm, looks back to Inara, who drops the act.

INARA
I guess we've lied enough.

Saffron drops the act as well.

SAFFRON
You're good.

INARA
You're amazing. Who are you?

SAFFRON
I'm Malcolm Reynold's widow.

All the color drains from Inara's face. (Okay, not all the color, she's from Future-Brazil so she still has a hue, but she's upset, okay?)

Saffron punches, hard, but Inara blocks — a spinning kick from Saffron and Inara rolls out of the way, Saffron moving to the shuttle and slamming the door behind her.

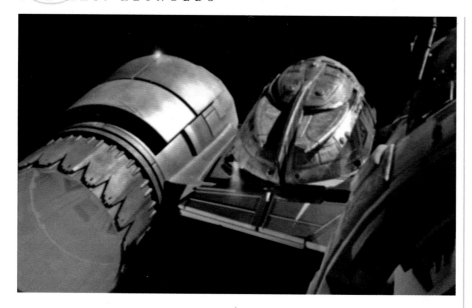

Inara is on her feet in a heartbeat, racing toward the foredeck hall...

INT. COCKPIT OF 2ND SHUTTLE - CONTINUOUS

Saffron pulls some chips from her dress and inserts them into the console, brings the shuttle to life.

EXT. SERENITY - CONTINUOUS

As the shuttle takes off and heads the opposite way.

INT. FOREDECK HALL - CONTINUOUS

Inara comes in as Zoe is at the entrance to the bridge, holding a dazed Wash. Jayne is trying to open the bridge door (it won't budge) as Kaylee is coming sleepily up out of her room. They all overlap:

ZOE
Baby wake up... He's bleeding...

JAYNE
There's nobody in there —

KAYLEE
What's going on?

Inara ignores them all, slams Mal's ladder in and drops down as fast as she can —

INT. MAL'S ROOM - CONTINUOUS

She finds Mal draped like the dead on the floor, rushes to him, fearing the worst —

INARA
Mal Mal Mal Mal —

She goes down, pulls up his head — and he moans — still alive. Unwanted wetness springs into her eyes as she gasps, relieved —

INARA (cont'd)
<Run-tse duh fwotzoo...> [Merciful buddha...]

And she kisses him, once, hard, then holds him to her, collecting herself — laying him back down and heading to the ladder as she calls out to above:

INARA (cont'd)
Get the Doctor! Mal's hurt... he...

She starts to sag. Puts a finger to her lips, recognizing the taste — she turns to Mal, scorn in her drooping eyes...

INARA (cont'd)
Oh, you stupid son of a —

And she collapses, unconcious, out of frame.

BLACKOUT AND FADE UP ON:

INT. - SAME - LATER

Fuzzy close on Mal awakening. Gets more focus as he looks about him, blinking.

MAL
Is it Christmas?

Reverse angle: The entire gang (minus River, Jayne and Kaylee) is staring at him. Simon closest, with his doctor bag, and Inara on his bed, propped up like a rag doll.

SIMON
Well, he's back...

ZOE
Yes, sir, it's Christmas. That special night when Nick the Saint comes down your chimney, changes your course, blows out the navcom, seals the bridge and takes off in your shuttle.

MAL
What happened about me...?

ZOE
Your blushing bride was a plant.
(re: him and Wash)
She took both of you out.

MAL
How did...

SIMON
A narcotic compound, probably spread over a seal on her lips. You get it on yours and pow.

ZOE
Lips, huh?

MAL
Well, no...

SIMON
We used to get a lotta guys brought in on the night shift at the E.R. — usually robbed and very groggy. Called it the "goodnight kiss".

ZOE
So you two were kissing.

BOOK
(pointedly, to Mal)
Well, isn't that special...?

MAL
(trying to change the focus)
Wash? How did —

WASH
Hey, I just got kicked in the head.

ZOE
My man would never fall for that <jien huo> [cheap floozy].

WASH
Most of my head wishes I had.

MAL
You guys don't understand...

BOOK
Seems pretty simple from here. You were taking advantage of a —

MAL
(standing clumsily)
I was the one being taken advantage of!

BOOK
My apologies, you were victimized, Wash was beaten and Inara found you here.

INARA
(defensively slurred and sleepy)
And then I fell. My head got hurt like Wash.

MAL
I don't get any of this.

INARA
I only fell is all.

MAL
What the hell is our status?

ZOE
We're shut down. Jayne and Kaylee are still trying to get on the bridge.

WASH
All we know is we're headed somewhere and it ain't Beaumonde.

Mal starts up the stairs, the others following. Hold on Inara, who says to Simon...

INARA
I'm fine. I don't need to be examined. I'm comfy.

INT. HALL - CONTINUOUS

As Mal and everyone files up (save Simon and Inara) to see Jayne firing up a blowtorch. Kaylee explains —

KAYLEE
She didn't just lock it, she fused it to something. Both entrances.

MAL
Why the big act? What the hell was she after?

BOOK
Besides molesting innocent captains?

MAL
You wanna stow it, Preacher? We're in some peril here.

ZOE
If she can fly this thing why just take the shuttle?

Simon is entering as well as:

WASH
Maybe she likes shuttles.

(off Mal's look)
Some people juggle geese...

RIVER
I told you.

They look at her.

RIVER (cont'd)
She's a thief.

A beat.

ANGLE: THE DOOR

as Jayne pulls it open.

INT. BRIDGE - LATER

Kaylee and Wash are lying side by side under the console, looking up at the wiring.

KAYLEE
She's a pro.

WASH
This is a masterful job of muck-up. See how she crossed the drive feeds —

KAYLEE
Yeah huh —

WASH
So we even try to reroute it'll lock down. <Jing tsai.> [Brilliant.]

KAYLEE
And she went straight for the thermal cap!

WASH
Yeah yeah! We're so humped!

They're starting just to admire it — a bit too much for Mal to take. He stands there with everyone else, waiting.

MAL
I'm glad you two are having a good time under there, you wanna progress to the making it right?

They poke their heads out.

WASH
That's not gonna happen for a good long while, Cap'n.

MAL
We don't have a good long while. We could be headed straight into a nice big solid moon for all we know, so hows about you get to work?

KAYLEE
Hey! You're the one whose big make-out session got us into this, sir.

MAL
I was poisoned!

INARA
You were drugged.

JAYNE
That's why I never kiss 'em on the mouth.

There is a moment for everyone's extreme silent horror.

MAL
Well, what CAN you do?

WASH
Give us some time we could get the Cortex and navcom back on line, at least see where we're headed.

MAL
That's fine, except for the part where I give you some time. What about steering?

INARA
What about stopping?

WASH
She humped us hard. We're gonna have to do a lot of —

MAL
Do it. It doesn't help me to see where I'm going if I can't change course.

KAYLEE
This girl really knows her ships.

INARA
That's not all she knows. She's well schooled.

SIMON
You mean the sedative? The Goodnight Kiss?

INARA
I only hit my head but Mal... went through that but no, I mean seduction, body language, signals... she had training. As in Companion, as in Academy.

BOOK
Our little Saffron's quite a wonder. I'm beginning to think she married beneath herself.

MAL
(to Inara)
How do you know? About the training?

INARA
She tried to seduce me too.

MAL
(trying not to sound too intrigued)
Really? Did she — did you —

INARA
You don't play a player. It was sloppy of her to try it, but I think she was in a rush.

MAL
But she had professional... so in my case, it was really...
(to Book)
You woulda kissed her too.

ZOE
Wash didn't.

MAL
But she was naked, and all articulate...

WASH
Okay. Everyone NOT talking about their sex lives, in here. Everyone else, elsewhere.

KAYLEE
Jayne, find me a splicer.

Jayne rummages through tools as everyone else save Book departs. Wash ducks back under with Kaylee.

WASH
Do you really think we have a hope in hell of fixing this?

KAYLEE
Not by talking 'bout it, darlin'.

INT. CHOP SHOP OFFICE - LATER

Breed is looking at a screen, call out of the room:

BREED
They're coming!

Corbin runs in.

CORBIN
How far out?

BREED
Ten minutes or so. Right on target, speed... a-1.

CORBIN
That girl is a wonder.

BREED
She gets it done. I'll tell the boys.

He starts out —

INT. BRIDGE - LATER

As Serenity's screens pop back to life:

WASH (O.S.)
YES!

He is looking at them, working them. Kaylee's still under the console, Jayne and Book at the ready.

Mal runs in.

MAL
You got it?

WASH
We got life. We got screens. It's a qualified "yes". A partial.

MAL
What about nav control?

Kaylee comes out to look miserable, shakes her head.

MAL (cont'd)
So where are we headed?

WASH
(working the screens)
Coordinates she entered... We're headed for something and it's not too far...

MAL
Did she signal anyone?

WASH
<Dung ee hwar...> [Hold on a second...] she did.
Same coordinates, no I.D.

JAYNE
Who's out there...?

WASH
Let me see if her signal wave can translate to visual, there might be a — <Aiya!> [Damn!] Heavy ionization, electrical interference bouncing the signal all... Look at that... It's like a circle.

Mal gets it. He looks at Book, who also does.

MAL
It's a net.

JAYNE
I don't get it. Where are we headed?

BOOK
The end of the line.

Off their looks:

EXT. CHOP SHOP RING - CONTINUOUS

As the electricity fires up and does in fact form a powerful net.

END OF ACT THREE

ACT FOUR

INT. BRIDGE - MOMENTS LATER

The same gang are there, as the explanation begins.

BOOK
It's a Carrion House. Scrap shop, takes ships, pulls 'em apart or fixes 'em up.

WASH
Doesn't sound that scary...

MAL
That pattern you're looking at is a net. We fly into that we're more than helpless. It'll turn the ship into one big electrical conduit, burn us all from the inside out.

BOOK
Some of the newer ones'll just hold you, then the scrappers'll override the airlocks, pull the oh-two, or just gas you. They're not looking to deal with survivors.

JAYNE
One day you're gonna tell us all how a preacher knows so damn much about crime.

MAL
Kaylee.

KAYLEE
I'm trying, sir, but...

MAL
Well you stay on it. We can't fall into that net.

He's thinking fast, looks about him.

MAL (cont'd)
We need a plan B.

He hits the com.

MAL (cont'd)
(into com)
Zoe, get our suits prepped, now.
(to the others)
I figure we got one shot at this.
(to Wash)
Give me visual as soon as we're close.

WASH
Won't be long...

JAYNE
What do I do?

Mal turns to him, waits just a hair of a beat.

MAL
You go get Vera.

INT. CARGO BAY/AIRLOCK - LATER

Mal and Jayne are suited up, save helmets and gloves. Jayne is loading big-ass bullets into Vera while Zoe checks his suit and Simon hooks his encyclopedia to the com console with Book's help.

WASH (O.S.)
(over the com)
We are two minutes out...

JAYNE
This thing needs oxygen around it to fire, and we don't have a case.

MAL
We're gonna use a suit.

SIMON
Here. We got it.

They look over at:

ANGLE: SIMON'S ENCYCLOPEDIA

has a visual of the ring on it.

JAYNE
What am I aiming for. The window?

MAL
That might kill some folk, but it won't disrupt the net. See these six points where it's brightest? Those're the breakers. Hit one and it should short it out.

JAYNE
What do you mean, should?

INT. BRIDGE - CONTINUING

Kaylee slams her wrench against metal, near tears.

KAYLEE
If I just had a stupid conductor cap...

She pauses a moment, then races out of the room.

EXT. CHOP SHOP RING - CONTINUING

As we can see Serenity tiny in the distance.

INT. AIRLOCK - CONTINUING

Mal opens the door, and we see him suited up, with Jayne as well. Jayne is sitting, holding the gun. It's in a suit, Jayne holding it through the sleeves (which are duct-taped to his), the barrel

pointing out through the helmet. The butt of the gun is braced up against containers against the airlock doors.

Angle: their pov

through the door, of the approaching ring.

MAL
You see it?

JAYNE
Clear as day.
(then, softer)
You see, Vera? You dress yourself up, then you get taken out somewhere fun.

INT. COCKPIT OF INARA'S SHUTTLE - CONTINUING

As Kaylee rips some wires and parts from it.

She comes up and looks out the window, stops — mezmerized.

EXT. CHOP SHOP RING - CONTINUOUS

As the ship approaches, the net forms fully, electricity silently flaring in a spider's web of power.

INT. EXT AIRLOCK/SPACE - CONTINUING

Mal waits. Jayne waits.

Jayne FIRES, a silent burst blowing through the helmet, air rushing out as the breaker EXPLODES, the crackling web disintigrating —

— and Jayne continues firing, aims up at the office itself:

INT. CHOP SHOP OFFICE - CONTINUING

Corbin and Breed duck and cover as the bullets rake across the window. We hear it crack and

groan — they look at each other in horror —

EXT. CHOP SHOP RING - CONTINUOUS

and the window and all the contents of the office are blow out into space — pan down to see Serenity blow through the sparking but harmless ring, continuing on in the distance.

INT. BRIDGE - LATER

Kaylee, Mal, Zoe. Wash is at the controls. We hear things hummming to life.

WASH
We got it. It's not pretty, but we can steer enough to turn the hell around.

MAL
Nice work, Kaylee.

KAYLEE
(despondent)
Weren't soon enough to help.

MAL
Lot easier to pull things apart than to put 'em right. You're still the best mechanic floating.

He kisses her on the top of her head. She waves him away, but didn't hate the compliment.

WASH
Captain, don't you know that kissing girls makes you sleepy?

MAL
Sometimes I just can't help myself. Let's go visiting.

INT. HOTEL ROOM - DUSK

Can something be rustically plush? 'Cause that best describes this little suite.

Saffron sits on the bed, pulling on her boots. She is nothing like the girl we've seen, much more modern and cool (though she still wears a skirt). And she's packing a sidearm in a shoulder holster.

She stops a moment, listening to something.

The door flies open, Mal having kicked it in. Before she can draw, he has his gun to her head.

MAL
Honey... I'm home...

A beat. She knocks his gun aside, it fires as she draws hers but he is in close, they tussel — he wrenches her gun from her hand as they collapse onto the bed, him on top.

MAL (cont'd)
Looks like you get your wedding night after all.

She pushes him, they go tumbling to the floor but he's still on top and this time he's got his gun to her chin.

MAL (cont'd)
It's the first time, darlin'. I think you should be gentle with me.

She lets out a breath, smiles at him unfathomably.

SAFFRON
Are you gonna kill me?

MAL
Can you conjure up a terribly compelling reason for me not to?

SAFFRON
I didn't kill you...

MAL
You handed me and my crew over to those that would kill us, that buys you nothing.

SAFFRON
I made you dinner...

MAL
Why the act? All the seduction games, the dancing about folk — there has to be an easier way to steal.

SAFFRON
You're assuming the payoff is the point.

MAL
I'm not assuming anything at this juncture.

He sits, gun still well on her. She gets up on her elbows, below but facing him.

SAFFRON
How'd you find me?

MAL
Only a few places that shuttle could make it to from where you left. Happy to find it intact. You always work for Elder Gommen?

A beat, and he leaves.

INT. INARA'S SHUTTLE

As she is turning off her vidscreen. Mal knocks, enters after:

INARA
Come in.

MAL
We're back on course, should be on Beaumonde just a day or two late. Hope that's all right.

INARA
It should be fine, thank you. And does the vixen live?

MAL
If you can call it that. All's well, I suppose.

INARA
Yes.

MAL
You're a very graceful woman, Inara.

INARA
(surprised)
I... thank you.

MAL
So here's where I'm fuzzy: you got by that girl, came and found me, and then you just happened to trip and fall?

INARA
Wh— what do you mean?

MAL
Come on, Inara, how's about we don't play. You didn't just trip, did you?

She holds his look, and aquiesces.

INARA
No.

He smiles, nodding.

MAL
Well isn't that something. I knew you let her kiss you.

Her look changes to one of stupified disbelief. He exits, chuckling. We hold on her expression for a long, long time.

END OF SHOW

SAFFRON
I work with lots of folk. He's thrown me a few choice fish. What'll become of the dear Elder?

MAL
Oh, he'll be laying eyes on me soon enough. And to think I saved his town from vicious bandits.

SAFFRON
(smiling sexily)
You're quite a man, Malcolm Reynolds. I've waited a long while for someone good enough to take me down.

MAL
(also smiles)
Saffron... you even think about playing me again I will riddle you with holes.

Her smile goes. This is the closest we're gonna get to seeing what's inside her, and there ain't much to warm your hands by.

SAFFRON
Everybody plays each other. That's all anybody ever does. We play parts.

MAL
You got all kinds a' learnin' and you made me look the fool without trying, yet here I am with a gun to your head. That's 'cause I got people with me, people who trust each other, who do for each other and ain't always looking for the advantage. There's good people in the 'verse. Not many, lord knows, but you only need a few.

SAFFRON
Promise me you're gonna kill me soon.

MAL
You already know I ain't gonna.

SAFFRON
You know, you did pretty well. Most men, hell, they're on me inside of ten minutes. Not trying to teach me to be strong and the like.

MAL
I got one question for you. Just one thing I'd like to know straight up.

SAFFRON
Ask me.

MAL
What's your real name?

She looks at him... looks away, considering the question...

— and he slams the butt of his gun into her chin, knocking her out cold. He stands, regards her genuinely vulnerable form. Says with a kind of sadness:

MAL (cont'd)
You'd only've lied, anyhow.